Young Lady's Guide

The
Young Lady's Guide

to the

Harmonious Development
of
Christian Character

HARVEY NEWCOMB

Solid Ground Christian Books
PO Box 660132 ~ Vestavia Hills AL 35266

SOLID GROUND CHRISTIAN BOOKS
PO Box 660132, Vestavia Hills, AL 35266
205-443-0311
sgcb@charter.net
http://www.solid-ground-books.com

The Young Lady's Guide
to the Harmonious Development of Christian Character

by Harvey Newcomb (1803-1863)

Taken from the 1843 edition by James B. Low, Boston, MA

Published by Solid Ground Christian Books

Classic Reprints Series

First printing October 2003

ISBN: 1-932474-07-2 (hardcover) - first edition June 2003
ISBN: 1-932474-29-3 (paperback) - first edition January 2004

Manufactured in the United States of America

PREFACE.

THIS book is addressed to those who are supposed to have commenced the Christian life. Its object is, to aid them in the harmonious development of all their powers, upon Christian principles; so as to produce the highest degree of cultivation, intellectual, social, moral, and religious, of which they are capable, in the circumstances where Providence has placed them. It is equally adapted to the various walks of life, having respect to a course of self-culture within the reach of all. It is addressed to a *particular class of persons*, whom it is especially designed to benefit. It is not intended, however, to be read exclusively by them. The greater portion of it is equally suited to any other class. It was originally written as a directory for a beloved sister of the author. It has since passed through two very thorough revisions; and in the present one, a considerable portion of it has been entirely rewritten, some parts of it condensed, and much new matter added. Those who have read the former editions will find this almost a new book, while the material substance of the original has been retained. Since it was first written, it has twice undergone a critical examination by learned and judicious friends; and, in the present revision, which is the last that is contemplated, the author has thrown out every sentence and every expression which has appeared to him of doubtful utility; so that those who read it, may rely upon its being a *safe guide*. Under a deep and solemn sense of responsibility for the influence which such a book is destined to exert, and with the humble hope of benefiting immortal minds, it is respectfully committed to the Christian public.

JANUARY, 1843.

CONTENTS.

1 *

CHAPTER III.

CHAPTER IV.

CHAPTER VII.

CHAPTER VIII.

CHAPTER IX.

CHAPTER X.

CHAPTER XI.

CHAPTER XII.

CHAPTER XIII.

CHAPTER XIV.

CHAPTER XV.

YOUNG LADY'S GUIDE.

CHAPTER I.

TRUE RELIGION ESSENTIALLY PROGRESSIVE.

THE great moral and spiritual change, which the Scriptures declare to be necessary to salvation, is compared by Christ and the apostles to a new birth, because it is the beginning of spiritual life. The term *regeneration*, however, only applies to this change in its commencement, which is instantaneous. The young convert, therefore, is very properly called by the apostle Peter a " new-born babe." It is a great mistake, then, to suppose that a true Christian, who is in a right state of mind, is to look back to the period of his conversion for his most lively and vigorous exercises of grace, or for his principal evidences of being in a gracious state. It may, indeed, be at that time more perceptible, because the change from a state of nature to a state of grace is very great. Yet this change is imperfect, and the greater part of the work of " putting off the old man," — of " bringing under the body and keeping it in subjection," remains yet to be done ; while the " new man " must grow up from the feebleness of

2

childhood to the " stature of a perfect man in Christ Jesus."

True religion must, therefore, be essentially pro- gressive. This is the clear implication of all the figures used in the word of God to describe the work of grace in the heart. It is compared to a mustard-seed, which is the least of all seeds. But, when it springs up, it rises and spreads its branches till it becomes the greatest of all herbs. The beauty and appropriateness of this figure will not be appreci- ated unless we take into consideration the luxuriant growth of plants in Eastern countries. The Jews have a fable of a mustard-tree whose branches were so extensive as to cover a tent. But we should never expect such a plant to spring up at once into full matu- rity. It is the *mushroom* which opens full grown to behold for the first time the morning sun ; but it as speedily withers away. Yet neither should we expect such a plant to become stationary in its growth, before it arrives at maturity. If it ceases to grow, there must be a worm at the root, or some fatal disease, which will cause it to shrivel and die. The operation of grace is also compared to leaven ; which is so little at first that its presence in the meal can scarcely be perceived. But when it begins to work, it increases and extends till the whole is leavened. Yet its progress may be impeded by cold ; and the process can rarely be restored, so as not to injure the production. So the Christian will rarely recover from the injurious effects of backsliding and growing cold in his religious affections.

Again, grace is compared to a living spring — a fountain, whose waters bubble up and send forth a constant stream. Christ says, "The water that I shall give him shall be *in him* a well of water, *springing up into everlasting life.*" When these words were uttered, our Lord was sitting on a deep well, in conversation with the woman of Samaria. As his custom was, he drew instruction from the objects around him. He directed her attention away from the water which could only quench natural thirst, to the living water, which refreshes the soul. But she, not understanding him, wished to know how he could obtain *living water* from a deep well, without any thing to draw with. In order to show the superiority of the water of life, he told her that those who drank of it should have it *in them*, constantly springing up of itself, as from an overflowing fountain. One of the most deeply-cherished recollections of the author's early life, is the living spring that flowed from a rock near the home of his childhood. The severest drought never affected it, and in the coldest season of a northern winter it was never frozen. Oft, as he rose in the morning, when the chilling blasts whistled around the dwelling, and every thing seemed sealed up with perpetual frost, the ice and snow would be smoking around the spring. Thus, like a steady stream, should our graces flow, unaffected by the drought or barrenness of others, melting the icy hearts around us.

"The righteous," says David, "shall flourish like a palm-tree; he shall *grow* like a cedar in Lebanon." The palm-tree continues to grow and increase, and retains its vigor and fruitfulness perhaps longer than any other tree. It is also renowned for its ability to multiply its own kind, its root producing a great number of suckers; and when it is planted by a living spring in the desert, soon there will be found a little forest of palm-trees growing up around it. This is one of the most useful of trees, every part of it being put to some profitable use. To " flourish like the palm-tree," therefore, is full of meaning. This can be realized by the Christian only when he is making progress in his own spiritual growth, contributing, by his influence, to the increase of the " trees of righteousness " in the garden of the Lord, and abounding in works of usefulness. The cedar is an evergreen. It does not, like many trees, shed its verdure, and remain apparently lifeless one half the year, and then shoot forth luxuriantly again for a little season; but its growth is steady and sure. It is *perpetually green*. To grow like a cedar, therefore, indicates a steady progress in the divine life.

The motives which urge us to seek and maintain an elevated standard of piety, are the highest that can be presented to our minds. *The glory of God requires it.* This is the greatest possible good. It is the manifestation of the divine perfections to his intelligent creatures. This manifestation is made by discovering to them his works of creation, providence, and grace, and by impressing his moral image upon their hearts. In this their happiness consists. In promoting his own glory, therefore, God exercises the highest degree of disinterested benevolence. Nothing can add to his happiness: nothing can diminish it. If the whole creation were blotted out, and God were the only being in the universe, he would still be perfectly glorious and happy in himself. There can be, therefore, no selfishness in his maintaining his own glory. The glory of the Creator is essential to the good of the creature. A desire to glorify God must, then, be the ruling principle of our conduct, the moving spring of our actions. But how is the glory of God promoted by our growth in grace?

1. It is manifested to us by impressing his image upon our hearts, and by giving us a spiritual discovery of the excellence, purity, and loveliness, of his moral nature.

2. It is manifested to others, so far as we maintain a holy life; for thereby the moral image of Christ is exhibited, as the glory of the sun appears by the reflected light of the moon.

3. The glory of God is promoted by making others acquainted with the riches of free grace, and bringing them to Christ; for, by that means, they receive spiritual light to behold the beauty and glory of the divine perfections, and his image is stamped upon their souls.

We have, likewise, great encouragement to aim at progress in divine things. The word of God is full of promises to such as seek after high attainments in divine knowledge and holiness. The prophet Hosea says, "Then shall we know, if we follow on to know the Lord: his going forth is prepared as the morning; and he shall come unto us as the rain, as the latter and former rain upon the earth." His going

2 *

forth, to those who follow on to know him, shall be as
certain, and as regular, and steady, as the daily return
of the morning; and as progressive as the sun, when
his beams break from the east, and increase in bright-
ness and intensity, till they pour down the burning
heat, and steady, clear light, of perfect day. "If we
follow on to know the Lord," our consolations shall be
as constant, and our experience of the goodness of the
Lord as certain, as the regular succession of night
and day; and our communion with God, and increase
of light, shall be as steady as the progress of the sun
from early dawn to mid-day. There may be occasional clouds; but they will quickly disperse, and the
Sun of Righteousness will break forth with sweeter
beams and more cheering lustre.

He shall also "come unto us as the rain, as the
latter and former rain upon the earth." In Palestine,
the rain does not fall, as in this country, at all seasons
of the year; but heavy rains descend, to water the
ground at seed-time, to cause the seed to spring up
and grow; and these rains are so plentiful as to
carry on vegetation with steady progress, till near the
harvest, when the "latter rain" falls, to perfect the
crop — to give body to the kernel, so that, when it shall
ripen, it may be plump and full. If this latter rain
fails, the kernel shrinks, and shrivels up, so that the
grain is deteriorated in quality, and diminished in
quantity. The "former rain," in the text quoted, then,
would seem to denote that "refreshing from on high,"
which the soul experiences when the "good seed" of
the word first springs up; and, if this be abundant,

and the young convert will " follow on to know the
Lord," the impulse which he then receives will carry
him on in a steady course of spiritual growth, till the
" latter rain " comes to perfect his fruits. In the experience of Christians who have made much progress
in the divine life, there is something very much resembling this " latter rain." They go on in a steady
course, after their conversion, always advancing,
though, perhaps, less perceptibly at some seasons
than others, as there are seasons in vegetation when
things seem to make no progress. But, at length,
after having faithfully followed on to know the Lord,
they receive a fresh unction from on high. The
Spirit of the Lord is poured out upon them anew, like
the " latter rain," to perfect the growth of the Christian graces. It may happen, in the growth of vegetation in the East, that, for a while before the " latter
rain," the drought may be such as to cause the grain
to droop, and, perhaps, to appear as though it were
going to dry up and wither away. So, often, previous
to this new experience of which I am speaking, the
Christian is brought through great trials, often exceeding, in the strength of temptation and the power of
conviction, that which preceded his first experience of
pardoning mercy. But, when light again breaks in
upon his mind, he is brought out into " a large place,"
and beholds the " beauty of the Lord," and the glories
of his grace, with clearer vision than ever before.
The riches of full assurance break in upon the soul,
and his peace flows as a river that is never dry. He
has new and clearer discoveries of the glory of God,

and of that divine and unspeakably-glorious mystery,
" God manifest in the flesh." His soul is lifted up in
God's ways, though exceedingly abased in himself,
and humbled before God. He has exchanged the
" spirit of bondage " for the " spirit of adoption."
His mind is in " perfect peace, stayed on God." And
this " latter rain " brings his fruits to maturity. His
love and joy, as well as all his religious affections, are
more pure and spiritual, with less mixture of human
passion; his faith is stronger, clearer, and more
steady; his patience is strengthened; he is more
forbearing, more gentle, more meek, more humble,
more consistent in his temper and conduct at all times.
He literally and truly " brings forth fruit with patience; " and his fruit remains, and is seen, to the
glory of God's grace. And, with many, this refreshing is often repeated, through a long Christian life,
causing them always to " bring forth fruit in their
season."

There is something like this " latter rain " in the
experience of Bible saints, as in that of Job, in his
trial, and of David and Peter, after their falls. So,
also, we find it in the memoirs of eminent Christians,
as of Bunyan, Mrs. Edwards, (wife of President Edwards,) Dr. Payson, James Brainerd Taylor, Dr.
Griffin, and many others. Mrs. Edwards, for a
long time, enjoyed, as she said, " THE RICHES OF
FULL ASSURANCE." She felt " an uninterrupted and
entire resignation to God, with respect to health or sickness, ease or pain, life or death, and an entire resignation of the lives of her nearest earthly friends." She

also felt a "sweet peace and serenity of soul, without
a cloud to interrupt it; a continual rejoicing in all the
works of nature and Providence; a wonderful access
to God by prayer, sensibly conversing with him, as
much as if God were here on earth; frequent, plain,
sensible, and immediate, answers to prayer; all tears
wiped away; all former troubles and sorrows of life
forgotten, except sorrow for sin; doing every thing for
God's glory, with a continual and uninterrupted cheerfulness, peace, and joy." At the same time she engaged in the common duties of life with great diligence, considering them as a part of the service of
God; and, when done from this motive, she said they
were as delightful as prayer itself. She also showed
an "extreme anxiety to avoid every sin, and to discharge every moral obligation. She was most exem-
plary in the performance of every social and relative
duty; exhibited great inoffensiveness of life and conversation; great meekness, benevolence, and gentleness of spirit; and avoided, with remarkable conscientiousness, all those things which she regarded as
failings in her own character."

But how did these persons arrive at this eminence in
the Christian life? Although by free, sovereign grace,
yet it was by no miracle. If we will use the same
means, we may attain the same end; and that without any disparagement to our dependence upon God,
or his sovereignty in the dispensation of his grace;
for he has appointed the *means*, as well as the *end*.
In speaking of the attainments of Mrs. Edwards, her

husband says, " Mrs. Edwards had been long, in an
uncommon manner, growing in grace, and rising, by
very *sensible degrees*, to higher love to God, weaned-
ness to the world, and mastery over sin and temptation, through *great trials and conflicts*, and long-
continued *struggling* and *fighting* with sin, and
earnest and *constant prayer* and *labor* in religion,
and engagedness of mind in the use of all means.
This growth had been attended, not only with a
great increase of religious affections, but with a
most visible alteration of outward behavior; particularly in living above the world, and in a greater degree of steadfastness and strength in the way of duty
and self-denial; maintaining the Christian conflict
under temptations, and conquering, from time to
time, under *great trials ;* persisting in an unmoved,
untouched calm and rest, under the *changes and ac-
cidents* of time, such as seasons of extreme pain, and
apparent hazard of immediate death."

We find accounts of similar trials and struggles in
the lives of others.   This is what we may expect.   It
agrees with the Christian life, as described in God's
word.   It is " through much tribulation that we enter
the kingdom of heaven."   This is the way in which
we must go, if we would ever enter there.   We must
make religion the great business of life, to which every
thing else must give place.   We must engage in the
work with our *whole souls*, looking to Christ for
strength against our spiritual enemies ; following the
example of Paul, " forgetting those things which are

behind, and reaching forth unto those things which
are before ; pressing toward the mark for the prize
of the high calling of God in Christ Jesus ; " and
then we shall come off conquerors at last, " through
him that hath loved us, and given himself for us."

CHAPTER II.

DOCTRINAL KNOWLEDGE.

It is common for persons to speak of *doctrine* with aversion, as though it were something abstract and dry, having no connection with practical life. This notion, however, is founded on a misapprehension, not only of the meaning of the term, but of the connection of actions with established principles of the mind. The general signification of the word *doctrine* is, the principles upon which any system is founded. As applied to Christianity, it means *divine truth;* for this is the foundation upon which the Christian religion rests. Although the truths of God's word are not reduced to a regular system in the Bible, yet, when brought together, they make the most beautiful and perfect of all systems. It is proper, therefore, that we should contemplate them *in a body*, as they appear with the most perfect symmetry in the plan of God's moral government. There is a disposition, with many, to undervalue doctrinal knowledge. They think it of little consequence what they *believe*, if they are only *sincere*, and manifest much *feeling* on the subject of religion. This is a ruinous mistake. There is an intimate connection between faith and practice. The principles which are believed, and received into the heart, govern and control the conduct. The doctrines which God has revealed in his word are the principles of his moral government. If we mistake these principles, we may be found in open rebellion, while we think we are doing God service. For example, God commands us to keep holy the Sabbath day. But, if we do not *believe* that he has given this commandment, we shall feel under no obligation to *obey* it. And every truth which God has revealed is as intimately connected with practice as this, although the duty enjoined may be, in itself considered, of less consequence. Christianity is called a spiritual building. " Ye are built up a spiritual *house*." " Whose *house* are we." " Ye are God's *building*." The *foundation* and *frame-work* of this building are the doctrines or truths of the Bible. Some of these doctrines are called *fundamental*, or *essential*, because they lie at the *foundation* of the whole building, and are so *essential* to it, that, if taken away, the edifice would fall to the ground. These are, *the existence of God* in the mysterious union of *Father, Son, and Holy Ghost ; the fall*, and consequent *depravity* and *condemnation*, of man ; the *atonement of Christ ; justification by faith* in him alone ; the *necessity of regeneration* by the Holy Spirit ; and the *eternal punishment* of those who finally reject the gospel. If any *one* of these were taken away, it would overturn the whole building. These may, therefore, well be called the *foundation*. But there are many other important parts of a *frame* besides the foundation. So there are many very important truths of Christianity besides

3

its essential doctrines. But some of these are of more consequence than others. If a *post* or a *beam* is taken away, the building is greatly marred, and in danger of falling; yet, if well *covered*, it may still be a comfortable dwelling. Again, although a *brace* or a *pin* is of service to strengthen the building, yet either may be taken away without very serious injury. But a *frame* may be *complete* in all its parts, and yet be no building. Without a *covering*, it will not answer a single design of a house; and in proportion as it is well covered, will it be a comfortable residence. Just so with Christianity. The covering of the house is the work of the Holy Spirit in the heart, producing gracious affections, which manifest themselves in a holy life. But the covering of a house cannot exist without some kind of frame-work. So experimental and practical piety cannot exist without a belief of the fundamental doctrines of the gospel. The Holy Spirit operates upon the heart *through the truth*. He gives it a personal application, brings it home to the heart and conscience, and exerts an efficacious influence in connection with it, changing the heart and life. "Of his own will begat he us, *with the word of truth*." "Seeing ye have purified your souls, in *obeying the truth through the Spirit*." Thus the agency of the Spirit is generally acknowledged in connection with the truth. Any religious feeling or experience, therefore, which is not produced by the truth, made effectual by the Holy Spirit, is not genuine. There is a kind of indefinite religious feeling, which many mistake for Christian experience. They *feel*, and, perhaps, deeply; but they know not *why* they feel. Such religious feeling is to be suspected as spurious. It may be a delusion of Satan. By persuading people to rest upon this spurious religious feeling, he accomplishes his purpose as well as if he had kept them in a careless state. The clearer our views of truth, the more spiritual and holy will be our religious affections. Thus godly sorrow arises from a sight of our own depravity, with a sense of the exceeding sinfulness of sin, as committed against a holy God, and against great light and mercy. Faith is produced by a view of the atonement of Christ, and of his infinite fulness as a complete and perfect Savior. Love is excited by a discovery of the excellence of God's moral perfections. Holy fear and reverence arise from a sight of the majesty and glory of his natural attributes, and a sense of his presence. Joy may come from a sense of the infinite rectitude of his moral government, from the sight of the glory of God in his works of providence and grace, or from a general view of the beauty and excellence of divine truth. Comfort may be derived from evidence of the divine favor; and confidence, from an appropriation of God's promises to ourselves.

But all religious feeling produced by *impulse*, without any rational view of the truth, is to be suspected. Every religious affection has its counterfeit. Thus sorrow may be produced by the fear of hell, without any sense of the evil of sin. A presumption of our own good estate may be mistaken for faith; and this will produce joy. We may exercise a carnal or selfish love to God, because we think he loves us, and has made us the objects of his special favor; and this may excite the natural passions to a high degree of fervor, without any spiritual affection. The promises of God, also, so far as they concern the personal good of the believer, may administer as much comfort to the self-deceived as to the real saint.

But as the frame-work of a building, though complete in all its parts, would be no house without a covering, so we may have a speculative knowledge of the doctrines of the Christian religion, and be no Christians. It is the experimental and practical application of these doctrines to the heart and life that makes the building complete. By regarding ourselves as subjects of God's moral government, and the doctrines of the Bible as the laws of his kingdom, we feel such a personal interest in them, that we cannot rest in abstract speculation. Let us, therefore, study these doctrines, that we may know how to live to the glory of God.

Directions for acquiring Doctrinal Knowledge.

I. *Become a little child.* "As new-born babes, desire the sincere milk of the word." "Except ye be converted, and *become as little children*, ye shall not enter into the kingdom of heaven." A little child believes the words of his father. "My father says so," is reason enough for him. He does not say, "I will not believe it, because I cannot understand it." In like manner should we submit to the teachings of God's holy word. We cannot expect to comprehend

the ways of an infinite Being. We can see but a very
small part of the system of his moral government.
Let us not, then, try to carry out difficult points beyond what is taught in the Scriptures. God has revealed all that is necessary for us to know in this life.
He knows best where to leave these subjects. If there
were no difficulties in the truths revealed, there would
be no trial of our faith. It is necessary that we should
take some things on trust. There are some truths
clearly revealed, which we find difficulty in reconcil-
ing one with the other. Be content to believe both on
the authority of God's word. He will reconcile them
hereafter. " What I do thou knowest not *now*," said
our Lord to Peter, " but thou shalt know hereafter."
Let this consideration always satisfy us: " Even so,
Father, for so it seemed good in thy sight." I am the
more particular here, because this is the point where
error begins. The setting up of feeble reason in opposition to the word of God, is the origin of most
mistakes in religion. And, if we determine to be satisfied of the reasonableness of the truth before we
believe it, and carry out the principle, we shall land in
downright atheism. I do not mean to say that any
truth is unreasonable. On the contrary, divine truth
is the perfection of reason. But there are some truths
which may appear unreasonable because we cannot
see the whole of them. Thus a fly on the corner of
a house cannot see the beauty and symmetry of the
whole building. So far as his eye extends, it may appear to be sadly lacking in its proportions. Yet this is

3 *

but a faint representation of our narrow views of God's moral government.

But a great many of the difficulties which are felt in regard to religious truth arise from mistaking the true province of reason. There are a multitude of *facts* in natural science which are capable of being demonstrated; and yet all philosophy is set at defiance to determine the *mode* or *manner* of their existence, or the *reasons why* they exist. Thus we can easily understand the fact of the attraction of the needle to the pole; but the cause of this attraction, or the manner in which it operates, is entirely beyond our apprehension. So we can understand the fact that the heat of the sun, with moisture upon the earth, will cause seed to vegetate; but we can explain neither the *reason why*, nor the *mode of operation;* nor can we tell the reason why every seed will produce its kind, or why every animal will propagate its own species; neither can we discover the *mode*, or *manner*, in either of these cases; and yet the *fact* is undeniable. To *determine the facts*, in all these cases, by an examination of the evidence by which they are substantiated, is the true province of reason; but it would be unphilosophical and absurd to deny the *fact*, because we cannot understand the *how* or the *why*. Apply this simple principle to divine truth, and half the difficulties with which it is surrounded will vanish. Thus we can understand the fact of the connection of Adam's fall with the depravity of all men; but the reasons which influenced the Divine Mind, in constituting the arrangement under which this takes place, are entirely out of our reach; nor can we explain the mode by which this depravity is inherited. So we can apprehend the fact of the Trinity of persons in the Godhead, and the union of the divine and human natures in Christ; but the *mode*, or *manner*, is above our comprehension. Reason is competent to judge of the evidence by which these truths are established; and no better evidence can be had or desired than the word of God, in ascertaining the meaning of which reason is to be employed. But, when that meaning is ascertained, reason is to bow with implicit faith. It is to be observed, however, that the word of God does not teach any thing which is obviously absurd, and repugnant to right reason, as the Papal notion of transubstantiation; and the fact that the meaning we attach to any passage of Scripture is absurd, and repugnant to reason, is presumptive evidence that we have mistaken its meaning.

II. *Avoid a controversial spirit.* Do not study for the sake of finding arguments to support your own opinions. Take the place of a sincere inquirer after truth, with a determination to embrace whatever you find supported by the word of God, however contrary it may be to your favorite notions. But, when objections arise in your mind against any doctrine, do not suppose you have made some new discovery, and therefore reject it without further inquiry. The same objections have, perhaps, occurred to the mind of every inquirer on the same subject; and, very probably, they have often been satisfactorily answered by able writers. This is a common error of young inquirers. They are apt to think others take things upon trust, and that they are the only persons who have thought of the difficulties which start up in their minds. But, when their reading becomes more extensive, they learn, with shame, that what appeared to them original thought, was only reviving old, cast-off opinions.

III. *Use such helps as you can obtain.* Read carefully-selected and judicious authors, on doctrinal subjects. Although the Scriptures are our only guide, yet we may profit by the experience of others. We may see how the difficulties which arise in our own minds appeared to them, and how they solved them. We may learn, also, that our difficulties with commonly-received opinions are not new, but that they have before occurred to the minds of others, who, nevertheless, after examination, have retained these opinions. This may prevent us from hastily rejecting any doctrine without thorough examination. We may also obtain much light upon many difficult passages of Scripture, by an acquaintance with the times and circumstances in which they were written ; and men who undertake to write on such subjects generally search deeply into these matters. Furthermore, it has pleased God, in every age, to raise up men "*mighty in the Scriptures.*" With their extraordinary powers of mind, and knowledge of the languages in which the Scriptures were originally written, it would be strange if they should not have clearer perceptions of their meaning, and more comprehensive views of divine truth, than those who have only read the English Bible; and to despise what they have written would be the height of self-conceited folly.

We may also employ the sermons which we hear for an increase of doctrinal knowledge, as well as an excitement to the performance of duty. But all which we read or hear must be brought to the test of God's word. We are commanded to " try the spirits, whether they be of God." Do not take the opinions of men upon trust. Compare them diligently with the word of God, and do not receive them till you are convinced that they agree with this unerring standard. Make this your text-book; and only use others to assist you in coming to a right understanding of this. Yet be not too confident in your own understanding; and be ever ready to suspect your judgment, where you find it opposed by the opinions of the mass of learned and pious men whom God has raised up for the instruction of his people.

IV. *In all your researches after doctrinal knowledge, seek the guidance of the Holy Spirit.* Pray that God would enable you to understand his word, that you may be " rooted and grounded in the faith." The influences of the Holy Spirit are twofold. He enlightens the understanding, to lead it into a correct knowledge of the truth; and he applies the truth, to the sanctification of the heart. Pray diligently that you may have both. If you persevere in the proper observance of this direction, you cannot fail to profit by the others; but, if you neglect this, your pursuit of doctrinal knowledge will serve only as food for your pride, self-confidence, and conceit, and exert a blighting influence upon your soul.

CHAPTER III.

NATURE AND EFFECTS OF TRUE RELIGION.

THE nature and effects of true religion are described in the Holy Scriptures, under the similitude of a tree planted by the side of a river. The Psalmist says the righteous " shall be like a tree planted by the rivers of water, that bringeth forth his fruit in his season: *his leaf shall not wither.*" The prophet Jeremiah, also, speaking of the man who trusts and hopes in the Lord, says, " He shall be as a tree planted by the waters, and that spreadeth out her roots by the river, and shall not see when heat cometh, *but her leaf shall be green;* and shall not be careful in the year of drought, *neither shall cease from yielding fruit.*"

The river, which is ever flowing, represents the abundant provision of God's grace. But a tree may stand so near a river as to be watered when it overflows its banks; and yet, if its roots only spread over the surface of the ground, and do not reach the bed of the river, it will wither in a time of drought. This aptly represents those who appear engaged and in earnest only during remarkable outpourings of the Spirit. They are all alive and full of zeal when the river overflows; but, when it returns to its ordinary channel, their leaf withers; and, if a long season of spiritual drought follows, they become dry and barren, so that no appearance of spiritual life remains. But mark how different the description of the true child of God: " He shall be as a tree *planted* by the rivers of water." This figure appears to have been taken from the practice of *cultivating* trees. They are removed from the wild state in which they spring up, and their roots firmly fixed in a spot of ground *cultivated* and *prepared* to facilitate their growth. So the Christian is taken from a state of nature, which is a wild, uncultivated state, and placed in a state of grace, by the side of the river, which flows from the throne of God and the Lamb. But this tree also " spreadeth out her roots by the river." When the roots of the tree are spread out along the bed of the river, it will always be supplied with water, even when the river is low. This steadiness of Christian character is elsewhere spoken of under a similar figure : " The *root* of the righteous *shall not be moved ;* " " He shall cause them that come of Jacob to *take root ;* " " Being *rooted* and grounded in love." Hence the prophet adds that the heat and the drought shall not affect it ; but its *leaf shall be green*, always growing ; and it *shall not cease to bring forth fruit*. And throughout the Scriptures the righteous are represented as bringing forth fruit : " And the remnant that is escaped out of the house of Judah shall again take root downward, and bear fruit upward." Here is first a taking deep root downward, or the sanctification of the faculties of the soul, by which new principles of action are adopted ; and a bearing fruit upward, or the exercise of those princi-

ples, in holy affections and corresponding outward
conduct. Again, " Israel shall blossom and bud, and
fill the face of the world with fruit." The bud and
blossom are the first exercises of Christian experience.
But every tree bears a multitude of false blossoms,
which, by the superficial observer, may not be distinguished from the true. They may for a time appear
even more gay and beautiful. As it appears in full
bloom, it would be impossible for the keenest eye to
discover them. But as soon as the season arrives for
the fruit to begin to grow, these fair blossoms are
withered and gone, and nothing remains but a dry and
wilted stem. So, in the first stages of Christian experience, there are many counterfeits. But the real
children of God shall not only bud and blossom, but
they shall "*fill the face of the world with fruit.*" In
the Song of Solomon, the church is compared to " an
orchard of pomegranates, with *pleasant fruits.*" The
pomegranate is a kind of apple. The tree is low, but
spreads its branches, so that its breadth is greater than
its height. So the true Christian is humble and lowly,
while his good works spread all around him. The
blossoms of this tree are large and beautiful, forming
a cup like a bell. But when the flowers are double,
no fruit follows. So the double-minded hypocrite
brings forth no fruit. The pomegranate apple is
exceedingly beautiful and delicious, and so the real
fruits of Christianity are full of beauty and loveliness.
Again, the church is said to lay up for Christ all manner of pleasant fruit, new and old. But *backsliding*
Israel is called an empty vine, bringing forth fruit *unto*

4

himself. Here we may distinguish between the *apparent* good fruits of the false professor and of the real
Christian. The latter does every thing for Christ.
He desires the glory of God and the advancement of
Christ's kingdom ; and this is his ruling motive. But
the former, though he may do many things good in
themselves, yet does them all with selfish motives.
His ruling desire is to gratify himself, and to promote
his own honor and interest, either in this world or in
that which is to come.

The *fruit* which his people bring forth is that on
which Christ chiefly insists, as a test of Christian
character. " Every good tree bringeth forth good
fruit ; but a corrupt tree bringeth forth evil fruit."
He compares himself to a vine, and his followers to
branches ; and informs them that every branch which
beareth not fruit shall be taken away. In the passage
quoted from the first Psalm, the righteous is said to
bring forth fruit *in his season.* And in the 92d Psalm
and 14th verse, it is said, " They shall still bring forth
fruit *in their old age ;* they shall be *fat and flourishing ;* " thus exhibiting a constancy of fruit-bearing,
and an uninterrupted growth, even down to old age.

But what is meant by bringing forth fruit *in his
season ?* Paul says, " The fruit of the Spirit is in *all*
goodness, and righteousness, and truth." Hence we
conclude that bringing forth fruit *in season* must be
carrying out the principles of the gospel into every
part of our conduct. In another place, the same
apostle informs us more particularly what are the
fruits of the Spirit : " love, joy, peace, long-suf-

fering, gentleness, goodness, faith, meekness, temperance." Let us, then, carry out these principles, and see what influence they will have upon the Christian character. *Love* is something that can be *felt.* It is an outgoing of heart towards the object loved, and a feeling of union with it. When we have a strong affection for a friend, it is because we see in him something that is lovely. We love his society, and delight to think of him when he is absent. Our minds are continually upon the lovely traits of his character. So ought we to love God. The ground of this love should be the infinite purity, excellence, and beauty of his moral perfections. He is infinite loveliness in himself. There is such a thing as feeling this love in exercise. In the Song of Solomon, love is said to be " *strong as death.*" Surely this is no faint imagery. Is it possible for a person to exercise a feeling " as strong as death," and yet not be sensible of it ? Love takes hold of every faculty of soul and body. It must, then, be no very dull feeling. Again, the warmth and the settled and abiding nature of love are represented by such strong language as this : " Many waters cannot quench love, neither can the floods drown it." Surely this can be no fitful feeling, which comes and goes at extraordinary seasons. It must be a settled and abiding principle of the soul, though it may not always be accompanied with strong emotion. We may sometimes be destitute of emotion towards the friends we love most. But the settled principle of esteem and preference is abiding ; and our attention

needs only to be called to the lovely traits in our
friend's character to call forth emotion.

David, under the influence of this feeling, breaks
forth in such expressions as these : " My soul *thirsteth*
for thee ; my flesh *longeth* for thee ; " " As the hart
panteth for the water-brooks, so *panteth* my soul after thee, O God ; my soul *thirsteth* for God, for the
living God ; " " My soul *longeth*, yea, even *fainteth*,
for the courts of the Lord ; my *heart and my flesh
crieth out* for the living God ; " " My soul *breaketh*
for the longing it hath unto thy judgments *at all
times*." Surely there is no dulness, no coldness, in
such feelings as these. They accord with the spirit
of the command, " Thou shalt love the Lord thy God
with all thine heart, and with all thy soul, and with *all
thy might*." And this was not, with the Psalmist, an
occasional lively frame. This soul-breaking longing
was the habitual feeling of his heart ; for he exercised it " *at all times*." And what was it that called
forth these ardent longings ? Was it the personal
benefits which he had received, or expected to receive,
from God ? By no means. After expressing an
earnest desire to dwell in the house of the Lord *all
the days of his life*, he tells us why he wished to be
there : " *To behold the beauty of the Lord, and to
inquire in his temple*." The object of his love was
" *the beauty of the Lord ; " * doubtless meaning his
moral perfections. Intimately connected with this was
his desire to know the will of the Lord. For this he
wished to " *inquire in his temple*." And whenever

the love of God is genuine, it will call forth similar
desire. The apostle John, whose very breath is love,
says, " This is the love of God, that we *keep his commandments*." The child that loves his parents will
delight in doing whatever pleases them. But the
child that cares for his parents only as he expects to
be benefited by them, will always do as little as
possible for them, and that little unwillingly. So in
our relations with God. The self-deceived may have
a kind of love to God, because he thinks himself a
peculiar object of divine favor, and because he still
expects greater blessings. But this does not lead him
to delight in the commands of God. He rather es-
teems them a *task*. His heart is not in the doing of
them; and he is willing to make them as light as
possible. But the true Christian *delights* in the law
of God; and the chief source of his grief is, that he
falls so far short of keeping it.

Again, if we love God, we shall love his image.
" Every one that loveth him that begat, loveth him
also that is begotten of him." Our love to Christians,
if genuine, must arise from the resemblance which
they bear to Christ; and not from the comfort which
we enjoy in their society, nor because they appear
friendly to us. This false professors also feel. If we
truly exercise that love, we shall be willing to make
personal sacrifices for their benefit. We are directed
to love one another *as Christ loved us*. And how did
Christ love us? *He laid down his life for us*. And
the beloved apostle says, we ought, in imitation of him,
" to lay down our lives for the brethren ; " that is, if

4 *

occasion require it. Such is the strength of that love,
which we are required to exercise for our Christian
brethren. But how can this exist in the heart, when we
feel unwilling to make the least sacrifice of our own
feelings or interests for their sakes?

But there is another kind of love required of us
— the love of compassion, which may be exercised
even towards wicked men. And what must be the
extent of this love? There can be but one standard.
We have the example of our Lord before us. So intense was his love, that it led him to sacrifice personal
ease, comfort, and worldly good, for the benefit of the
bodies and souls of men; and even to lay down his
life for their salvation. " While we were yet sinners,
Christ died for us." Thus must we lay ourselves out
for doing all we can to relieve the sufferings and save
the souls of our fellow-men.

Another fruit of the Spirit is JOY. We are commanded to rejoice in the Lord *at all times.* If we
have a proper sense of the holiness of God's moral
character, of the majesty and glory of his power, of
the infinite wisdom which shines through all his works,
the infinite rectitude of his moral government, and especially of that amazing display of his love in the work
of redemption, it will fill our hearts with " JOY UN-
SPEAKABLE AND FULL OF GLORY." Nor is rejoicing in
God at all inconsistent with mourning for sin. On the
contrary, the more we see of the divine character, the
more deeply shall we be abased and humbled before
him. Says Job, " I have heard of thee by the hearing
of the ear; but now *mine eye seeth* thee. *Wherefore,*

I abhor myself, and repent in dust and ashes." It was a *sight* of God which brought this holy man so low before him.

Another fruit of the Spirit is PEACE — peace with God, and peace with man. The impenitent are at war with God ; there is therefore no peace for them. God is angry with them, and they are contending with him. But the Christian becomes reconciled to God through Christ. He finds peace in believing in him. The Lord is no longer a God of terror to him, but a " God of peace." Hence the gospel is called the " way of peace," and Christ the " Prince of peace." Jesus, in his parting interview with his beloved disciples, says, " Peace I leave with you; *my peace* I give unto you." Righteousness, or justice, and peace, are said to have met together, and kissed each other. " We have peace with God, through our Lord Jesus Christ." We are brought into a state of reconciliation with God, attended with' a settled feeling of complacency towards his government. This begets a serene and peaceful disposition of heart. But this gracious work of the Holy Spirit does not stop with these exercises of the mind. It must be carried out in our intercourse with others, and our feelings towards them. Whatever is in our hearts will manifest itself in our conduct. If we exercise a morose, sour, and jealous disposition ; if we indulge a censorious spirit, not easily overlooking others' faults ; if we are easily provoked, and irritated with the slightest offence ; if we indulge in petty strife and backbiting, — surely the peace of God does not rule in our hearts.

MEEKNESS is a twin-sister of PEACE. It is a temper
of mind not easily provoked to resentment; or, as the
word signifies, *easiness of mind.* The term for a
meek man, used by the Romans, signified *used to hand*,
in allusion to the taming of wild animals, which the
cultivation of this grace truly resembles. It is the
bringing of our wild and turbulent passions under control. It is an eminent work of the Spirit; and we may
judge of our spiritual attainments by the degree of it
which we possess. The Scriptures abound with exhortations to the cultivation of it. It is preëminently
lovely in the female character. Hence Peter exhorts
women to put on the ornament of a meek and quiet
spirit, which is, in the sight of God, of great price.

LONG-SUFFERING and GENTLENESS are twin-daughters
of meekness. Long-suffering is godlike; it is an imitation of the forbearance of God towards his rebellious
creatures. He is long-suffering and slow to anger.
He does not let his anger burn hot against sinners till
all means of bringing them to repentance have failed.
O, how should this shame us, who cannot bear the least
appearance of insult or injury from our fellow-sinners
without resentment! But, if we would be the children
of our Father in heaven, we must learn to bear ill-
treatment with a forbearing and forgiving temper.
Gentleness is one of the most lovely of all the graces
of the Spirit. It is a " softness or mildness of disposition and behavior, and stands opposed to harshness and
severity, pride and arrogance." " It corrects whatever
is offensive in our manner, and, by a constant train of
humane attentions, studies to alleviate the burden of

common misery." The constant exercise of this spirit
is of the greatest importance to the Christian who
would glorify God in his life, and do good to his
fellow-creatures.

GOODNESS is another fruit of the Spirit. I suppose
the apostle here means the same that he expresses in
another place by " bowels of mercies and kindness."
It is doing good both to the bodies and souls of others,
as we have opportunity. " Be kindly affectioned one
to another." " Be ye kind one to another, tender-
hearted." This is a distinguished trait in the Christian
character. It shone forth in all its loveliness in our
divine Redeemer. He *went about* doing good. So
ought we to imitate his example. It should be our
chief aim and study to make ourselves useful to others ;
for we thereby glorify God. If we have the Spirit of
Christ, this will be our " meat and drink."

Another fruit of the Spirit is FAITH. " Faith is
credit given to a declaration or promise, on the authority of the person who makes it ; " including the idea of
confidence in such person, and reliance upon his word.
It is a common principle of action in the ordinary
affairs of life, in the transaction of which people act
according to their faith. If a person believes that his
house is on fire, he will make haste to escape. If a
man believes a bank note is good, he will receive it for
its professed value. If the merchant believes that his
customer is able to pay, he will give him goods upon
credit. That faith which is the fruit of the Spirit is a
hearty belief of all the truths of God's word, including
not only the idea of confidence in him, but a love of

the truth, and a hearty acquiescence in the will of God declared in it. Faith in Christ includes also the idea of trust, or reliance upon him for salvation. In proportion as we believe the truths of God's word, in the sense here specified, we shall act accordingly. One reason why the sinner does not repent and turn to God is, that he does not fully believe the word of God as it applies to himself. He may believe some of the abstract truths of the Scriptures; but he does not really believe himself to be in the dreadful danger which they represent him; or, if his understanding is convinced, his heart is so opposed to the truth that he will not yield to it. The reason why Christians live so far from the standard of God's word is, that their belief in the truths contained in it is so weak and faint. We all profess to believe that God is every where present; yet we often complain that we have no lively sense of his presence. The reason is, we do not fully and heartily believe this truth. So strong and vivid is the impression, when this solemn truth takes full possession of the soul, that the apostle compares it to " *seeing him that is invisible.*" Now, but for our unbelief, we should always have such a view of the divine presence. O, with what holy awe and reverence would this inspire us! On examination, we shall find that all the graces of the Spirit arise from faith, and all our sins and short comings from unbelief. It is a belief of the moral excellence of God's character which inspires love. It is a belief of our own depravity, and the exceeding sinfulness of sin, which creates godly sorrow. It is a strong and lively faith in all the truths of the Bible

which overcomes the world. "This is the victory
that overcometh the world, even our faith." It is an
unshaken belief in these truths, presenting the glories
of heaven just in view, which supports the Christian in
the dark and trying hour of death. It is the same belief which makes him " as bold as a lion " in the performance of his duty. This is what supported the
martyrs, and enabled them cheerfully to lay down their
lives for Christ's sake. It is this which must support
us in the Christian warfare ; and our progress will be
in proportion to our faith.

TEMPERANCE is another fruit of the Spirit. This
consists in the proper control of all our desires, appetites, and passions. The exercise of this grace is of
vital importance, not only as it concerns the glory of
God, but our own health and happiness.

Thus we see the beautiful symmetry of the Christian character, as it extends from the heart to all our
actions, in every relation of life.

CHAPTER IV.

CHARITY.

ALTHOUGH I have dwelt at considerable length upon the fruits of the Spirit, yet so deeply do I feel impressed with the excellency and amiable sweetness of the grace of *charity*, that I am constrained to commend it to my readers in a distinct chapter. Charity is the queen of the graces, excelling even faith and hope, and enduring when all those gifts which add brilliancy to the character shall cease their attractions; and, though you may not possess great personal charms, superior accomplishments, or great powers of mind, yet, if you do but " put on charity," you will, like the blessed Savior, " grow in favor both with God and man."

The apostle calls charity the " bond of perfectness; " " alluding to the girdle of the Orientals, which was not only ornamental and expensive, but was put on last, serving to adjust the other parts of the dress, and keep the whole together." It is a bond which holds all the Christian graces in harmonious union, and, by keeping them together, secures a permanent completeness and consistency of character. Without the girdle, the flowing robes of Oriental dress would present a sad appearance, hardly serving the purposes of decency. So the apostle concludes that the most brilliant gifts and heroic actions are all nothing without charity.

Charity, however, is not to be understood in the popular sense of *almsgiving*. It is the same word which is elsewhere rendered *love*. It means a benevolent disposition of heart, — love to God, and good-will to man, — diffused through the whole character and conduct. But my principal object, in this chapter, will be to consider it in its manifestations, in our intercourse with our fellow-men; taking Paul's description of this grace in the thirteenth chapter of First Corinthians, and applying it so as to discover *negatively* what conduct is inconsistent with charity, and *positively* the effect of charity on the human character.

The apostle says, " Charity suffereth long, and is kind; charity envieth not; charity vaunteth not itself; is not puffed up; doth not behave itself unseemly; seeketh not her own; is not easily provoked; thinketh no evil; rejoiceth not in iniquity, but rejoiceth in the truth; beareth all things, believeth all things, hopeth all things, endureth all things."

I. Charity *suffereth long.* It will endure ill treatment, and prefer suffering to strife. It will not resent the first encroachments, but patiently bear with injuries as long as they can be borne. If charity reigns in your heart, you will consider how many and aggravated are your own offences against God, and yet that his long-suffering bears with your perverseness, and he is daily loading you with benefits; and shall you

5

be impatient of the slightest offences from a fellow-worm? Consider, also, how liable you are to encroach upon the rights of others, and to try their patience by your infirmities. Do not, therefore, be hasty in the indulgence of hard thoughts of others, nor impatient of their faults and infirmities. How much contention and strife might be avoided by a little forbearance! And who is there so perfect as not sometimes to need it to be extended toward himself? The ills of social life are greatly mitigated by the exercise of mutual forbearance; and they find no place under the sweet reign of charity.

II. But charity not only *suffereth long*, but *is kind.* "It is benign, bountiful, courteous, and obliging." But why did the apostle couple these two dispositions together? " *Charity suffereth long*, AND IS KIND." Evidently, because long-suffering, without kindness, would be unavailing. If you bear with the injuries or supposed offences of another, and yet suffer your mind to be soured, and your kind offices remitted, the wound will corrode and inflame till it breaks out with tenfold violence. But benignity of temper, and the constant practice of friendly offices and benevolent actions, will disarm ill-nature, and bring the offender to see the folly of his conduct. " A soft answer turneth away wrath, and the kind treatment of an enemy will pour coals of fire on his head." What can be more lovely than a kind and obliging disposition, which delights in occasions and opportunities of contributing to the comfort and happiness of others? This disposition adorns with peculiar grace the female character. Solomon, describing a virtuous woman, says, "In her tongue is the law of kindness." If you cultivate this disposition at all times, and in all places, your presence will add a charm to every circle; you will honor your Master, and your ability to advance his cause will be greatly enhanced. In your efforts to do good, with the law of kindness in your lips, you can penetrate where, without it, you could gain no admittance; and, in your expostulations with the impenitent, you can reach the heart by the exhibition of a kind and tender spirit, where otherwise you would be repulsed, like the seven sons of Sceva, who presumptuously attempted, in imitation of Paul, to cast out devils in the name of Jesus. Especially is this disposition requisite in a Sabbath school teacher. Without it he can accomplish very little. Children cannot be won without kindness. If, then, you would be successful in this enterprise of love, cultivate a tender regard for the "little lambs," and be kind to them whenever you meet them. Never see a child in trouble without relieving him; or, if you can do no more, show your sympathy for his sufferings by such kind offices as are within your power.

III. Charity *envieth not*. It is not grieved, but gratified, to see others more prosperous and wealthy, more intelligent and refined, or more holy. The extension of holiness and happiness is an object of rejoicing to the benevolent mind, without regard to self.

There are some persons who are always complaining of the rich, and fretting about the aristocratic spirit of those whose rank and station, education, or mental endowments, place them in any respect above themselves. This is a sure indication of an envious spirit. There may be, in these respects, some ground of complaint. But place these persons in the situation of those of whom they complain, and, where the latter are proud, the former would probably be aristocratic; and, where these are aristocratic, those would be tyrannical.

An envious disposition argues, 1. *A want of self-respect.* If we respect ourselves, we shall not desire the factitious importance arising from wealth, so much as to grieve that others have more of it than ourselves; nor shall we be willing to concede so much merit to the possession of wealth, as to suspect those who have it of esteeming us the less because we have it not. 2. It argues a *want of benevolence.* The truly benevolent mind desires the increase of rational enjoyment, and will therefore rejoice in the happiness of others, without respect to his own. 3. It argues a *want of magnanimity.* The truly great will rejoice in the intellectual and moral elevation of others, as adding so much to the sum of human excellence. But the envious person cannot bear to see any other one elevated above himself. This is the spirit that brought Haman to the gallows, and Satan from the seat of an archangel to the throne of devils. 4. It argues a *narrow, selfish spirit, — a little and mean mind.* The law of God requires us to love our neighbor as ourselves; and reason sanctions the requisition. But the envious person will hate his neighbor, because he is not permitted to love him less than himself.

If you regard your own happiness, I conjure you to suppress the first motions of this vile and hateful temper; for, while indulged, it will give you no peace; its envenomed darts will rankle and corrode in your bosom, and poison all your enjoyments. It is a disposition which can never be satisfied, so long as there is a superior being in the universe. It is aimed ultimately at the throne of God; and the envious person can never be happy while God reigns. The effects of this disposition upon human character and happiness are strikingly illustrated in the story of Haman, which I commend to your serious attention. Cultivate, then, the habit of being pleased and gratified with the happiness and prosperity of others; and constantly seek the grace of God, to enable you to exercise benevolent feelings toward all, but especially those who are elevated in any respect above you.

IV. *Charity vaunteth not itself,* (or, as in the margin, *is not rash,*) *is not puffed up.* "It does not act precipitately, inconsiderately, rashly, thoughtlessly." Some people mistake a rash and heedless spirit for genuine zeal; and this puffs them up with pride and vainglory, and sets them to railing at their betters in age, experience, or wisdom, because they will not fall into their views and measures. There is scarcely any trait of character more unlovely, especially in a young person, than self-conceit. If the youth who is puffed up with a sense of his own consequence could but see the mingled emotions of pity and disgust which his conduct excites in the bosom of

5 *

age and wisdom, he would be filled with confusion and shame.

You will hear such persons prating much of independence of mind. They profess to think for themselves, and form their own opinions, without respect to what others have thought, and said, and written. They would scorn to consult a commentary, to assist them in determining a difficult passage of Scripture, or the writings of a learned divine, to help them out of a theological difficulty. That would be subjecting their minds to the influence of prejudice, or betraying a want of confidence in their own infallible powers! — which is the last idea they would think of entertaining. The long-cherished opinions of great, and wise, and good men, are disposed of with a sneer. You will hear them delivering their opinions pragmatically, and with strong assurance, on points of great difficulty, which good men, of the greatest learning and ability, have approached with diffidence; and boldly advancing ideas which they suppose to have originated in the depths of their own recondite minds, which they are afterwards mortified to learn are but some old, cast-off, crude theories or speculations, which had been a hundred times advanced, and as many times refuted, before they were born. But the matters appear so plain to them, that they cannot imagine how any honest mind can come to any other conclusions than those to which they have arrived. Hence they are ready to doubt the piety of all who differ with them, if not to assume the office of judge, and charge them with insincerity or hypocrisy. But their strong confidence in their opinions arises from superficial and partial examination, and overlooking objections and difficulties which readily occur to the well-balanced and discriminating mind, which has thoroughly investigated the subject in hand.

Yet I would not be understood to recommend implicit submission to the judgment and opinions even of the greatest and best of men. This is Popery. The mind must be convinced before it yields assent to any position. But it would be the height of self-conceited arrogance for any person, but especially for a youth, to presume himself too wise to gain instruction from the writings of men who have devoted their lives to the investigation of truth; or summarily to set aside, as unworthy of his attention, opinions which have been embraced by the greatest and best of men for successive generations. Nor does it argue any uncommon independence of mind; for you will generally find such persons arranged under the banner of some one of the various schools of theology, morals, philosophy, or politics, and following on with ardor the devious course of their leader, receiving whatever falls from his lips as the voice of an oracle, and running with enthusiasm into all his extravagances. Like the vane upon the spire, that lifts up itself with proud eminence to the clouds, they are ready to be carried about by every wind of doctrine. Whereas true independence of mind consists in weighing evidence and argument impartially, and forming a decision independent of prejudice, party feeling, pride of opinion, or self-will;

and, when coupled with humility, it will always rejoice to receive instruction from any source. The person who knows himself will be deeply humbled under a sense of his own weakness and ignorance, and will advance his opinions with modesty, while he treats the opinions of others with becoming respect.

V. Charity *doth not behave itself unseemly.* It does not disregard the courtesies of life, nor break over the bounds of decency and decorum, but pays a strict regard to propriety of conduct, in all circumstances. There are many unseemly things which render the conduct of any person repulsive and disgusting.

Forwardness, or a disposition to be conspicuous, is unseemly, especially in a young person. It is, indeed, the duty of every one to be always ready to engage in every good work; and it is wrong to be backward, and refuse to coöperate with others in carrying on any useful enterprise. But the heart is deceitful; and, while we satisfy our consciences with the idea that we are going forward in the discharge of duty, we may be but feeding our own vanity, by bringing ourselves into notice. An humble Christian has a low estimate of his ability to do good, and is generally disposed to prefer others, as better qualified than himself, to occupy any conspicuous post. "In honor preferring one another." He will therefore be modest and retiring; though, when the course of duty is plain, he will by no means shrink from it. "The righteous are bold as a lion." There are several characteristics, however, which distinguish the forward, unseemly spirit. He is jealous and testy. You will hear him complaining of the aristocratic spirit of others ; and, if he is not noticed as much as he thinks he deserves, he will take offence. He will rarely be found cordially coöperating with others in any good work, unless he is foremost in it himself. If you wish to secure his aid, or forestall his opposition, you must be careful to consult him before you undertake any enterprise. Should you neglect to do so, however good your object, or well chosen your measures, you may expect him to find fault and throw obstacles in the way at every step of your progress. Such persons often exhibit a fiery zeal and a restless activity ; but they are never roused except for the promotion of an object with which *self* is in some manner identified.

To assume, in a dictatorial manner, to catechize others, as to their views on any subject, especially if they are older than yourself, is unseemly. You will meet with some persons who seem to take it for granted that they have a right to call you to account for your opinions, and to determine authoritatively your claim to the character which you profess. I do not question the propriety of kind and modest inquiries as to the opinions and views of others; nor of endeavoring, by fair and candid arguments, to convince them of what we suppose to be their errors. But, then, we must never forget that they are our equals, possessing the same right to judge of the truth with ourselves, and accountable for their errors to the same tribunal. This will leave no ground for the exercise of a dogmatical or a dictatorial spirit.

It is unseemly for young persons to be foremost in

speaking, in company, or to give advice with confidence, in regard to any thing which is to influence the conduct of their superiors in age, wisdom, or experience. Elihu, although a man of superior knowledge and abilities, did not presume to speak to Job till his aged friends had ceased; for he said, "Days should speak, and multitude of years should teach wisdom." Young persons sometimes render themselves ridiculous by such unseemly conduct. The prophet Isaiah gives this as one of the marks of a degenerate age, that "the child shall behave himself proudly against the ancient, and the base against the honorable."

Fierce contention about personal rights is unseemly. It begets a selfish, jealous spirit. You never hear this where love reigns; for love is a yielding spirit. The spirit that can never brook the least encroachment upon his rights is an unseemly spirit, which will always be embroiled in some difficulty or other.

All coarseness, grossness, or rudeness, of character is unseemly; and the declaration that charity doth not behave unseemly, conveys the idea of an exquisite propriety of deportment, free from every thing indelicate, obtrusive, repulsive, or unamiable.

VI. Charity *seeketh not her own.* It is not selfish. The temper here described is inculcated in a beautiful manner in Paul's Epistle to the Philippians. He exhorts them, in lowliness of mind, each to esteem other better than themselves; and not to look exclusively on their own things, but also on the things of others; and then commends to them the example of our Lord, who, though King of kings, humbled himself to the condition of a servant, enduring hardship, contumely, and an ignominious death, for our sakes. This does not mean that we are not to love ourselves at all, nor be entirely regardless of our own interests; for the rule which requires us to love our neighbor *as ourselves*, recognizes the right of self-love; and the command, " Thou shalt not steal," establishes the right of private property. But it forbids us to make our own interest and happiness our chief concern, to the disregard of the rights of others and the general good; and requires us to make sacrifices of feeling and interest for the benefit of others, and even sometimes to prefer their happiness and interest to our own. This is the spirit of genuine benevolence; and the exercise of it will impart far more elevated enjoyment than can be derived from private advantage.

Were this disposition in exercise, it would cut off all ground of envy and jealousy; it would remove the cause of most of the contentions that arise in society, and mitigate, in a wonderful degree, the ills of life. It lies at the foundation of all social enjoyment. The reciprocity of mutual affection depends upon the exercise of a self-sacrificing disposition; and the society where this does not exist is intolerable. Nor is it feeling or interest alone that must be given up. There is yet a more difficult sacrifice to be made, before we can be, in any considerable degree, comfortable companions. *It is the sacrifice of the will.* This is the last thing the selfish heart of man is disposed to yield. He has taken his stand, and the pride of his heart is committed to maintain it. He deceives .himself, and compels conscience to come to his aid; while, in reality, it is a matter with which conscience has nothing to do; for the point might have been yielded without doing violence to that ever-wakeful monitor, whose office is thus perverted, and made to subserve the purposes of stiff-necked obstinacy. A disposition to yield to the judgment and will of others, so far as can be done conscientiously, is a prominent characteristic of that charity which seeketh not her own; while an obstinate adherence to our own plans and purposes, where no higher principle than expediency is concerned, is one of the most repulsive and uncomfortable forms of selfishness.

A selfish person never willingly makes the smallest sacrifice of feeling or interest to promote the welfare or happiness of others. He wraps himself up in his own interests and pursuits, a cheerless and forbidding object. He would gladly know no law but his own will. He has a little world of his own, in which he lives, and moves, and has his being. He makes every one with whom he comes in contact contribute something to his own selfish purposes. His overweening desire to promote his own interests disposes him constantly to encroach upon the rights of others; or, if not to encroach upon their rights, to take advantage of their good nature, to drag them into his service. You might as well walk for pleasure in a grove of thorn-bushes, or seek repose on a bed of nettles, as to look for comfort in the society of selfish persons.

VII. Charity *is not easily provoked.* "It corrects

a sharpness of temper, and sweetens and softens the mind." It does not take fire at the least opposition or unkindness, nor "make a man an offender for a word." One of the servants of Nabal described his character in this significant manner: "He is such a son of Belial that a man cannot speak to him." There are many such sons and daughters of Belial. They are so sulky and sour, so fretful and peevish, that you can hardly speak to them but they will snap and snarl like a growling watch-dog; and if they were equally dangerous, it might not be less necessary to chain them. All this is the opposite of charity. The quality here negatively described may be summarily comprehended in the term *good nature;* but in a more elevated sense than this term is usually employed, it being the fruit, not of natural amiableness, but of gracious affection. This temper is essential to any considerable degree of usefulness. If you are destitute of it, your Christian character will be so marred as in a great measure to counteract the influence of your positive efforts. A bad temper, even in connection with many excellent qualities, may render a person an uncomfortable companion, and an intolerable yoke-fellow; thus bringing great reproach upon the cause of Christ. Nor need any one excuse himself on the ground of natural disposition; for the Lord has said, "My grace is sufficient for thee." The gospel of Jesus Christ is a remedy for all our natural corruptions; and we are required to lay aside *every weight,* even the sin that most easily besets us.

6

VIII. Charity *thinketh no evil*, is not suspicious, does not lay up slight expressions, or equivocal conduct, and reason out evil from them, and suffer it to corrode and sour the mind against an individual, but puts the best construction upon the words and conduct of others that they will bear, not yielding to an ill opinion of another but upon the most indisputable evidence. There is, perhaps, no more fruitful source of disquiet and unhappiness, both to ourselves and others, than a suspicious disposition. " Jealousy," says Solomon, " is cruel as the grave ; the coals thereof are the coals of fire which hath a most vehement flame." A jealous person always sees a " snake in the grass ; " he is afraid to trust his most intimate friend. He puts the worst construction upon the language and conduct of others that they will bear. Hence he conceives himself grossly insulted, when no ill was designed ; and a gentle rebuke, or a good-humored repartee, constitutes an unpardonable offence. He always looks on the dark side of human character ; so that a single foible, or one glaring fault, will eclipse a thousand real excellences. He is incessantly complaining of the degeneracy of the times, and especially of the corruption of the church ; for he can see nobody around him who is perfect, and therefore he comes to the conclusion that there is very little piety in the world, forgetting that, were he to find a church of immaculate purity, his own connection with it would introduce corruption. Should such a person conceive it to be his duty to tell you all your faults, wo betide you ! For, desirable as self-knowledge is, it is no kindness to have our faults aggravated a hundred-fold, and concentrated before our minds, like the converging rays of the sun, in one focal blaze, nor poured upon our heads like the sweeping torrent, nor eked out like the incessant patterings of a drizzling rain. Thus did not Paul. When he felt it his duty to reprove, he was careful to commend what was praiseworthy, and to throw in some expressions of kindness along with his censures. And here, though it be a digression, let me conjure you never to undertake the unthankful office of censor. You will find some inexperienced persons who will desire you, as an office of friendship, to tell them all their faults. Be sure, if you undertake this with a friend, your friendship will be short. It will lead you to look continually at the dark side of your friend's character; and, before you are aware, you will find yourself losing your esteem for him. Very soon, you will beget the suspicion that you have conceived some dislike. If the cause is continued, this suspicion will corrode and increase; and the result will be a mutual alienation of affection. However sincerely such an experiment may be entered upon, it can hardly fail, in the nature of things, to produce this result.

It may, however, be said that we are bound, by our covenant obligations, to *watch over our brethren*. But there can scarcely be a greater misapprehension than to understand this duty in the sense of an incessant lookout for the little faults and foibles, or even the more marked and glaring defects of character in our brethren. The injunction is, " If thy brother trespass

against thee, go and tell him his fault," &c. But we
are not required to procure a magnifying-glass, and go
about, making a business of detecting and exposing
the faults of our brethren.   On the contrary, there are
many cautions against a meddlesome disposition, and
against being busybodies in other men's matters.   We
are admonished, with great frequency and solemnity,
to watch ourselves ; but where is the injunction,
" Watch thy brethren " ?   Even the Savior himself
did not thus attempt to correct the faults of his disciples.   He rebuked them, indeed, and sometimes sharp-
ly ; but he was not continually reminding them of their
faults.   He was not incessantly browbeating Peter for
his rashness, nor Thomas for his incredulity, nor the
sons of Zebedee for their ambition ; but he " taught
them *as they were able to bear it ;* " and that rather
by holding up before their minds the truth, than by
direct personal lectures.

Our covenant obligations unquestionably make it
our duty to watch, and see that our brethren do not
pursue a course of life inconsistent with their Christian
profession, or which tends to backsliding and apostasy ;
and, if they are true disciples, they will be thankful
for a word of caution when they are in danger of
falling into sin.   And, when they do thus fall, we are
required to rebuke them, and not to suffer sin upon
them.   But this is a very different affair from that of
setting up a system of espionage over their conduct,
and dwelling continually upon their faults and deficiencies — a course which cannot long be pursued without
an unhappy influence upon our own temper.   The

human mind is so constituted as to be affected by the objects it contemplates, and often assimilated to them. Show me a person who is always contemplating the faults of others, and I will show you a dark and gloomy, sour and morose spirit, whose eyes are closed to every thing that is desirable and excellent, or amiable and lovely, in the character of man; a grumbling, growling misanthrope, who is never pleased with any body, nor satisfied with any thing; an Ishmaelite, whose hand is against every man, and every man's hand against him. If there is nothing in the human character, regenerated by the grace of God, on which we can look with complacency and delight, then it is impossible for us to obey the sacred injunction, " Love the brethren."

IX. *Charity rejoiceth not in iniquity*, but *rejoiceth in the truth*. One mark by which the people of God are known is, that they " sigh and cry over the abominations that are done in the land," and weep rivers of water, because men keep not the law of God; while the wicked " rejoice to do evil, and delight in the frowardness of the wicked." But we may deceive ourselves, and be indulging a morbid appetite for fault finding and slander, while we suppose ourselves to be grieving over the sins of others. Grief is a tender emotion; it melts the heart, and sheds around it a hallowed influence. Hence, if we find ourselves indulging a sharp, censorious spirit, — eagerly catching up the faults of others, and dwelling on them, and magnifying them, and judging harshly of them, — we may be sure we have another mark, which belongs

6 *

not to the fold of the good Shepherd. One of the prominent characteristics of an impenitent heart is a disposition to feed upon the faults of professors of religion. Those who indulge this disposition will not admit that they take delight in the failings of Christians. They will condemn them with great severity, and lament over the dishonor they bring upon religion. Yet they catch at the deficiencies of Christians as eagerly as ever a hungry spaniel caught after his meat. This is the whole of their spiritual meat and drink. It is the foundation of their hopes. They rest their claim for admittance into the celestial paradise on being as consistent in their conduct as some of those who profess to be God's people; hence, every deficiency they discover gives them a new plea to urge at the portals of heaven. Thus they secretly, though perhaps unwittingly, "rejoice in iniquity." But it is to be feared, if we may judge from the exhibition of the same spirit, that many who make high pretensions to superior sanctity rest their hopes, to a great extent, on a similar foundation. With the Pharisaical Jews, they think if they judge them that do evil, even though they do the same, they shall escape the judgment of God. They are as eager to catch up and proclaim upon the house-top the deficiencies of their brethren, as the self-righteous moralist, who prides himself on making no profession, and yet being as consistent as those that do. If such persons do not rejoice in iniquity, it is, nevertheless, " sweet in their mouth," and they " drink it in like water." Their plea is, that they do not speak of it with pleasure, but with grief bear their testimony against it. But grief is solitary and silent. "He sitteth alone, and keepeth silence." Who ever heard of a man's proclaiming his grief to every passing stranger? The harsh and bitter spirit, which palms itself on the conscience as a testimony against sin, is but an exhibition of impenitent pride. It bears not the most distant semblance of Christian humility and fidelity. "Brethren," says the apostle, "if a man be overtaken in a fault, restore such an one in the spirit of meekness; *considering thyself, lest thou also be tempted*." But, from the faultfinding and censorious spirit of some people, one would suppose it never came into their minds to consider whether it might not be possible for them to fall into the same condemnation; although an examination of the lamentable falls that have taken place might show a fearful list of delinquents from this class of persons. David, while in his fallen state, pronounced sentence of death upon the man in Nathan's parable, whose crime was but a faint shadow of his own. The Scribes and Pharisees were indignant at the wretched woman who had been taken in sin; yet they afterwards, by their own conduct, confessed themselves guilty of the same crime. Judas was one of your censorious fault finders. He was the disciple that found fault with the tender-hearted Mary, for her affectionate tribute of respect to the Lord of life, before his passion. He thought it a great waste to pour such costly ointment on the feet of Jesus, and that it would have been much better to have it sold, and the money given to the poor. He was very compas-

sionate to the poor, and a great enemy of extravagance;
but, a little while afterwards, he sold his Lord for thirty
pieces of silver.   So, in every age, if you examine into
the character of apostates, you will find that they have
been noted for their severity against the sins of others,
and particularly in making conscience of things indifferent, and pronouncing harsh judgment against those
who refuse to conform to their views.   Especially will
such persons be grieved with their brethren on accoun
of their dress, or style of living, or their manner of
wearing the hair, or some such matter, that does not
reach the heart.

The humble Christian, who looks back to the " hole
of the pit whence he was digged," and remembers
that he now stands by virtue of the same grace that
took his feet out of the " horrible pit and miry clay,"
will be the last person to vaunt over the fallen condition
of his fellow-creatures.   He will look upon them with
an eye of tender compassion, and his rebukes will be
administered in a meek, subdued, and humble spirit,
remembering the injunction of Paul : " Let him that
thinketh he standeth, take heed lest he fall."   But the
spirit of which I have been speaking is not only *carnal*,
but *devilish*.   The devil is the *accuser of the brethren*.

Charity not only rejoiceth not in iniquity, but *positively* rejoiceth in the truth — is glad of the success of
the gospel, and rejoices in the manifestation of the
grace of God, by the exhibition of the fruits of his Spirit
in the character and conduct of his people.   Hence it
will lead us to look at the bright side of men's characters, and, if they give any evidence of piety, to rejoice

in it, and glorify God for the manifestation of his grace in them, while we overlook, or behold with tenderness and compassion, their imperfections. And this accords with the feelings of the humble Christian. He thinks so little of himself, and feels such a sense of his own imperfections, that he quickly discerns the least evidence of Christian character in others; and he sees so much to be overlooked in himself, that he is rather inclined to the extreme of credulity, in judging the character of others. He is ready, with Paul, to esteem himself " less than the least of all saints; " and, where he sees any evidence of piety in others, he can overlook many deficiencies.

I am persuaded that we are greatly deficient in the exercise of joy and gratitude for the grace of God manifested in his children. The Epistles of Paul generally commence with an expression of joy and thanksgiving for the piety of those to whom he was writing. Even in regard to the Corinthians, among whom so many evils existed, he says, " I thank my God always on your behalf, *for the grace of God which is given you by Jesus Christ.*" But how seldom are we heard thanking God for the piety of our brethren !

X. Thus far, with the exception of the first two heads, and a part of the last, we have had the *negative* character of charity. We now come to its *positive* manifestations.

Charity *beareth all things ;* or, as it may be rendered, *covereth all things.* The latter seems to be more

agreeable to the context ; for otherwise it would mean
the same as *endureth all things*, in the latter clause of
the verse, and thus make a tautology ; while it leaves
a deficiency in the description, indicated by the passage
in Peter, " Charity shall cover the multitude of sins."
" Charity will draw a veil over the faults of others, so
far as is consistent with duty," in accordance with the
spirit of the golden rule, which requires us to do unto
others as we would they should do to us ; for who
would like to have his faults made the subject of common conversation among his acquaintances ?   And, if
it is contrary to charity thus to speak of the faults of
individuals, it is not the less so to speak of the faults of
masses of men, as of the clergy, or of the church.
The injustice is the more aggravated, because it is con-
demning by wholesale.   A member of the church of
Christ, who speaks much of its corruptions, is guilty of
the anomalous conduct of *speaking evil of himself ;* for
the members of Christ's body are *all one in him.*   It may
sometimes be our duty to speak of the faults of others ;
but, where charity reigns in the heart, this will be done
only in cases of unavoidable necessity, and then with
great pain and sacrifice of feeling.   The benevolent
heart feels for the woes of others, and even com-
passionates their weakness and wickedness.   It will
desire, therefore, as much as possible, to hide them
from the public gaze, unless the good of others should
require their exposure ; and even then, will not do it
with wanton feelings.   But these remarks apply with
much greater force to the practice of Christians speak-

ing of one another's faults. Where is the heart that
would not revolt at the idea of brothers and sisters
scanning each other's faults in the ears of strangers?
Yet the relation of God's children is far more endear-
ing than the ties of consanguinity. Suppose a family
of children, all of them in some manner deformed, yet
each possessing many excellences of person. What
would be thought of them, if they were always worry-
ing themselves and complaining about each other's
deformities? And what would be the effect on their
individual dispositions and feelings, and on the peace
and happiness of the family?

Charity *believeth all things, hopeth all things.* This
is the opposite of jealousy and suspicion. It is a readi-
ness to believe every thing in favor of others; and
even when appearances are very strong against them,
still to hope for the best. This disposition will lead us
to look at the characters of others in their most favorable
light; to give full weight to every good quality, and
full credit for every praiseworthy action; while every
palliating circumstance is viewed in connection with
deficiencies and misconduct. Charity will never attribute an action to improper motives or a bad design,
when it can account for it in any other way; and,
especially, it will not be quick to charge hypocrisy and
insincerity upon those who seem to be acting correctly.
It will give credit to the professions of others, unless
obviously contradicted by their conduct. It does not,
indeed, forbid prudence and caution — "The simple
believeth every word; but the prudent man looketh

well to his going "— but it is accustomed to repose
confidence in others, and it will not be continually
watching for evil.

A charitable spirit is opposed to the disposition to
discuss private character. It will not willingly listen
to criticisms upon the characters of others, nor the
detail of their errors and imperfections; and it will
turn away with disgust and horror from petty scandal
and evil-speaking, as offensive to benevolent feeling.
It is a kind of *moral sense*, which recoils from detrac-
tion and backbiting.

Charity *endureth all things*. This is nearly sy-
nonymous with long-suffering; and yet it is a more
comprehensive expression. Charity will endure with
patience, and suffer, without anger or bitterness of
feeling, every thing in social life which is calculated to
try our tempers, and exhaust our patience. It is not
testy, and impatient at the least opposition or the
slightest provocation; but endures the infirmities, the
unreasonableness, the ill-humor, and the hard language
of others, with a meek and quiet spirit.

XI. Finally, charity is the practical application of
the golden rule of our Savior, and the second table of
the law, to all our intercourse with our fellow-men,
diffusing around us a spirit of kindness and benevolent
feeling. It comprehends all that is candid and gener-
ous, bland and gentle, amiable and kind, in the human
character, regenerated by the grace of God. It is
opposed to all that is uncandid and disingenuous,
coarse and harsh, unkind, severe, and bitter, in the

disposition of fallen humanity. It is the bond which holds society together, the charm which sweetens social intercourse, the UNIVERSAL PANACEA, which, if it cannot cure, will at least mitigate, all the diseases of the social state.

7

CHAPTER V.

HARMONY OF CHRISTIAN CHARACTER.

NOTHING delights the senses like harmony. The eye rests with pleasure on the edifice which is complete in all its parts, according to the laws of architecture ; and the sensation of delight is still more exquisite, on viewing the harmonious combination of colors, as exhibited in the rainbow, or the flowers of the field. The ear, also, is ravished with the harmony of musical sounds, and the palate is delighted with savory dishes. But take away the cornice, or remove a column from the house, or abstract one of the colors of the rainbow, and the eye is offended ; remove from the scale one of the musical sounds, and give undue prominence to another, and harmony will become discord ; and what could be more insipid than a savory dish without salt ? So it is with the Christian character. Its beauty and loveliness depend on the harmonious culture of all the Christian graces in due proportion. If one is deficient, and another too prominent, the idea of deformity strikes the mind with painful sensations, like harsh, discordant musical sounds, or like the disproportionate combination of colors.

The apostle Peter, after exhorting to growth in

grace, says, " And besides this, giving all diligence, add to your faith virtue ; and to virtue, knowledge ; and to knowledge, temperance ; and to temperance, patience ; and to patience, godliness ; and to godliness, brotherly kindness ; and to brotherly kindness, charity." He would have the new man grow up with symmetrical proportions, so as to form the " stature of a perfect man in Christ Jesus," not having all the energies concentrated in one member, but having the body complete in all its parts, giving a due proportion of comeliness, activity, and strength, to each. Thus he says, *Add to your faith virtue.* By *faith* I suppose we are to understand the elementary principle of the Christian character, as exhibited in regeneration ; or the act which takes hold of Christ. But we are not to rest in this. We are to add *virtue,* or strength and courage, to carry out our new principle of action. But this is not all. We may be full of courage and zeal ; yet, if we are ignorant of truth and duty, we shall make sad work of it, running headlong, first into this extravagance, and then into that, disturbing the plans of others, and defeating our own, by a rash and heedless course of conduct.

Young Christians are in danger of making religion consist too exclusively in emotion, which leads them to undervalue knowledge. But, while emotion is inseparable from spiritual religion, knowledge is no less essential to intelligent emotion. Ignorance is not the mother of devotion ; and though a person may be sincerely and truly pious, with only the knowledge of a few simple principles, yet, without a thorough and

comprehensive knowledge of religious truth, the Christian character will be weak and unstable, easily led
astray, and "carried about by every wind of doctrine."
Knowledge is also essential to a high degree of usefulness. It expands and invigorates the mind, and
enables us, with divine aid, to devise and execute
plans of usefulness with prudence and energy.

But knowledge alone is not sufficient; nor even
knowledge added to faith. *Temperance* must be
added, as a regulator, both of soul and body. All
the appetites and passions, desires and emotions, must
be brought within the bounds of moderation. And to
temperance must be added *patience*, that we may be
enabled to endure the trials of this life, and not to faint
under the chastening hand of our heavenly Father.
As it is through much tribulation that we are to enter
into the kingdom of heaven, we have need of patience,
both for our own comfort and for the honor of religion.
Indeed, no grace is more needful in the ordinary affairs
of life. It is the little, every-day occurrences that try
the Christian character; and it is in regard to these
that patience works experience. Many of these things
are more difficult to be borne than the greater trials of
life, because it is more difficult to see the hand of God
in them. But patience enables us to endure those
things which cross the temper, with a calm, unruffled
spirit; to encounter contradictions, little vexations, and
disappointments, without fretting or repining; and
saves us from sinking under severe and protracted
afflictions.

To patience must be added *godliness*, "which is

profitable unto all things, having promise of the life
that now is, and of that which is to come." To be
godly, is to be, in a measure, *like God*. It is to be
" renewed in knowledge, after the image of him that
created us," and to have the same mind in us that was
in Christ Jesus. This is the fruit of that patience
which works experience, and results in hope, which
maketh not ashamed.

To godliness must be added brotherly kindness ;
which is but acting out the state of heart expressed
by *godliness*, which indicates a partaking of divine
benevolence.

Then comes the crowning grace of CHARITY,
" which is the bond of perfectness," comprehending
the whole circle of social virtues.

Where all these qualities exist in due proportion,
they will form a lovely character, harmonious and
beautiful as the seven colors of the rainbow ; yea,
with the addition of an eighth, of crowning lustre.
But, if any one suffers his religious feelings to concentrate on one point, as though the whole of religion
consisted in zeal, or devotional feeling, or sympathy, or
the promotion of some favorite scheme of benevolence,
you will find an exhibition of character as unlovely
and repulsive as though the seven colors of the rainbow should concentrate in one, of livid hue, or pale
blue, or sombre gray ; as disagreeable as though the
sweet melody of a harmonious choir were changed
into a dull, monotonous bass ; and as unsavory as a
dish of meats seasoned only with bitter herbs.

This disproportionate development of Christian char-

7 *

acter is more frequently seen in young converts, especially such as have not received a thorough Christian education, and are, consequently, deficient in religious knowledge. They find themselves in a new world, and become so much absorbed in the contemplation of the new objects that present themselves to their admiring gaze, that they seem almost to forget that they have any other duties to perform than those which consist in devotional exercises. If these are interrupted, they will fret and worry their minds, and wish for some employment entirely of a religious nature. They wonder how it is possible for Christians to be *so cold*, as to pursue their worldly employments as diligently as they do who take this world for their portion; and often you will hear them breaking out in expressions of great severity against older Christians, because they do not sympathize with them in these feelings. Their daily employments become irksome; and they are tempted even to neglect the interests of their employers, with the plea that the service of God has the first claim upon them. But they forget that the service of God consists in the faithful performance of every social and relative duty, " *as unto the Lord, and not to men*," as well as the more direct devotional exercises; and that the one is as essential to the Christian character as the other. The Bible requires us to be " diligent in business," as well as " fervent in spirit; " and the religion of the Bible makes us better in all the relations of this life, as well as in our relations with God.

Young Christians are also prone to undervalue *little*

things. The greater things of religion take such strong possession of their souls, that they overlook many minor things of essential importance. In seasons of special religious awakening, this mistake is very common; in consequence of which many important interests suffer, and the derangement which follows makes an unfavorable impression as to the influence of revivals. The spirit of the Christian religion requires that every duty should be discharged in its proper time.

The beauty of the Christian character greatly depends on its symmetrical proportions. A person may be very zealous in some things, and yet quite defective in his Christian character; and the probability is, that he has no more religion than shows itself in its consistent proportions. The new energy imparted by the regenerating grace of God may unite itself with the strong points of his character, and produce a very prominent development; while, in regard to those traits of character which are naturally weak, in his constitutional temperament, grace may be scarcely perceptible. For instance, a person who is naturally bold and resolute will be remarkable, when converted, for his *moral courage;* while, perhaps, he may be very deficient in *meekness.* And the one who is naturally weak and irresolute will, perhaps, be remarkable for the mild virtues, but very deficient in strength and energy of character. The error lies in cultivating, almost exclusively, those Christian graces which fall in with our prominent traits of character. We should rather bend our energies, by the grace of God, chiefly to the development of those points of character which are naturally weak, while we discipline, repress, and bring under control, those which are too prominent. This will prevent deformity, and promote a uniform consistency of character.

There is, perhaps, a peculiar tendency to this *one-sided* religion in this age of excitement and activity; and the young convert, whose Christian character is not matured, is peculiarly liable to fall into this error. The mind becomes absorbed with one object. The more exclusively this object is contemplated, the more it is magnified. It becomes, to his mind, the *main thing*. It is identified with his ideas of religion. He makes it a *test of piety*. Then he is prepared to regard and treat all who do not come up to his views on this point as destitute of true religion, however consistent they may be in other respects. This leads to denunciation, alienation of feeling, bitterness, and strife. But one of God's commands is as dear to him as another; and we cannot excuse ourselves before him for disobeying one of them, on the ground that all our energies are absorbed in securing obedience to another. The perfection of Christian character consists in the harmonious development of the Christian graces. This is the " stature of a perfect man in Christ Jesus," — a man who has no deformity, who is complete in all his faculties and members.

CHAPTER VI.

To a true child of God, nothing is so precious as
the volume of inspiration. It is like a mine of all
sorts of metals and precious stones, overlaid with gold
and silver. That which is most necessary for the
common purposes of life lies on the surface. These
are the simple truths of the gospel, which are essential to salvation. But below these are the iron, the
tin, the copper, — the strong truths, the doctrines, the
practical principles, which tax the powers of the
mind to develop, but which give strength and consistency to the Christian character. Yet beyond
these is an inexhaustible treasure of precious stones,
every examination of which discovers new gems of
surpassing lustre and surprising beauty.

The Bible is the charter of the Christian's hopes,
the deed of his inheritance. Is he a wayfaring man
in a strange land? This book contains a description
of the country to which he is bound, with a map of
the way, on which all the cross-ways and by-paths are
designated. Is he a mariner on the stormy ocean of
life? This is both his chart and compass. Here he
finds all the shoals and reefs distinctly marked, and

monuments placed upon many dangerous places, where others have made shipwreck.

Seeing, then, we have such a treasure put into our hands, it cannot be a matter of surprise that we should be directed to *search* after the precious things it contains, nor that Christians should love to ponder its sacred pages. "Thy word," says the Psalmist, "is a lamp unto my feet, and a light unto my path." It is like a lantern, which sheds light on our path, amid the darkness of the night, to direct the steps of our feet. The sincere Christian will therefore search the word of God, for a knowledge of his will, with more eagerness than he would search for hidden treasures of gold and silver. In obedience to the command of God, he will *set his heart* to the work. After the giving of the law, Moses says, " *Set your hearts* unto all the words which I testify among you this day." To *set our hearts* upon any object, implies such a love for it, and desire after it, as leads to a strong determination to make every possible effort to obtain it ; and this ought to be the settled and permanent feeling of our hearts, in regard to a knowledge of the will of God, as revealed in his word. And, as we obtain this knowledge, we should imitate the Psalmist, who said, " Thy word have I *hid in my heart*, that I might not sin against thee." His object, in hiding the word in his heart, was to know how to regulate his conduct so as not to sin against God. So must we hide the word of God in our hearts, and for the same reason. We must study it as the directory of life. Whenever we open this blessed book, this should be the sincere inquiry

of our heart: " Lord, what wilt thou have *me* to *do* ? "
Let us come to it with this childlike spirit of obedience, and we shall not fail to learn the will of God.
But when we have learned our duty in God's word,
the next thing is, to *do it without delay.* First, there
must be an earnest desire to know present duty, and
then a steadfast and settled determination to *do it as
soon as it is known.* The pressure of obligation rests
upon the present moment; and, when present duty is
ascertained, the delay of a single moment is *sin.*

With these remarks, I submit a few practical directions for the profitable reading and study of the Holy
Scriptures.

I. *Read the Bible in your closet, or under circumstances which will secure you from interruption, either
by the conversation of others, or the attraction of other
objects.* Do not attempt to fill up little broken intervals of time with the reading of God's word. Leave
these seasons for lighter reading. Reading the Scriptures is conversing with God, who speaks to us when
we read his holy word. His all-seeing eye rests upon
our hearts; and he knows whether we are engaged in
solemn trifling. If we read his word so carelessly
as not to understand its meaning, and drink in its
spirit, we treat him as we should disdain to be treated
by an earthly friend. Let us, then, never approach
the word of God but with feelings of reverence and
godly fear.

II. *Go to the word of God with a preparation of
heart.* If we were going to visit some person of great
consequence, whose favor and esteem we wished to

secure, we should take care to have every thing about our persons adjusted in the most becoming manner. So let it be with our minds when we come to converse with God.   Let us shut out all worldly thoughts, and strive to secure a tranquil, holy, and tender frame, so that the truths we contemplate may make their proper impression upon our hearts.

III. *Seek the aid of the Holy Spirit.*   Christ promised his disciples that, when the Holy Spirit should come, he would "*guide* them into all truth."   Without his enlightening influences, we cannot understand the word of God; and without his gracious influences, we shall not be disposed to obey it.   But we have the most abundant encouragement to seek the aid of this divine Instructor.   Christ assures us that God is more willing to give his Holy Spirit to them that ask him, than earthly parents are to give good gifts to their children.   Before opening God's word, therefore, we should pray that he would show us the truth, the rule of our duty, and incline our hearts to obey it; and, as we proceed, keep our hearts silently lifted up to God for the same object.

IV. *Read with self-application.*   Whenever you have discovered any truth, ask what bearing it has upon *present duty.*   If it relates to spiritual affections, compare with it the state of your own heart.   If it relates to the spirit and temper of Christians, in their intercourse with one another, or with the world, compare it with your own conduct.   If it relates to some positive duty, inquire whether you have done it.   And, wherever you find yourself deficient, endeavor to exercise repentance, and seek for pardon through the blood of Christ, with grace to enable you to correct what is wrong.

V. *Read the Scriptures regularly.* A daily supply of refreshment is no less necessary for the soul than for the body. The word of God is the bread of eternal life, " the food of the soul." Take, then, your regular supplies, that your soul may not famish. Choose for this purpose those seasons when you are least liable to interruption; when you can retire and shut out the world; when you can best command the energies of your mind. There is no time more fit and suitable for this than the morning. Then the mind is clear, vigorous, unencumbered, and prepared to receive impressions. There is also a propriety in consulting God's word at the close of the day. But this depends much on the state of the body. If you become exhausted and dull, after the labors of the day, I would rather recommend taking the whole time in the morning. But by no means confine yourself to these stated seasons. Whenever the nature of your pursuits will admit of your seclusion for a sufficient length of time to fix your mind upon the truth, you may freely drink from this never-failing fountain the water of life.

VI. *Study the Scriptures systematically.* If you read at random, here a little and there a little, your views of divine truth will be partial and limited. This method may, indeed, be pursued in regard to reading *strictly devotional;* but only when other time is taken for obtaining a connected view and a critical under-

8

standing of the whole Bible. The Holy Scriptures are like a dish of savory meats. There is almost every variety of style and matter. There is *history, biography, argumentative and didactic essays, and poetry.* Although these various kinds of writing are contained in a great number of books, written by various authors, at different times, without concert, yet a remarkable unity of design pervades the whole ; and perfect harmony of sentiment prevails throughout. Every thing, from the very beginning, points to the glorious plan of redemption revealed in the gospel. Although we may, at first view, feel the want of a regular system of divinity, yet a careful attention to the subject will discover Divine Wisdom in the present arrangement. We have here the principles of his government exhibited in *living examples ;* which give us a clearer view, and more vivid impression of them, than we could obtain from the study of an abstract system. In the systematic and thorough study of the Bible, the following hints may be of use : —

1. *Keep before your mind the grand design of the Scriptures ;* which is, to convince mankind of their lost and ruined condition, make known the way of salvation, and persuade them to embrace it.

2. *Make it your constant aim to ascertain what is the plain and obvious meaning of the writer ; for this is the mind of the Spirit.* To aid you in this, observe the following particulars : —

(1.) Endeavor to become acquainted with the peculiarity of each writer's style. Although the Scriptures were dictated by the Holy Spirit, yet it

was so done that each writer employed a style and
manner peculiar to himself. This does not invalidate
the evidence of their divine origin, but the rather
shows the wisdom of the Spirit; for, if the whole
Bible had been written in a uniform style, it would
have given opposers a strong argument against its
authenticity; while the want of that uniformity furnishes conclusive evidence that it could not have been
the work of a single impostor. Again, a continued
sameness of style would make the reading of so large
a book as the Bible tedious and unpleasant; but the
rich variety presented by the various authors of this
blessed book, helps our infirmities, and makes the
reading of it pleasing and delightful.

(2.) "Inquire into the character, situation, and
office of the writer; the time, place, and occasion of
his writing; and the people for whose immediate use
he intended his work." This will enable you to understand his allusions to particular circumstances and
customs, and to see the practical application of the
principles he advances.

(3.) Consider the principal scope or aim of the
book; or what was the author's object, design, or
intention, in writing it. Notice, also, the general plan
or method which he has pursued. This will enable
you to discover his leading ideas, if it be an argumentative work; or the particular instructions of God's
providence, if it be historical.

(4.) Where the language is difficult to be understood, pay strict attention to the context, and you will
generally find the author's meaning explained. But,

if not, consider whether the difficult phrase is a peculiarity of the writer's style. If so, look out the place where he has used it in a different connection, and see what meaning is attached to it there. But if this does not satisfy you, examine the passages in other parts of the Scriptures which relate to the same subject, and compare them with the one under consideration. This will generally clear up the darkest passages. But if you still feel in doubt, you may find assistance from consulting commentators, who have made themselves acquainted with the particulars I have mentioned; which, with a knowledge of the language in which the book was originally written, may have enabled them to remove the difficulty. But, in reading commentaries, always bear in mind that they are the productions of fallible men, whose *opinions* are not to be taken for Scripture. You may, however, avail yourself of their knowledge, without submitting your mind implicitly to their judgment; and this you will be compelled to do, because, on many points, they differ in opinion.

3. *Do not task yourself with a certain quantity of reading at the regular seasons devoted to the study of the Bible.* This may lead you to hurry over it, without ascertaining its meaning or drinking into its spirit. You had better study one verse thoroughly, than to read half a dozen chapters carelessly. The nourishment received from food depends less on the quantity than on its being perfectly digested. So with the mind : one clear idea is better than a dozen confused ones ; and the mind, as well as the stomach, may be

overloaded with undigested food. Ponder upon every portion you read, until you get a full and clear view of the truth which it teaches. Fix your mind and heart upon it, as the bee lights upon the flower; and do not leave it till you have extracted the honey it contains.

4. *Read in course.* By studying the whole Bible in connection, you will obtain a more enlarged view of its contents, and perceive more distinctly its unity of purpose. But I would not have you confine yourself entirely to the regular reading of the whole Bible in course. Some portions of the historical parts do not require so much *study* as that which is more argumentative and doctrinal; and some parts of the word of God are more devotional than others, and therefore better fitted for daily practical use. A very good plan is, to read the Old and New Testaments in course, a portion in each every day. If you begin at Genesis, Job, and Matthew, and read a chapter every day, at each place, omitting the first and reading three Psalms on the Sabbath, you will read the whole Bible in a year, while on every day you will have a suitable variety. Besides this, the more devotional and practical books should be read frequently. The Psalms furnish a great variety of Christian experience, and may be resorted to with profit and comfort, in all circumstances. This is the only book in the Bible which does not require to be read in course. The Psalms are detached from each other, having no necessary connection. The other books were, for the most part, originally written like a sermon or a letter. They

8 *

have, for convenience, since been divided into chapters and verses. If you read a single chapter by itself, you lose the connection; as, if you should take up a sermon and read a page or two, you would not get a full view of the author's subject. I would therefore recommend that, in addition to your daily reading in the Old and New Testaments, you always have in a course of thorough and critical study some one of the most difficult and fruitful of these books. But, if you attend the Sabbath school, either as teacher or pupil, the lessons there studied will be sufficient for this purpose. Before beginning the *study* of a book, you ought to take an opportunity to read the whole of it rapidly at one sitting, in order to learn the author's scope and design. You will find this a profitable practice, whenever you have time for it; and you will be especially interested to review, in this way, the books you have studied; and the more thoroughly they have been studied, the more deeply will you be interested in the review. You will find great advantage from the use of a reference Bible and concordance. By looking out the parallel passages, as you proceed, you will see how one part of the Scriptures explains another, and how beautifully they all harmonize. But, for the reading of the Scriptures, a paragraph Bible, without the divisions of chapters and verses, when you become accustomed to it, will be more pleasant and profitable than the common Bible.

5. In reading the Scriptures, there are some subjects of inquiry which you should carry along with you constantly : —

(1.) *What do I find here which points to Christ?*
Unless you keep this before your mind, you will lose
half the interest of many parts of the Old Testament;
and much of it will appear to be almost without
meaning. It is full of types and prophecies relating
to Christ, which, by themselves, appear dry, but, when
understood, most beautiful and full of instruction.

(2.) *The Bible contains a history of the church.*
Endeavor, then, to learn the state of the church at the
time of which you are reading. For the sake of convenience, and a clearer view of the subject, you may
divide the history of the church into six periods:
1. From the fall to the flood; 2. From Noah to
the giving of the law; 3. From Moses to David
and the prophets; 4. From David to the Babylo-
nish captivity; 5. From the captivity to Christ;
6. From Christ to the end of time, which is called
the gospel dispensation. From the commencement
you will see a gradual development of God's designs
of mercy, and a continually-increasing light. Take
notice of what period of the church you are reading;
and from this you may judge of the degree of obligation of its members; for this has been increasing with
the increase of light, from the fall to the present day;
and it will continue to increase to the end of time.
Note, also, the various declensions and revivals of
religion which have occurred in every period of the
church, and endeavor to learn their causes and consequences. By this, you will become familiar with
God's method of dealing with his people; from which

you may draw practical lessons of caution and encouragement for yourself.

(3.) Inquire what doctrinal truth is taught, illustrated, or enforced, in the passage you are reading; and also what *principle* is recognized. Great and important principles of the divine government and of practical duty are often implied in a passage of history which relates to a comparatively unimportant event. Let it be your business to draw out these principles, and apply them to practice. Thus you will be daily increasing your knowledge of the great system of divine truth.

(4.) Note every promise and every prediction; and observe God's faithfulness in keeping his promises, and fulfilling his prophecies. This will tend to strengthen your faith. You will find it profitable, as you proceed, to take notes of these several matters particularly; and, at the close of every book, review your notes, and sum them up under different heads.

6. Read the Gospels with great care, for the purpose of studying the character of the blessed Jesus. Dwell upon every action of his life, and inquire after his motives. By this course you will be surprised to find the Godhead shining through the manhood in little incidents which you have often read without interest. Look upon him at all times in his true character, as Mediator between God and man. Observe his several offices of Prophet, Priest, and King. See in which of these characters he is acting at different times; and inquire what bearing the particular action

you are considering has upon his mediatorial character. Observe, also, the particular traits of character
which appear conspicuous in particular actions ; — as,
power, energy, manly hardihood, dignity, condescension, humility, love, meekness, pity, compassion, tenderness, forgiveness, &c. Take notes ; and when
you have finished the course, draw from them, in
writing, a minute and particular description of his
character. This will be of great service to you as a
pattern. You will also, by this means, see a peculiar
beauty and fitness in Christ for the office he has
undertaken, which you would not otherwise have
discovered. But do not stop with going through this
course once. Repeat it as often as you can consistently with your plan of a systematic study of the
Holy Scriptures. You will always find something
new ; and upon every fresh discovery, you can revise
your old notes.

7. In reading the historical and biographical parts
of Scripture, observe, —

(1.) The histories contained in the Bible are the
histories of God's providence. Notice his hand in
every event, and inquire what principle or law of
his moral government is exemplified, carefully observing its application to nations, communities, and
individuals.

(2.) When you read of particular mercies or
judgments, look back for the cause ; that you may
discover the principles on which God administers his
most holy, wise, and just government.

(3.) In the biographies of the Bible, study the

motives and conduct of the characters described. If
they are unconverted men, you will learn the workings
of human depravity, and discover what influence a
correct religious public sentiment has in restraining
that depravity. If they are good men, you will see,
in their good actions, living illustrations of the great
doctrines of the Bible. Endeavor to learn by what
means they made such attainments in holiness, and
strive to imitate them. If any of their actions are
bad, look back and inquire into the cause of their
backslidings. If you discover it, you will find a way-
mark, to caution you against falling into the same pit.

8. The poetical and didactic parts of the Scriptures
are scattered throughout the whole Bible. These
abound with highly-wrought figures. This is probably
owing partly to the insufficiency of ordinary language
to express the lofty and sublime ideas presented to the
minds of the writers by the Spirit of truth, and partly
to the method of communicating ideas which always
prevails in the infancy of language. Endeavor to
understand the figures used. They are often taken
from prevailing habits and customs, and from circumstances peculiar to the countries where the Scriptures
were written. These habits and circumstances you
must understand, or you will not see the force of the
allusions. Others are taken from circumstances peculiar to particular occupations in life. These must also
be thoroughly studied, in order to be understood. But
where the figures are drawn from things perfectly
familiar, you will not perceive their surprising beauty
and exact fitness to express the idea of the sacred

penman, until you have carefully studied them, and noted the minutest circumstances. Beware, however, that you do not carry out these figures so far as to lead you into fanciful and visionary interpretations.

9. The books of the prophets consist of reproofs, exhortations, warnings, threatenings, predictions, and promises. By carefully studying the circumstances and characters of those for whom they were written, you will find the principles and laws of God's government set forth, in their application to nations, communities, and individuals. From these you may draw practical rules of duty, and also learn how to view the hand of God, in his providence, in different ages of the world. The predictions contained in these books are the most difficult to be understood of any part of the Bible. In reading them you will notice, —

(1.) Those predictions whose fulfilment is recorded in the Bible, and diligently examine the record of their fulfilment. You will see how careful God is to fulfil every jot and tittle of his word.

(2.) There are other prophecies, the fulfilment of which is recorded in profane history ; and others still which are yet unfulfilled. To understand these, it will be necessary to read ancient and modern history, in connection with the explanation of the prophecies, by those writers who have made them their study. Attention to this, so far as your circumstances will admit, will be useful in enlarging your views of the kingdom of Christ. But beware of becoming so deeply absorbed in these matters as to neglect those of a more practical nature ; and, especially, be cautious of advancing far into the regions of speculation, as to what is yet future.

10. You will find it an interesting and profitable employment, occasionally to read a given book through for the purpose of seeing what light it throws upon some particular point of Christian doctrine, duty, practice, or character. For example, go through with Acts, with your eye upon the doctrine of Christ's divinity. Then go through with it a second time, to see what light it throws on the subject of Revivals of Religion. Pursue the same course with other books, and in respect to other subjects. In this way, you will sometimes be surprised to find how much you have overlooked in your previous reading.

The foregoing suggestions may appear formidable, on account of the time and study requisite to carry them into execution. But it is to be remembered that the young Christian has his lifetime before him, and that his great business is to obtain a knowledge of divine things. The plan is not sketched with the expectation that every thing here recommended will be accomplished in a single year; but with the view of laying out business for life.

CHAPTER VII.

CHRIST and the apostles insist much on the duty of prayer; and this service has ever been the delight of the true children of God. In ancient times, it was considered the distinguishing mark of the pious that they "called upon God." All the holy men of God, of whom we read in the Scriptures, abounded in prayer. Abraham, Isaac, and Jacob, erected altars to the Lord wherever they pitched their tents. Moses, David, Elijah, Daniel, and other eminent saints, under the Old Testament, were mighty in prayer. The Jews regarded this as so essential to a pious life, that their houses were furnished each with an apartment for private devotion; and, in the mountains and desert places, little oratories were erected, to which devout persons retired, for more protracted seasons of communion with God. The Lord Jesus, our great Pattern, has set before us a life of prayer. The spirit of devotion characterized all that he did. He observed special seasons of prayer, before engaging in matters of importance. After having been employed in the work of his ministry, in the most laborious manner, during the day, we find him retiring to the mountains, or to some desert place, to commune with his Father;

9

sometimes spending the whole night in prayer to God.
And his example was followed by his apostles, whom
he endowed with inspiration and miraculous gifts, to
qualify them for settling the order of the Christian
dispensation. But, if it became inspired apostles, and
even the Lord of life and glory, to spend much time
in prayer, how much more such weak and sinful creatures as we are, who are surrounded with temptations
without, and beset with corruptions within!

The advantages of prayer are twofold. It secures
to us the blessings which we need, and also brings us
into a proper attitude for receiving them. The Lord
does not need to be informed of our wants, for they
are open to his view before they are known to us;
but he has been pleased to require us to ask for the
things which we desire, as one condition of granting
them. And surely it is a reasonable requirement, that
we should thus acknowledge our dependence upon
Him "from whom cometh down every good and
perfect gift." Moreover, the necessity of so doing
leads us to a sense of our need, to feel our unworthiness, and to keep in view our dependence upon
God. It likewise exercises our faith in his existence,
and confidence in his promises. This is the great
channel of intercourse between man and his Maker,
and should, therefore, be esteemed not merely a duty,
but a most blessed privilege.

As to the *nature of prayer*, it is the offering up of
the sincere desires and devout emotions of the heart
to God. It consists of the several parts of *adoration,
confession, supplication, intercession,* and *thanksgiv-*

ing. The first of these is an expression of a sense of the infinite majesty and glory of God. *Confession* is an humble acknowledgment of our sins and unworthiness. *Supplication* is pleading for blessings upon ourselves. *Intercession* is prayer for others. *Thanksgiving* is an expression of gratitude to God for his goodness and mercy towards us and our fellow-creatures. All these several parts are embraced in the prayers recorded in Scripture, though all of them are not generally found in the same prayer. The prayer of Solomon, at the dedication of the temple, commences with adoration, and proceeds with supplication and intercession. The prayer of Daniel, in the time of the captivity, commences with adoration, and proceeds with confession, supplication, and intercession. The prayer of the Levites, in behalf of the people, after the return from captivity, commences with thanksgiving and adoration, and proceeds with confession, supplication, and intercession. The prayers of David are full of penitential confession and thanksgiving. The prayer of Habakkuk consists of adoration, supplication, and thanksgiving. The prayer of the disciples, after the joyous return of the apostles from the council of their persecutors, consists of adoration, a particular rehearsal of their circumstances, and supplication. Paul particularly enjoins " prayer and supplication, with thanksgiving." The prayers recorded in Scripture, though probably but the substance of what was said on the several occasions when they were offered, are excellent models. Their simplicity, fervor, and directness, show them to have been the language of the heart; and this is prayer. The Lord's prayer furnishes a comprehensive summary of the subjects of prayer; and the prominent place assigned to the petition, " Thy kingdom come," shows that, in all our prayers, the glory of God should be our leading desire. But it is evident that Christ did not intend this as a particular form of prayer, to be used on all occasions; although it includes all that is necessary. We are affected with a *particular* consideration of the subjects in which we are interested; and therefore it is necessary to specify our particular circumstances, wants, and desires. We find our Lord himself using other words, to suit particular occasions; and so did the apostles and early Christians. This is only intended as a general pattern; nor is it necessary that all the petitions contained in the Lord's prayer should ever be made at the same time.

Prayer must always be offered in the name of Christ. There is no other way of approach to God; neither is there any other channel through which we can receive blessings from him. Jesus is our Advocate with the Father. He stands on the right hand of God, to make intercession for us. If you were desirous of obtaining the favor of some exalted person, you would not go directly to him yourself; but you would endeavor to enlist the kind offices of some one who had influence with him, to intercede for you. And especially, if a criminal desires pardon of a king or a governor, he will not send a petition in his own name, but endeavor to obtain the intercession of others. We are all condemned criminals before God, and in the eye of his law; and therefore we cannot come directly to him in our own name. But with Jesus he is ever well pleased. Him he always hears. And Jesus will intercede for all who come unto God by him. But this does not forbid us to pray directly to Christ, as God manifest in the flesh, which was a common practice with the apostles.

It is truly wonderful that the Infinite God should condescend to be influenced in his administration by the creatures which his own hand has made; and much more so, that he should listen to the petitions, and grant the requests, of such unworthy and sinful creatures as we are. Yet no one who attentively considers the promises which he has made to his people, can doubt the fact. Nor does this interfere with the immutability of God; since, in the counsels of eternity, his determinations were formed in view of the prayers of his saints; so that his administration is eternally and unchangeably affected by them.

David addresses God as the *hearer of prayer*, as though that were a distinguishing trait in his character. He says, also, " He will *regard* the prayer of the destitute, and *not despise* their prayer." Solomon says, " The prayer of the upright is *his delight;*" and, " He heareth the prayer of the righteous." The apostle James declares that " the effectual, fervent prayer of a righteous man *availeth much.*" Peter says, " The eyes of the Lord are over the righteous, and his ears are open unto their prayers." And Christ himself has assured us, in the strongest possible terms, of the disposition of God to give spiritual bless-

9 *

ings to those that ask for them. He says, "Ask, and it shall be given you; seek, and ye shall find; knock, and it shall be opened unto you. For *every one* that asketh, receiveth; and he that seeketh, findeth; and to him that knocketh, it shall be opened." And then, anticipating the difficulty of our believing a truth so wonderful and glorious, he appeals to the tenderest sympathies of our natures, and asks if any father would insult the hungry cries of his beloved son, when fainting for a morsel of bread, by giving him a stone; or, if he ask an egg, to gratify his appetite, will he give him a venomous scorpion, to sting him to death? * He then argues that, if sinful men exercise tender compassion towards their children, how much more shall our heavenly Father, whose very nature is love, regard the wants of his children who cry unto him!

These promises are confirmed by striking examples, in every age of the church. Thus Abraham prayed for Sodom; and, through his intercession, Lot was saved. Jacob wrestled all night in prayer, and prevailed, and received the blessing which he sought. Moses prayed for the plagues to come upon Egypt, and they came; again, he prayed for them to be removed, and they were removed. It was through his prayers that the Red Sea was divided, the manna and the quails were sent, and the waters gushed out of the rock. And through his prayers, many times, the arm of the Lord was stayed, which had been lifted up to destroy his rebellious people. Samuel — that lovely

* The scorpion is a little animal, of the shape of an egg, whose sting is deadly poison.

example of early piety, and the judge and deliverer of Israel — was given in answer to the prayer of his mother. When the children of Israel were in danger of being overcome by the Philistines, Samuel prayed, and God sent thunder and lightning, and destroyed the armies of their enemies. Again, to show their rebellion against God, in asking a king, he prayed, and God sent thunder and lightning upon them in the time of wheat-harvest. In order to punish the idolatry and rebellion of the Israelites, Elijah prayed earnestly that it might not rain ; and it rained not for three years and six months. Again, he prayed that it might rain, and there arose a little cloud, as a man's hand, which spread, and covered the heavens with blackness, till the rain descended in torrents. Hezekiah, when about to die, had fifteen years added to his life, in answer to prayer ; and, when Jerusalem was invaded by the army of Sennacherib, and menaced with destruction, he prayed, and the angel of the Lord entered the camp of the invader, and, in one night, slew one hundred and eighty-five thousand men. When all the wise men of Babylon were threatened with death, because they could not discover Nebuchad-nezzar's dream, Daniel and his companions prayed, and the dream and its interpretation were revealed. It was in answer to the prayer of Zacharias that the angel Gabriel was sent to inform him of the birth of John the Baptist. It was after ten days of united prayer that the Holy Ghost came down, on the day of Pentecost, " like a mighty rushing wind." Again, while the disciples were praying, the place was shaken where they were assembled, to show that God heard their prayers. It was in answer to the prayers of Cornelius that Peter was sent to teach him the way of life. When Peter was imprisoned by Herod, the church set apart the night of his expected execution for special prayer in his behalf. The Lord sent his angel, opened the prison doors, and restored him to the agonizing band of brethren. And when Paul and Silas were thrown into the dungeon, with their feet fast in the stocks, they prayed, and there was a great earthquake, which shook the foundations of the prison, so that all the doors were thrown open.

But the faithfulness of God to his promises is not confined to Scripture times. Although the time of miracles is past, yet every age of the church has furnished examples of the faithfulness of God in hearing the prayers of his children. These, however, are so numerous, that a selection only can be here referred to. When the Arians, who denied the Deity of Christ, were about to triumph, the bishop of Constantinople, and one of his ministers, spent a whole night in prayer. The next day, Arius, the leader of his party, was suddenly cut off by a violent and distressing disease. This prevented the threatened danger. Augustine was a wild youth, sunk in vice, and a violent opposer of religion. His mother persevered in prayer for him nine years, when he was converted, and became the most eminent minister of his age. The life of Francke exhibits many signal answers to prayer. His orphan-house was literally built up and sustained by prayer. Mr. West (afterwards Dr. West) became pastor of the

Congregational church in Stockbridge, Massachusetts, while destitute of piety. Two pious females of his congregation often lamented to each other that they received no edification from his preaching. At length, they agreed to meet once a week, to pray for him. They continued this for some time, under much discouragement. But, although the Lord tried their faith, yet he never suffered them both to be discouraged at the same time. At length their prayers were heard. There was a sudden and remarkable change in his preaching. " What is this ? " inquired one of them. " God is the hearer of prayer," replied the other. The Spirit of God had led Mr. West to see that he was a blind leader of the blind. He was converted, and changed his cold morality for the cross of Christ, as the basis of his sermons. A pious slave in Newport, R. I., was allowed, by his master, to labor for his own profit whatever time he could gain by extra diligence. He laid up all the money he earned in this way, for the purpose of purchasing his freedom, and that of his family. But, when some of his Christian friends heard what he was doing, they advised him to spend his *gained* time in fasting and prayer. Accordingly, the next day that he gained he set apart for this purpose. But, before the close of the day, his master, not knowing how he was employed, sent for him, and gave him a written certificate of his freedom. This slave's name was Newport Gardner. He was a man of good character and ardent piety ; and, in 1825, he was ordained deacon of a church of colored people who went out from Boston to Liberia. Instances of surprising answers to prayer, no less striking than these, are continually occurring at the present day. But of these I will mention only one. A few years ago, a pious widow had a son at college, who was a wild youth, and a great trial to her. On a certain occasion, he visited the metropolis, where there was, at the time, a religious awakening. Going out, one evening, to seek his pleasure, he strolled into the theatre; but, without being conscious of the cause, he began to feel uneasy in his mind, lost his interest in the play, and went out into the street. Seeing lights in the vestry of a church not far distant, he went in, and there was deeply affected. In the course of a few days, he became, as was believed, a "new creature." Soon after, he received a letter from his mother, who stated that, having heard of his intended visit to the city, and knowing that there was an awakening there, she had called together some of her friends to pray for him; and it appeared, from the date, that *this meeting for prayer in his behalf was held the evening when he was at the theatre!*

With the evidence here presented, who can doubt that God hears and answers prayer? But the objection arises, " If this doctrine be true, why is it that Christians offer up so many prayers without receiving answers?" The apostle James gives some explanation of this difficulty. " Ye ask, and receive not, *because ye ask amiss.*" It becomes us, then, seriously and diligently to inquire how we may *ask aright*, so as to secure the blessings so largely promised in answer to prayer. In relation to this subject, there are several things to be observed.

1. *We must sincerely desire the things which we ask.* If a child should ask his mother for a piece of bread, when she knew he was not hungry, but was only trifling with her, instead of granting his request, she would have cause to punish him for mocking her. And do we not often come to the throne of grace when we do not really feel our perishing need of the things we ask? God sees our hearts; and he is not only just in withholding the blessing we ask, but in chastising us for solemn trifling.

2. *We must desire what we ask, that God may be glorified.* "Ye ask amiss, *that ye may consume it upon your lusts.*" We may possibly ask spiritual blessings for self-gratification; and, when we do so, we have no reason to expect that God will bestow them upon us.

3. *We must ask for things* AGREEABLE TO THE WILL OF GOD. "And this is the confidence that we have in him, that if we ask any thing *according to his will*, he heareth us." The things that we ask must be such, *in kind*, as he has indicated his disposition to bestow upon us. Such are spiritual blessings on our own souls, the supply of our necessary temporal wants, and the extension of his kingdom. These are the *kind* of blessings that we are to ask; and the degree of confidence with which we are to look for an answer must be in proportion to the positiveness of the promises. Our Lord assures us that our heavenly Father is more willing to give good things, and particularly his Holy Spirit, to them that ask him, than earthly parents are to give good gifts to their children;

and he declares, expressly, that our sanctification is agreeable to the will of God. The promises of the daily supply of our necessary temporal wants are equally positive. We may also pray for a revival of religion in a particular place, and for the conversion of particular individuals, with strong ground of confidence, because we know that God has willed the extension of Christ's kingdom, and that the conversion of sinners is, *in itself*, agreeable to his will. But we cannot certainly know that he intends to convert a particular individual, or revive his work in a particular place, at a particular time; nor can we be sure that the particular temporal blessing that we desire is what the Lord sees to be needful for our present necessities; though our hope and expectation of receiving these blessings may be greatly strengthened by the freedom of access to the mercy-seat, and the sweet and confiding acquiescence in the will of God, which we experience in asking for them.

4. *We must ask in faith.* "But let him ask in faith, nothing wavering. For he that wavereth is like a wave of the sea, driven with the winds, and tossed. For let not that man think that he shall receive any thing of the Lord." Much has been said and written respecting the "*prayer of faith;*" and different opinions have been expressed in relation to the exercise of the soul which is so designated by the apostle James. I shall advance no theory on the subject. The main thing is, to maintain such a nearness to God as shall secure an experimental knowledge of it. Two things, however, are essential to the prayer of

faith. There must be *strong confidence in the existence and faithfulness of God.* " He that cometh unto God must believe *that he is,* and that *he is a rewarder of them that diligently seek him.*" The prayer of faith must also be *dictated by the Holy Spirit.* Faith itself is declared to be " the *gift of God ;* " and the apostle says, " The Spirit also helpeth our infirmities ; for we know not what we should pray for as we ought, but the Spirit itself maketh intercession for us, with groanings which cannot be uttered." " He maketh intercession for the saints, according to the will of God." When this is understood, we are no longer astonished that God should assure us, by so many precious promises, that he will hear and answer our prayers. Christians are called the Temple of the Holy Ghost ; and if the Holy Ghost dwell in us, to guide and direct us in all our ways, will he forsake us in so important a matter as prayer ? O, then, what a solemn place is the Christian's closet, or the house of prayer ! There the whole Trinity meet in awful concert. The Holy Spirit there presents to the Everlasting Father, through the Eternal Son, the prayers of a mortal worm ! Is it any wonder that *such a prayer* should be heard ? With what holy reverence and godly fear should we approach this consecrated place !

5. We must ask in a *spirit of humble submission,* yielding our will to the will of the Lord, committing the whole case to him, in the true spirit of our Lord's agonizing prayer in the garden, when he said, " *Not my will, but thine, be done.*" It is often the case that

10

a blessing is delayed until we come into just this frame of spirit — when we seem to have no will of our own, but are willing that God should exercise his holy and wise sovereignty, and dispose of the whole case according to his good pleasure ; and then the blessing comes, often with greater measure than we had dared to ask.

PRACTICAL DIRECTIONS.

1. *Maintain a constant spirit of prayer.* " Continuing instant in prayer." " Praying always, with all prayer and supplication in the Spirit." " And he spake a parable unto them, to this end, that men ought always to pray, and not to faint." The meaning of these passages is, not that we should be all the time exclusively engaged in prayer, to the neglect of every thing else ; but that we should maintain such a prayerful frame, that, the moment our minds are disengaged, our hearts will rise up to God. Intimately connected with this is the practice of *ejaculatory prayer*, which consists of a short petition, silently and suddenly sent up from the heart. This may be done any where, and under all circumstances. Nehemiah offered up a silent prayer to God, as he presented the cup to the king of Persia, that he might find favor, in the request which he was about to make ; and so may we do, in all circumstances of difficulty. This kind of prayer is indispensable to the Christian warfare. It helps us in resisting temptation ; and by means of it we can seek divine aid in the midst of the greatest emergencies.

But to maintain this incessant spirit of prayer is a very difficult work. It requires unwearied care and watchfulness, labor and perseverance. Yet no Christian can thrive without it.

2. *Observe stated and regular seasons of prayer.* Some make so much of the foregoing, as to neglect all audible and formal prayer. This is evidently unscriptural. Our Savior directs us to enter into our closet, and, when we have shut the door, to pray to our Father who is in secret. And to this precept he has added the sanction of his own example. In the course of his history, we find him often retiring to solitary places, to pour out his soul in prayer. Other examples are also recorded in Scripture. David says, " Evening, and morning, and at noon, will I pray." And again, " Seven times a day do I praise thee." It was the habitual practice of Daniel to kneel down in his chamber, and pray three times a day. But this practice is so natural, and so agreeable to Christian feeling, that no argument seems necessary to persuade those who have any piety to observe it. It has been the delight of the saints in all ages to retire alone, and hold communion with God.

No very definite rule can be given, as to the particular time of prayer. There is a peculiar propriety in visiting the throne of grace in the morning, to offer up the thanksgiving of our hearts for preservation, and to seek grace for the day ; and also in the evening, to express our gratitude for the mercies we have enjoyed, to confess the sins we have committed, seek for pardon, and commit ourselves to the care of a covenant-keep-

ing God, when we retire to rest. It is also very
suitable, when we suspend our worldly employments
in the middle of the day to refresh our bodies, to renew our visit to the fountain of life, that our souls may
also be replenished. The twilight of the evening is
likewise a favorable season for devotional exercises.
But it is of the greatest importance that every one
should set apart stated and regular seasons, every day,
for private devotion. This is necessary in order to
secure the end — to " pray without ceasing; " which
means that we should pray, not occasionally, as we
happen to feel disposed, but habitually. These seasons should be regarded as *engagements with God;*
and when unavoidably interrupted, the first time at
our command should be observed instead of the regular season. But, when our souls delight in communion
with God, we shall be disposed, in addition to these
regular and stated seasons, to retire often to pour out
our hearts before him, and receive fresh communica-
tions of his grace. This we need, to prevent our
hearts from coming under the power of sensible
objects, and clinging to earth.

For devotional exercises, we should select those
times and seasons when we usually find our minds
vigorous and our feelings lively. As the morning
is, in many respects, most favorable, it is well to
spend as much time as we can in the closet before
engaging in the employments of the day. An hour
spent in reading God's word, and in prayer and praise,
early in the morning, will give a heavenly tone to the
feelings; which, by proper watchfulness, and frequent

draughts at the same fountain, may be carried through all the pursuits of the day.

As already remarked, our Lord, in the pattern left us, has given a very prominent place to the petition, " THY KINGDOM COME." This is a large petition. It includes all the instrumentalities which the church is putting forth for the enlargement of her borders and the salvation of the world. All these ought to be distinctly and separately remembered ; and not, as is often the case, be crowded into one general petition, at the close of our morning and evening prayers. General truths do not much affect the heart ; and therefore we need to particularize, in order to interest our feelings. I would therefore recommend the arrangement of these subjects under general heads for every day of the week, and then divide the subjects which come under these heads, so as to remember one or more of them at stated seasons, through the day, separate from your own personal devotions. Thus you will always have your mind fixed upon one or two objects ; and you will have time to enlarge, so as to remember every particular relating to them. This, if faithfully pursued, will give you a deeper interest in every benevolent effort.

3. *Observe special seasons of prayer.* Before engaging in any important matter, make it a subject of special prayer. For this you have the example of the blessed Jesus. When he was baptized, before entering upon his ministry, he prayed. Before choosing his twelve apostles, he went out into a mountain, and spent a whole night in prayer. The Old Testament

10 *

saints were also in the habit of "inquiring of the Lord," before engaging in any important enterprise. And Paul enjoins upon the Philippians, "in every thing, by prayer and supplication, with thanksgiving," to let their requests be made known to God. Also, whenever you are under any particular temptation or affliction; whenever you are going to engage in any thing which will expose you to temptation; whenever you perceive any signs of declension in your own soul; when the state of religion around you is low; when your heart is affected with the condition of individuals who are living in impenitence; or when any subject lies heavily on your mind,— make the matter, whatever it is, a subject of special prayer. There is a peculiar fitness in this which must commend itself to every pious heart.

In seasons of peculiar difficulty, or when earnestly seeking any great blessing, you may find benefit from setting apart days of fasting, humiliation, and prayer. This is especially suitable whenever you discover any sensible decay of spiritual affections in your own heart. Fasting and prayer have been resorted to on special occasions, by eminent saints, in all ages of the world. The practice was very common among the Old Testament saints. Nor is the New Testament without warrant for the same. Our Lord himself set the example by a long season of fasting, when about to endure a severe conflict with the Tempter. And he has further sanctioned the practice by giving directions respecting its performance. We have examples also in the Acts of the Apostles. The prophets and

teachers in the church at Antioch fasted before sepa-
rating Barnabas and Paul as missionaries to the
heathen. And when they ordained elders in the
churches, they prayed, *with fasting.* Paul, in his
Epistle to the Corinthians, speaks of their giving
themselves to *fasting and prayer*, as though it were
a frequent custom. You will find, also, in examining
the lives of persons of great spiritual attainments, that
most of them were in the habit of observing frequent
seasons of fasting and prayer. There is a peculiar
fitness in this act of humiliation. It is calculated to
bring the body under, and to assist us in denying self.
The length of time it gives us in our closets also enables us to get clearer views of divine things. But
there is great danger of trusting in the outward act of
humiliation, and expecting that God will answer our
prayers for the sake of our fasting. This will evidently bring upon us disappointment and leanness of soul.
This is the kind of fasting so common among Roman
Catholics and other nominal Christians. But it is no
better than idolatry.

When you set apart a day of fasting and prayer,
you ought to have in view some definite objects. The
day should be spent in self-examination, meditation,
reading the Scriptures, confession of sin, prayer for
the particular objects which bear upon your mind, and
thanksgiving for mercies received. Your self-examination should be as practical as possible ; particularly
looking into the motives of your prayers for the special
objects you are seeking. Your confession of sin
should be minute and particular ; mentioning every

sin you can recollect, whether of thought, word, or
deed, with every circumstance of aggravation. This
will have a tendency to affect your heart with a sense
of guilt, produce earnest longings after holiness, and
make sin appear more hateful and odious.   Moreover,
confession of sin is one of the conditions of pardon.
Your meditations should be upon those subjects which
are calculated to give you a view of the exceeding
sinfulness of sin, and the abounding mercy of God in
Christ. Your reading of the Scriptures should be
strictly devotional. Your prayers should be very
particular ; mentioning every thing relating to the
object of your desires, and all the hinderances you
have met in seeking it. Carry all your burdens to
the foot of the cross, and there lay them down.   Your
thanksgiving, also, should be very minute and particular ; mentioning every mercy and blessing which you
can recollect, with your own unworthiness, and every
circumstance which may tend to magnify the love,
condescension, and mercy of God.

4. *Come to the mercy-seat with preparation of heart.*
We ought, indeed, to maintain so habitually a devout
spirit, as to be always prepared to approach the throne
of grace. But our minds are so liable to be injured by
contact with the world, that it seems becoming in us to
spend some time in collecting our thoughts and stirring
up our affections, before approaching the Majesty of
heaven. When you enter your closet, shut out the
world, that you may be alone with God. Bring your
mind into a calm and heavenly frame, and endeavor to
obtain a deep sense of the presence of God, " *as seeing*

him who is invisible." Think of the exalted nature of
the transaction in which you are about to engage ;
think of your own unworthiness, and of the way God
has opened to the mercy-seat ; think of your own
wants, or of the necessities of those for whom you
intercede ; think of the exhaustless fulness of Christ ;
think of the many precious promises of God to his
children, and come with the spirit of a little child to
present them before him.

5. *Persevere in prayer.* In the eleventh and eigh-
teenth chapters of Luke, our Lord shows, by two
impressive parables, the importance of importunity in
prayer. In the first, he presents the case of a man
who was prevailed upon to do his friend a kindness,
because of his importunity, when he would not have
done it for friendship's sake ; and in the other, of an
unjust judge, who was persuaded by importunity to do
justice. And from these he argues that God, who is
disposed, by his own benevolence and mercy, to listen
to the cries of his children, will much more be affected
by the importunity of those whom he loves. He adds,
with emphasis, " And shall not God avenge his own
elect, which cry day and night unto him, *though he
bear long with them ?* I tell you he will avenge them
speedily." But the delay of a blessing which has
been earnestly sought should lead to self-examination.
If the thing sought is agreeable to the will of God, you
may have been asking amiss, perhaps with selfish
desires, and too little regard for the glory of God ;
perhaps you have not sufficiently felt your dependence,
or have not humbled yourself enough to receive the

blessing; or perhaps you have *regarded iniquity* in your heart, in which case the Lord will not hear you. Still, it is possible the blessing may be delayed for the further trial of your faith. Look at the woman of Syro-Phœnicia, who came to beseech Jesus to heal her daughter. Here is an example of faith, worthy of imitation. She continued to beseech Jesus to have mercy on her, although he did not answer her a word. The disciples entreated Christ to send her away, because she troubled them with her cries; yet she persevered. And even when Christ himself told his disciples that he was only sent to the lost sheep of the house of Israel, and compared her to a dog seeking for the children's bread, yet, with all these repulses, she would not give up her suit, but begged even for the dog's portion, the children's crumbs. When by this means our Lord had sufficiently tried her faith, he answered her prayer. So likewise persevere in your prayers, and "in due time you shall reap, if you faint not."

CHAPTER VIII.

TEMPTATION.

THERE is, in the Holy Scriptures, abundant evidence of the existence of an evil spirit, who is permitted, in various ways, to tempt mankind. This appears in the very beginning of the history of our race; for, according to the apostle John, in the Revelation, "that old serpent," which deceived our first parents, was "the Devil and Satan." The same malicious being was also permitted to tempt the "second Adam," in the beginning of his mediatorial work for the recovery of lost man. He is represented as the father of the wicked, and as putting evil designs into the hearts of men. "The tares are the children of the wicked one." "Thou child of the devil." "Ye are of your father the devil." "And Satan stood up against Israel, and provoked David to number Israel." "The devil having now put into the heart of Judas Iscariot, Simon's son, to betray him." "Ananias, why hath Satan filled thine heart to lie to the Holy Ghost?" Wicked men are spoken of as being carried captive by him at his will; and he is also represented as the adversary of the people of God, seeking to lead them into sin, and, if possible, to destroy them. "Your adversary, the devil, as a roaring lion, walketh about, seeking whom he may devour." These, with numerous other passages, fully establish the fearful truth that we are continually beset by an evil spirit, who is seeking to injure and destroy our souls; and that, in some mysterious manner, which we cannot explain, he has access to our minds. It is of great importance, then, that we should know something of the character of our great adversary, and of his devices to deceive and ruin our souls. From the representations of Scripture, we learn the following things respecting him : —

1. *He is powerful.* He is called " prince of this world," " prince of darkness," and " the god of this world." These titles denote the possession of power, and the exercise of dominion. The persons over whom he exercises dominion are, other fallen spirits, called " his angels," and all mankind in their natural state. Paul, in writing to the Ephesians, represents that, in their former state, before their conversion, they walked " according to the prince of the power of the air, *the spirit that now worketh in the children of disobedience;*" and all unconverted men are children of disobedience. Hence, when any are converted, they are said to be turned " from the power of Satan unto God." But, besides exercising dominion over natural men, he is permitted to tempt and try the true children of God. This is evident from the numerous cautions that are given them against his devices. He is also called *Destroyer;* and is said to walk about, seeking whom he may devour. So great was his power, and so mighty his work of ruin and destruction, that it became necessary for the Son of God to come

into the world to destroy his works. "For this purpose was the Son of God manifested, that he might
destroy the works of the devil."

But, although he is powerful, yet his power is limited.
This you see in the case of Job. No doubt his malice
would have destroyed that holy man at once. But he
could do nothing against him till he was permitted;
and then he could go no farther than the length of his
chain. God reserved the life of his servant. Jude
speaks of the devils as being " reserved *in chains;*"
which means that they are kept perfectly under the
control of the Almighty, so that they can do nothing
without his permission. But the question arises, "Why
is Satan permitted to exercise any power at all?"
Perhaps it is not consistent with proper reverence for
the Supreme Being to entertain this objection; for he
is a righteous Sovereign, in no wise accountable to us,
or to any being but himself, for the measures of his .
administration; and "he giveth not account of any
of his matters." Nevertheless, it appears, from the
Scriptures, that the temptations of Satan, and the
power which he is permitted to exercise, are wisely
overruled for good. The children of God on earth
are in a state of trial and discipline; and these are
among the means which the Lord uses to prove and
develop their characters. Instance the case of Job.
Satan had slandered that holy man, by accusing him
of serving God from selfish motives. By suffering
him to take away all he had, the Lord proved this
accusation to be false; and Job came out of the
furnace greatly purified. The apostle James says,

11

"My brethren, count it all joy when ye fall into divers temptations; knowing this, that the trying of your faith worketh patience." If the children of God were never tempted, they would never have an opportunity to prove the sincerity of their faith. But they have the blessed assurance that God will not suffer them to be tempted above what they are able to bear, but will, with the temptation, also make a way to escape, that they may be able to bear it. Satan is likewise permitted to exercise his power for the discovery of hypocrites, and for the punishment of sinners. "These have no root, which for a while believe, and in time of temptation fall away." "But, if our gospel be hid, it is hid to them that are lost: in whom the god of this world hath blinded the minds of them that believe not."

2. *Satan has much knowledge.* He knew the command of God to our first parents, and therefore tempted them to break it. When those that were possessed with devils were brought to Christ, they cried out, "We *know* thee, who thou art; the Holy One of God." He has also a knowledge of the Bible; for he quoted Scripture in his temptation of Christ. And, as he has had a long experience in this world, he must have much knowledge of human nature, so as to be able to suit his temptations to the peculiar constitutions of individuals.

3. *He is wicked.* "The devil sinneth from the beginning." He is called the *wicked one;* or, by way of eminence, "*the wicked.*" He is altogether wicked. There is not one good quality in his character.

4. *He is crafty, and full of deceit and treachery.*

He lays snares for the unwary. That he may the more readily deceive the people of God, he appears to them in the garb of religion. " Satan himself is transformed into an angel of light." In consequence of his cunning and craft, he is called the *serpent*.* He is likewise represented as deceiving the nations.† Hence we are cautioned against the *wiles* of the devil.‡

5. *He is a liar.* The first thing recorded of him is the lie which he told our first parents, to persuade them to disobey God. Hence our Savior calls him a " liar from the beginning."

6. *He is malicious.* As Satan is the enemy of God, so he hates every thing good. He is continually bent on mischief. If his power were not restrained, he would introduce general disorder, anarchy, and confusion into the government of God. He loves to ruin immortal souls, and takes delight in vexing the people of God. Hence he is called *destroyer*,§ *adversary*, *accuser*, *tormentor*, and *murderer*.||

Now, since we are beset by an adversary of such knowledge and power, so sly and artful, so false and so malicious, it becomes us to be well acquainted with his arts, that we may be on our guard against them. Paul says, " For we are not ignorant of his devices." O that every Christian could say so ! How many sad falls would be prevented ! I will mention a few of the devices of Satan, which are manifest both from Scrip-

---

* Gen. iii. 1 ; Isa. xxvii. 1 ; Rev. xii. 9.   † Rev. xx. 8.
‡ Eph. vi. 11.   § *Abaddon* signifies *destroyer*.
|| Rev. ix. 11 ; 1 Pet. v. 8 ; Rev. xii. 10 ; Matt. xviii. 34 ; John viii 44.

ture and experience. It is the opinion of some great and good men, that the devil can suggest thoughts to our minds only through the *imagination*. This is that faculty of the mind by which it forms ideas of things communicated to it through the senses. Thus, when you see, hear, feel, taste, or smell any thing, the image of the thing is impressed upon the mind by the imagination. It also brings to our recollection these images when they are not present. It is thought to be only by impressing these images upon the imagination, that he can operate upon our souls. Hence we may account for the strange manner in which our minds are led off from the contemplation of divine things by a singular train of thought, introduced to the mind by the impression of some sensible object upon the imagination. This object brings some other one like it to our recollection, and that again brings another, until our minds are lost in a maze of intellectual trifling.

Satan adapts his temptations to our peculiar tempers and circumstances. In youth, he allures us by pleasure, and bright hopes of worldly prosperity. In manhood, he seeks to bury up our hearts in the cares of life. In old age, he persuades to the indulgence of self-will and obstinacy. In prosperity, he puffs up the heart with pride, and persuades to self-confidence and forgetfulness of God. In poverty and affliction, he excites discontent, distrust, and repining. If we are of a melancholy temperament, he seeks to sour our tempers, and promote habitual sullenness and despondency; if naturally cheerful, he prompts to the indulgence of levity. In private devotion, he stands between us and God, to prevent us from realizing his presence, and seeks to distract our minds, and drive us from the throne of grace. In public worship, he disturbs our minds by wandering thoughts and foolish imaginations. When we enjoy a comfortable and happy frame of mind, he stirs up pride in our hearts, and leads us to trust in our own goodness, and forget the Rock of our salvation. Even our deepest humiliations he makes the occasion of spiritual pride. Thus we fall into darkness, and thrust ourselves through with many sorrows. If we have performed any extraordinary acts of self-denial, or of Christian beneficence, he stirs up in our hearts a vainglorious spirit. If we have overcome any of the corruptions of our hearts, or any temptation, he excites a secret feeling of self-satisfaction and self-complacency. He puts on the mask of religion. Often, during the solemn hours of public worship, he beguiles our hearts with some scheme for doing good ; taking care, however, that *self* be uppermost in it. When we are in a bad frame, he stirs up the unholy tempers of our hearts, and leads us to indulge in peevishness, moroseness, harshness, and anger, or in levity and unseemly mirth.

There is no Christian grace which Satan cannot counterfeit. He cares not how much religious feeling we have, or how many good deeds we perform, if he can but keep impure and selfish motives at the bottom. There is great danger, therefore, in trusting to impulses, or sudden impressions of any kind. We ought to " try the spirits, whether they be of God." The Spirit of grace does not reveal truth or duty directly

11*

to us. He has finished his work of Revelation, and
put the record of it into our hands, as our only rule of
truth and duty.   His office now is, to enlighten our
minds to perceive the truth, and to stir us up to perform the duties required in his word.   If, therefore,
we find a secret impulse operating upon our minds *to
persuade us to perform known duty*, we may know it
is from the Spirit of God.   But, if our conviction of
duty arises from *the impression upon our mind*, we
shall be liable to be led astray, and carried about by
every wind.   The fact that our religious feelings are
not produced by ourselves, but that they arise in our
mind in a manner for which we cannot account, is no
evidence, either that they come from the Spirit of
God, or that they do not.   Satan is sometimes transformed into an angel of light.   He is often the author
of false comforts and joys, very much resembling
those which are truly gracious.   Nor is it certain that
religious feelings are holy and spiritual because they
come with texts of Scripture, brought to the mind in
a remarkable manner.   If the feeling is produced by
the truth contained in the Scriptures so brought to the
mind, and is, in its nature, agreeable to the word of
God, it may be a spiritual and holy affection.   But, if
it arises from the application of the Scripture to our
own case, on account of its being so brought to our
mind, it is probably a delusion.   Satan has power to
bring Scripture to our minds ; and he can apply it
with dexterity, as we see in his temptations of the
blessed Savior.   Besides, our hearts are exceedingly
deceitful, and our indwelling corruptions are in league

with the adversary. How easily, then, may he succeed in cheating our souls with false peace and selfish
joys! Satan, no doubt, often brings the most sweet
and precious promises of God to the minds of those he
wishes to deceive. But he misapplies the promises,
as he did to our Lord, when he attempted to persuade
him to cast himself down from a pinnacle of the temple, on the strength of the promise, "He shall give his
angels charge concerning thee; and in their hands
they shall bear thee up, lest at any time thou dash thy
foot against a stone." We must be satisfied that the
promises belong to us, before we take them to ourselves. We have "a more sure word of prophecy,"
by which we are to try every impulse, feeling, and impression, produced upon our minds. Any thing which
does not agree with the written word of God, does not
come from him; for he "cannot deny himself."

Satan manages temptation with the greatest subtlety
and adroitness. He asks so little at first, that, unless
our consciences are very tender, we do not suspect
him. If he can persuade us to parley, he perhaps
leaves us for a while, and returns again, with a fresh
and more vigorous attack. He is exceedingly perse-
vering; and, if he can induce us to give place to him
at all, he is almost sure to overcome us at last. So it
was with Eve. She parleyed at first; then listened
to the suggestions of the tempter; then lusted after
the fruit of the forbidden tree; then took and ate.
Such is the progress, and such the end, of those who
parley with temptation.

We are also liable to temptation from the world

without, and from the corruptions of our own hearts
within. "They that will be rich fall into temptation
and a snare." The riches, honors, pleasures, and
fashions, of this world are great enemies to serious
piety. "Every man is tempted when he is drawn
away of his own lusts, and enticed." Remaining
corruption is the sorest evil that besets the Christian.
The temptations of Satan alone would be light, in
comparison with the inward conflict he is compelled
to maintain against the lusts of his own heart. But
the devil makes use of both these means of temptation
to accomplish his ends. The former he uses as outward enticements, and the latter act as traitors within.
Thus you may generally find a secret alliance between the arch deceiver and the corruptions of your
own heart. It is not sin to be tempted; but it is sin
to give place to temptation. "Neither give place to
the devil."

The heart is very properly compared to a castle or
fort. Before conversion, it is in the possession of the
great enemy of souls, who has fortified himself there,
and secured the allegiance of all our moral powers.
But, when Jesus enters in, he "binds the strong man
armed," and takes possession of the heart himself.
Yet Satan, though in a measure bound, loses no opportunity to attempt regaining his lost dominion.
Hence we are directed to "keep the heart *with all
diligence.*" Now, we know how a castle, fort, or city,
is kept in time of war. The first thing done is to *set
a watch,* whose business is to keep constantly on the
look out, this way and that way, to see that no enemy

is approaching from without, and no traitor is lurking within. Hence we are so frequently exhorted to *watch.* " Watch and pray, that ye enter not into temptation." " Take heed, watch and pray ; for ye know not when the time is." " And what I say unto you, I say unto all, Watch." " Watch ye, stand fast in the faith, quit you like men, be strong." " Continue in prayer, and watch *in* the same, with thanksgiving." " Praying always, with all prayer and supplication in the Spirit, and *watching thereunto* with all perseverance." " Let us watch and be sober." " Watch, then, *in all things.*" " Watch *unto* prayer." " Blessed is he that *watcheth*, and keepeth his garments, lest he walk naked, and they see his shame." " Set a watch, O Lord, before my mouth ; keep the door of my lips." If we were in a house surrounded by a band of robbers, and especially if we knew there were persons in it who held a secret correspondence with them, we should be continually on our guard. Every moment we should be *watching*, both within and without. But not unlike this is our case. It is therefore with good reason that we are so frequently cautioned on this point, and directed to *watch in all things.* But there are particular seasons when we should set a *double watch.*

1. We are directed to watch *unto* prayer. When you approach the mercy-seat, watch against a careless spirit. Suffer not your mind to be drawn away by any thing, however good and important in itself, from the object before you. If the adversary can divert your mind, on the way to that consecrated place, he

will be almost sure to drive you away from it without a blessing.

2. We are required to watch not only *unto*, but *in*, prayer. Satan is never more busy with Christians than when he sees them on their knees. He well knows the power of prayer; and this makes him tremble.

> "Satan trembles when he sees
> The weakest saint upon his knees."

You should, therefore, with the most untiring vigilance, watch in prayer against all wandering thoughts and distraction of mind. You will often experience, on such occasions, a sudden and vivid impression upon your mind, of something entirely foreign from what is before you; and this, we have reason to believe, is the temptation of Satan. If you are sufficiently upon your watch, you can banish it without diverting your thoughts or feelings from the subject of your prayer, and proceed as though nothing had happened. But, if the adversary succeeds in keeping these wild imaginations in view, so that you cannot proceed without distraction, turn and beseech God to give you help against his wiles. You have the promise, that if you resist the devil, he will flee from you. These remarks apply both to secret prayer and public worship.

3. We have need of special watchfulness when we have experienced any comfortable manifestations of God's presence. It is then that Satan tempts us to consider the conflict over, and relax our diligence.

If we give way to him, we shall bring leanness upon our souls.

4. We have need of double watchfulness, when gloom and despondency come over our minds; for then the adversary seeks to stir up all the perverse passions of the heart.

5. Watch, also, when you feel remarkably cheerful. Satan will then, if possible, persuade you to indulge in levity, to the wounding of your soul, and the dishonor of religion.

6. We have need of special watchfulness in prosperity, that we forget not God; and in adversity, that we murmur not at his dealings with us.

7. Set a watch over your tongue, especially in the presence of the unconverted. "The tongue is a fire, a world of iniquity." David says, "I will keep my mouth with a bridle, while the wicked is before me." I do not mean that you should *ever* engage in any sinful conversation in the presence of Christians. Some professors of religion will indulge in senseless garrulity among themselves, and put on an air of seriousness and solemnity before those whom they regard as unconverted. This they pretend to do for the *honor of Christ.* But Christ says, "Out of the abundance of the heart the mouth speaketh." God abhors lip-service. However, in the company of sinners and formal professors, we are peculiarly exposed to temptation, and have need, therefore, to set a double guard upon our lips. A single unguarded expression from a Christian may do great injury to an unconverted soul.

8. Watch over your heart, when engaged in doing good to others. It is then that Satan seeks to stir up pride and vainglory.

9. Set a *double* watch over your easily-besetting sin. " Let us lay aside every weight, and the sin which doth so easily beset us." Most persons have some constitutional sin, which easily besets them. Satan takes the advantage of this infirmity, to bring us into difficulty.

10. Finally, keep a constant watch over the *imagination.* Since this is the medium through which temptation comes, never suffer your fancy to rove without control. If you mortify this faculty, it may be a great assistance to your devotion. But, if you let it run at random, you will be led captive by Satan at his will. Strive, then, after a sanctified imagination, that you may make every power of your soul subservient to the glory of God.

CHAPTER IX.

SELF-DENIAL.

THE duty of self-denial arises from the unnatural relation which sin has created between us and God. The first act of disobedience committed by man was a setting up of himself in opposition to God. It was a declaration that he would regard his own will in preference to the will of his Creator. *Self* became the supreme object of his affections. And this is the case with all unregenerate persons. Their own happiness is the object of their highest wishes. They pursue their own selfish interests with their whole hearts. When any thing occurs, the first question which arises in their minds is, "How will this affect *me?*" It is true they may often exercise a kind of generosity towards others; but, if their motives were scanned, it would appear that self-gratification is at the bottom of it. The correctness of these assertions no one will doubt, who is acquainted with his own heart. All unconverted persons live for themselves. They see no higher object of action than the promotion of their own individual interests. The duty in question consists in the denial of this disposition. And a moment's attention will show that nothing can be more reasonable. We belong to a grand system of being,

12

of which God is the Sun and Centre ; and no individual has a right to attach to himself any more importance
than properly belongs to the place he occupies in this
system. It is by this place that his value is known.
If he thinks himself of more consequence than the
station he occupies will give him, it leads to discontent and murmuring; and this is setting up the
wisdom and will of the creature in opposition to
the Creator. This was probably the origin of the
first act of disobedience. Satan thought himself entitled to a higher station in the system of being than
God gave him; therefore he rebelled against the
government of the Most High. This act of rebellion
was nothing more than setting up his own selfish
interests against the interests of the universe. And
what would be the consequence, if this selfish principle were carried out in the material universe ?
Instance our own planetary system : if every planet
should set up an interest separate from the whole,
would they move on with such beautiful harmony ?
No ; every one would seek to be a sun. They would
all rush towards the common centre, and universal
confusion would follow. God is the Sun and Centre
of the moral universe ; and the setting up of private,
individual interests as supreme objects of pursuit, if
permitted to take their course, would produce the
same general confusion. This it has done, so far as
it has prevailed. Its tendency is to create a universal
contention among inferior beings for the throne of the
universe, which belongs to God alone. But the interests of God — if I may be allowed the expression —

are identified with the highest good of his intelligent creation. Hence we see the perfect reasonableness of the first commandment — "Thou shalt have no other gods before me." There can be no selfishness in this ; because the best interests of the universe require it. But, by pursuing our own selfish interests as the chief good, we make a god of *self*.

The religion of Jesus Christ strikes at the root of this selfish principle. The very first act of the new-born soul is a renunciation or giving up of self, — the surrender of the whole soul to God. The entire dedication which the Christian makes of himself, soul, body, and property, to the Lord, implies that he will no longer live to himself, but to God. "Present your bodies a living sacrifice, holy and acceptable unto God." "For none of us liveth to himself." "They which live should not henceforth live unto·themselves, but unto Him which died for them, and rose again." "Whether, therefore, ye eat or drink, or *whatsoever ye do*, do all *to the glory of God*." Self-denial, then, is the surrendering of our will to the will of God. It is an adoption of the revealed will of God as the rule of duty, and a steadfast, determined, and perse-vering denial of every selfish gratification which comes between us and obedience to this rule. It is seeking the glory of God and the good of our fellow-creatures, as the highest objects of pursuit. In short, it is to "love the Lord our God with all our heart, soul, might, mind, and strength, and our neighbor as ourselves."

By carrying out this principle, in its application to our feelings and conduct, we learn the practical duty of *self-denial;* which Christ declares to be an indispensable term of discipleship. " If any man will come after me," says he, " let him *deny himself,* and take up his cross daily, and follow me ; " and, " He that loveth father or mother more than me, is not worthy of me ; and he that loveth son or daughter more than me, is not worthy of me." " If any man will come after me, let him *deny himself,* and take up his cross and follow me. For whosoever will save his life shall lose it ; and whosoever will lose his life for my sake shall find it." " If any man come to me, and hate not his father and mother, and wife and children, and brethren and sisters, yea, and his *own life* also, he *cannot be my disciple.*" " He that loveth his life, shall looo it ; and ho that hateth his life in this world shall keep it unto life eternal." " If thy right eye offend thee, [or cause thee to offend,] pluck it out, and cast it from thee." *We must follow Christ.* Here we are taught that, unless we put away self-seeking, and willingly surrender the dearest objects of affection on earth, yea, and *our own lives also,* if need be, we have no claim to the character of disciples of Christ. The glory of God, and the general good, must be our ruling principle of action ; and we must not gratify ourselves, in opposition to the will of God or the interest of our fellow-beings. Every action must be brought to this test. Here is heart work, and life work. Self must be denied in all our spiritual feelings, and in all our devotions, or they will be abominable in the sight of God. Here is work for self-examination. Every exercise of our minds should be tried by this

standard. We must likewise deny self in our conduct.
And here we have the examples of many holy men,
recorded in Scripture, with a host of martyrs and
missionaries, but especially of our Lord himself, to
show what influence the true spirit of self-denial exerts
upon the Christian life. Our Lord declares that, in
order to be his disciples, we must *follow* him. And
how can this be done, but by imitating his example?
He was willing to make *sacrifices* for the good of
others. He led a life of toil, hardship, and suffering,
and *gave up his own life*, to save sinners. His immediate disciples did the same. They submitted to
ignominy, reproach, suffering, and death itself, for the
sake of promoting the glory of God in the salvation
of men. Cultivate, then, this spirit. Prefer the glory
of God to every thing else. Prefer the general good
to your own private interest. Be willing to make
sacrifices of personal interest, ease, and feeling, for
the benefit of others. Carry this principle out in all
your social intercourse, and it will greatly increase
your usefulness. It will likewise promote your own
interest and happiness. Nothing renders a person
more amiable and lovely in the sight of others than
disinterested benevolence. Think no sacrifice too
great to make, no hardship too painful to endure, if
you can be the means of benefiting perishing souls.
Remember, it was for this that Jesus gave up his life;
and he requires you to be ready to give up every
thing you have, and even life itself, if the same cause
shall require it.

But let me caution you against placing self-denial

12 *

chiefly in outward things. We are not required to
relinquish any of the comforts and enjoyments of this
life, except when they come in competition with our
duty to God and our fellow-creatures. " Every creature of God is good, and nothing to be refused, if it be
received with thanksgiving ; " and godliness has the
promise of this life as well as of that which is to come.
The religion of some people seems to consist chiefly
in denying themselves of lawful enjoyments ; and you
will find them very severe and censorious towards
others, for partaking freely and thankfully of the
bounties of God's providence. This, however, is but
a species of self-righteous mockery, characterized by
Paul as a " voluntary humility." Instead of being self-
denial, it is the gratification of *self* in maintaining an
appearance of external sanctity. It may, however, be
not only proper, but obligatory upon us, to sacrifice
these lawful enjoyments, when we may thereby promote the interests of Christ's kingdom, which requires
the exercise of a self-sacrificing spirit.

CHAPTER X.

PUBLIC WORSHIP. SABBATH EMPLOYMENTS.

THE duty of public worship is clearly taught in the Holy Scriptures. From the appointment of one day in seven, to be set apart exclusively for the service of God, we may argue the propriety of assembling together, to acknowledge and worship him in a social capacity. God has made us social beings; and all the institutions of his appointment contemplate us as such. The public worship of the Sabbath is preéminently calculated to cultivate the social principle of our nature. It brings people of the same community regularly together, every week, for the same general purpose. In the house of God all meet upon a level. If we look forward from the institution of the Sabbath to the organization of the Jewish church, we find that God established a regular system of public worship. An order of men was instituted, whose special business was to conduct the public worship of God. After the return of the Jews from captivity, social meetings, called *synagogues*,* or *assemblies*, held every

---

* The term *synagogue* was applied both to the place of meeting and to the congregation assembling for public worship, as the term *church* is now used.

Sabbath, for public religious worship, became common all over the land. Although we have no particular account of the divine origin of these assemblies, yet it is supposed they were instituted by Ezra, who was commissioned, by divine authority, to reëstablish the worship of the true God, and complete the canon of the Old Testament; and they were sanctioned by the presence of Christ, who often took part in the public exercises.

Under the gospel dispensation, the plan of synagogue worship is continued, with such modifications as suit it to the clearer and more complete development of God's gracious designs towards sinful men. A new order of men has been instituted, to conduct public worship, and impart public instruction. As religion consists very much in the exercise of holy affections, God has appointed the preaching of the word as a suitable means for stirring up these affections. Our desires are called forth, our love excited, our delight increased, and our zeal inflamed, by a faithful, earnest, and feeling representation of the most common and familiar truths of the Bible from the pulpit. It is evident, then, that the private reading of the best books, though highly useful, cannot answer the ends of public worship.

The duty of public worship may also be inferred from the fitness and propriety of a public acknowledgment of God by a community in their social capacity. It is befitting dependent beings, whom God has created, and constituted into societies and communities, to acknowledge their dependence, and engage in solemn acts of worship, *in their associated capacity.*

This duty is enforced by the example of holy men of old, but especially of Christ and his apostles. David took great delight in the public worship of God's house, which he expressed in such language as this: " My soul thirsteth for thee ; my flesh longeth for thee in a dry and thirsty land, where no water is, to see thy power and glory, *so as I have seen thee in the sanctuary."* " *I went into the sanctuary of God* ; then understood I their end." " Lord, *I have loved the habitation of thy house,* and the place where thine honor dwelleth." " *I went with them to the house of God,* with the voice of joy and praise, with a multitude that kept holy day." " We took sweet counsel together, *and walked to the house of God in company."* " *I will dwell in the house of the Lord* forever." " One thing have I desired of the Lord, that will I seek after, — that I may *dwell in the house of the Lord all the days of my life,* to behold the beauty of the Lord, and to inquire in his temple." Such were the feelings of the man who has expressed, in strains of sweetest melody, the experience of Christians in all ages. But the example of Jesus is very clear on this point: " And he came to Nazareth, where he had been brought up, and, *as his custom was,* he went into the synagogue on the Sabbath day, and stood up for to read." From this it appears that Jesus, even before entering upon his ministry, was in the habit of attending regularly upon the public worship of God in the synagogue of Nazareth, where he had been brought up. This was the first time he had been there after the commencement of his ministry; yet he went into the synagogue on the Sabbath day, *as his custom was;* showing that he had always been in the habit of doing so.

After the crucifixion of our Lord, we find the disciples regularly assembling together upon the *first day of the week,* which is the Christian Sabbath. And Jesus himself honored these assemblies by his presence, after his resurrection. That this practice continued to be observed by the churches founded by the apostles, is evident from the frequent allusions to it in the Acts, and in the writings of Paul, who preached at Macedonia upon the first day of the week, when the disciples came together to break bread. In the sixteenth chapter of his First Epistle to the Corinthians, he gives directions for taking up collections for the poor saints *on the first day of the week,* which evidently means the time when they were in the habit of meeting for public worship; and, in the eleventh chapter of the same Epistle, he tells them how to regulate their conduct when they "*come together in the church.*" Again, he exhorts the Hebrews "*not to forsake the assembling of themselves together.*" It appears clear, then, that, under the direction of the apostles, the public worship of God upon the Sabbath was observed in the primitive churches. And this is confirmed by the fact that the same practice has since been uniformly observed by the church in all ages.

From the foregoing arguments I draw the following conclusions : —

1. It is the imperative duty of every person, who has it in his power, to attend regularly upon the public worship of God. He has appointed public worship, consisting of devotional exercises, and the preaching of his word, as the principal means of grace for edifying his people, and bringing lost sinners to himself. We cannot, therefore, excuse ourselves for not waiting upon these means ; nor can we expect the blessing of God upon any others which we may substitute in their place.

2. The duty of attending upon the public worship of God is not diminished by the existence of things in the ministry, church, or congregation, with which we are connected, which we do not approve, provided the essential truths of the gospel are preached, and the regular forms of worship maintained. This conclusion is drawn from the practice of Christ himself. He attended habitually upon the regularly-constituted public worship of the Jews, although there appears to have been scarce any signs of spiritual worship among them. The Scriptures were read, the truth was declared ; yet all was cold formality, — a mere shell of outside worship. But this principle does not hold good where there is an essential departure from fundamental truth. We are not at liberty to attend upon the ministry of false teachers ; for of these Christ has warned us to beware ; and the apostle John, in his epistle to the elect lady, says, " If there come any unto you, and bring not this doctrine," (i. e., the doc-

trine of Christ,) "receive him not into your house, neither bid him God-speed; for he that biddeth him God-speed is a partaker of his evil deeds." And is not sitting under their ministry bidding them God-speed? And do we not thus become partakers of their evil deeds?

3. No person who neglects public worship upon the Sabbath, when it is in his power to attend, can expect a blessing upon his soul. When preaching is of an ordinary character, and not very full of instruction, or when the manner of the preacher is disagreeable, people are frequently tempted to think they can improve their time better at home, in reading, meditation, and prayer. But this is a great mistake, unless they can spend the Sabbath profitably without the presence of God. If it is the *duty* of every one to attend upon the regularly-instituted public worship of the Sabbath, when we neglect it we are out of the way of duty. And God will never bless us in the neglect of any positive duty, even if our whole time be spent upon our knees. Obedience is one condition of the promise. "*If ye abide in me, and my words abide in you,*" says the Savior, "ye shall ask what ye will, and it shall be done unto you." Those who cherish sin, or live in the neglect of known duty, have, therefore, no reason to expect that God will hear their prayers. "If I regard iniquity in my heart," says the Psalmist, "the Lord will not hear me." Besides, it is the regular ministration of his word in the sanctuary that God chiefly blesses for the growth of Christians and the conversion of sinners. And when the appointed

means of grace are slighted, can any one expect the blessing of God? Will he bless the means which you have devised and preferred to those of his own appointment? Do not, then, neglect the habitual and regular attendance upon the public worship of God, whenever there is a properly-conducted assembly of orthodox * Christians within your reach. I would not dare neglect this, even if the reading of a sermon were substituted for preaching.

PRACTICAL HINTS IN RELATION TO PUBLIC WORSHIP.

1. *Attend on the stated ministrations of your pastor.* If there is more than one church professing your own sentiments in the place where you reside, select the pastor who is most spiritual, and will give you the best instruction. But, when you have made this selection, consider yourself bound to wait on his ministry. Do not indulge yourself in going from place to place, to hear this and that minister. This will give you " *itching ears,*" and cultivate a love of novelty, and a critical mode of hearing, very unfavorable to the practical application of the truth to your own soul. If you wish to obtain complete views of truth, — if you wish your soul to thrive, — attend, as far as possible, upon *every* appointment of your pastor. Ministers generally adopt some plan of instruction,

---

* I use the term *orthodox* in its general signification, as applying to all evangelical denominations who hold the fundamental doctrines of the Bible.

13

which they believe to be adapted to the state of their people, and frequently pursue a chain of subjects in succession, so as to present a complete view of the great doctrines of the Bible. Whenever you absent yourself, you break this chain, and lose much of your interest and profit in your minister's preaching. I do not say but, on special occasions, when some subject of more than usual importance is to be presented at another place, it may be proper for you to leave your own church. But, in general, the frequent exchange of pulpits between neighboring ministers, and the occasional appearance of a stranger in the pulpit, will furnish as great variety as you will find profitable.

2. *Be punctual in attending at the stated hour of public worship.* This, though of great importance, is sadly neglected by many congregations. Punctuality is so necessary in matters of business, that a man is hardly considered honest when he fails to meet his friend at the hour of engagement. And why should it be thought of less consequence to be exact and punctual in our engagements with God than with man? The person who enters the house of God after the service has commenced, embarrasses the preacher, and disturbs the devotions of others. Besides, he shows great want of reverence for the sacredness of the place, time, and employment. "God is greatly to be feared *in the assembly of his saints,* and to be had in reverence of all them that are about him." Always calculate to be seated in the sanctuary a few

minutes before the time appointed for the commencement of worship; that you may have time to settle
your mind, and to lift your soul in silent prayer to God
for his blessing.

3. *Go to the house of God with a preparation of
heart.* First visit your closet, and implore the influences of the Holy Spirit, both upon yourself and your
fellow-worshippers, that your and their hearts may be
prepared to receive the truth ; and, if possible, go immediately from your closet to the house of worship.
On the way, shut out all thoughts except such as are
calculated to inspire devotional feelings; and, if in
company, avoid conversation. Whatever may be the
nature of such conversation, it will be very likely to
produce a train of thought which will distract and disturb your mind during public worship.

4. *When you approach the house of worship, remember that the Lord is there in a peculiar manner.*
He has promised to be where two or three shall meet
in his name. It is in the *assembly of his saints* that
he makes known the power of his Spirit. As you
enter his house, endeavor to realize the solemnity of
his presence, and walk softly before him. Avoid carelessness of demeanor, and let your deportment indicate
the reverence due to the place where "God's honor
dwelleth." " Keep thy foot when thou goest to the
house of God." I do not like to specify any particular acts which are unbecoming in the house of God,
lest I should seem to imply that a young lady may be
guilty of a public breach of the rules of good breed-
ing ; but, if you bear in mind continually that you are

a guest in the house of the Lord, and that the Lord of
Hosts is there to witness all you do, you will be likely
to be serious and circumspect.   When seated in the
place of worship, set a watch over the senses, that
your eyes and ears may not cause your mind to
wander upon forbidden objects.   There is great danger that the attraction of persons, characters, and
dress, may dissipate the serious thoughts with which
you entered the sanctuary, so that you will lose the
benefit of the means of grace.   Set a watch, also,
over your imagination.   This is a time when Satan is
peculiarly busy in diverting the fancy; and, unless
you are doubly watchful, he may lead away your
mind by some phantom of the imagination, before you
are aware of it.   Keep these avenues of temptation
guarded, and seek to bring yourself into a prayerful
frame of mind, that you may be suitably affected by
the various exercises of public worship.

5. *Unite in spirit with the devotional part of the
service.*   " God is a Spirit; and they that worship him
must worship in spirit and in truth."   Sing with the
spirit and with the understanding, and see that you do
not mock God with an empty song of praise, which
finds no response in your heart. · Endeavor, also, in
prayer, to follow the words of the person who leads,
applying the several parts of the prayer to yourself in
particular, when they suit your case, and yet bearing
in mind the various subjects of petition which relate to
the congregation and the world; remembering that
God abhors hypocritical worship, in which men appear
outwardly as worshippers, but have no spiritual appre-

hension of the meaning of the solemn service in which
they are engaged. In all the exercises of public worship, labor and strive against wandering thoughts.
This is the time when Satan will beset you with all
his fury. Now you must be well armed, and fight
manfully. Be not discouraged, though you may be
many times foiled. If you persevere in the strength
of Jesus, you will come off conqueror at last.

6. " *Take heed* HOW *you hear*." Consider the
speaker as the ambassador of Christ, sent with a
message from God to yourself. " Now, then," says
the apostle, " we are ambassadors for Christ, as
though God did beseech you by us : we pray you, in
Christ's stead, be ye reconciled to God." The figure
here used is borrowed from the practice of one government sending a person on a particular errand to
another. The analogy, however, does not hold good
throughout. It is like a sovereign sending an ambassador to persuade rebels against his government to submit to him, and accept of pardon. But, in such a
case, it would be possible, either for some person who
was not sent, to deliver a false message in the name
of the king, or for one who was really sent, to deliver
a different message from the one sent by him. So it
is in relation to preachers of the gospel. There are
many whom Christ has never sent, who are spreading
abroad lies over the land ; and there are others, really
sent by Christ, who have, in some respects, misappre-
hended their instructions, and therefore do not deliver
his message just as he has directed. But our blessed
Lord, foreseeing this, has wisely and kindly given us

13 *

a *check-book*, by which we may discover whether those who speak in his name tell the truth. Hence we are commanded to "search the Scriptures," and to "try the spirits, whether they be of God." And the Bereans were commended as more noble, because they searched the Scriptures daily, to know whether the things preached by the apostles were so. If, then, they were applauded for trying the preaching of the apostles by the word of God, surely we may try the preaching of uninspired men by the same standard.

But beware of a fault finding spirit. There are some persons who indulge such a habit of finding fault with preaching, that they never receive much benefit from it. Either the matter of the sermon, the apparent feeling of the preacher, or his style, or manner of delivery, does not suit them ; and therefore they throw away all the good they might have obtained from his discourse. Remember that preachers of the gospel are but men. So weak are they, that the apostle compares them to "earthen vessels." Do not, then, expect perfection. Bear with their infirmities. Receive their instructions as the bread which your heavenly Father has provided for the nourishment of your soul. Do not ungratefully spurn it from you. What would you think to see a child throwing away the bread his mother gives him, because it does not suit his dainty appetite ? But the instruction delivered to you by the ministers of Christ, if it agrees with the word of God, is the bread which your heavenly Father has provided as the food of your soul. It may not suit your taste. It may not be savory enough. It may be coarse food. It may not have any such dressings as render it palatable to a capricious appetite. Or it may be, in your estimation, too strong meat. Still it is the food which God has provided for your soul; and you will suffer incalculable loss, if you are so dainty as to throw it away. But, if there appears really to be a deficiency in your minister's preaching, pray for him, that he may preach better. See to it, however, that the fault be not with yourself, in not keeping your heart in such a state as to be able to appreciate good preaching. Many sermons, which appeared dry and dull the first time they were delivered, on being repeated in a time of awakening, and heard with a new ear, have been pronounced excellent, and full of instruction.

Hear, also, with self-application. From almost any passage in the Bible the Christian may draw a practical lesson for himself. Some truths may not be immediately applicable to your present circumstances; yet you ought to be affected by them. Even a sermon addressed exclusively to impenitent sinners is calculated to excite the most intense feelings of the Christian's soul. It reminds him of the exceeding wickedness of his past life; it shows him what an awful gulf he has escaped; it leads him to mourn over his ingratitude; and it calls forth his prayers and tears in behalf of the perishing. Strive to bring home the truth, so far as it is applicable to yourself, in the most searching manner. Examine your own heart diligently, that you lose nothing which belongs to you. *Do not hear for others.* Let every one make his own application of the truth. Many are so intent on finding garments for others, that they lose their own. *Hear with a prayerful frame of mind.* If any part of the discourse is intended for professors of religion, let your heart continually ascend to God for the Holy Spirit to apply it to yourself and to every Christian present. If any part of it is designed for impenitent persons, let your soul put forth an agony of prayer, that it may be blessed for their conversion. *Remember and practise what you hear.* We are exhorted to give earnest heed to the things which we have heard, lest at any time we should let them slip. James tells us, " If any be a hearer of the word, and not a doer, he is like unto a man beholding his natural face in the glass ; for he beholdeth himself, and goeth his way, and straightway forgetteth what manner of man he was." Alas, how many thus hear ! But, in regard to them, our Savior likens them to a man that built his house upon the sand, which, when the storm came, was swept away with a terrible destruction. How many, who have paid a decent respect to the worship of God, without practising the self-denying duties inculcated in his word, will find their foundation swept from under them in the terrible storm which is at hand, none can tell. Let us see to it that we are not among the many who will say, in that day, " Lord, Lord," without having obeyed his word ; that he should say to us, " Depart from me, ye that work iniquity."

MEETINGS FOR PRAYER.

Intimately connected with public worship are social meetings for prayer. We have examples of these in the primitive church. The disciples held a *ten days'* prayer-meeting, before the advent of the Holy Spirit on the day of Pentecost. When the apostles returned from before the council, they held a prayer-meeting, and the place was shaken where they were assembled. When Peter was imprisoned, the church held a prayer-meeting *in the night*, and an angel delivered him out of the prison. We read of a place by the river side, where prayer was " wont to be made." And at Miletus, Paul held a precious prayer-meeting with the elders of the church of Ephesus. These meetings have been maintained among evangelical Christians in every age. They are the life of the church. They are the mainspring of human agency in revivals of religion. Without a spirit of prayer, sufficient to bring God's people together in this way, I see not how vital piety can exist in a church. The feelings of a lively Christian will lead him to the place of prayer. But it will not do to follow our feelings at all times, because they are variable. If you suffer yourself to be guided by the mere impulse of feeling, you can never be depended on as a stable and consistent Christian. We ought the rather to be guided in all things by settled and permanent principle. Those who are so governed are the only Christians that can be relied on in an

emergency.   The follower of Christ is called a soldier;
but the main thing with a soldier, and without which
he would be good for nothing, is, that he is always
to be found at his post.   But what would become of
an army, or of the country which they defend, if,
when called to duty, but a small proportion of them
should be found there?   And what will become of the
cause in which the great Captain of our salvation is
engaged, if but few of the soldiers of the cross are to
be found at the place of rendezvous?   Let it be a
settled principle with you, then, to be *always at your
post*.   Let nothing but absolute necessity keep you
from the place of prayer.

As females are forbidden, by the dictates of nature and
the word of God, to bear a part in the exercises of promiscuous and public meetings, it is highly proper, and
very profitable, for them to hold meetings for prayer by
themselves alone.   We have reason to believe they did
so in primitive times; for we read of a place by the
river side, where prayer was wont to be made, and of
the women who resorted thither.   Such meetings exercise the gifts and graces of those who attend them,
and serve to keep alive the flame of piety, as two or
more brands placed together will preserve the fire,
when, if left alone, they would all go out.   Such
meetings have been greatly blessed of God; and sometimes the flame of piety is kept alive in the female
prayer-meeting, after it has apparently gone out on
every other altar.

THE SABBATH SCHOOL.

I cannot persuade myself, in this connection, to pass over an institution which occupies so prominent a place in the employments of the holy Sabbath, as the Sabbath school; and I think I may presume on the interest which those for whom I am writing feel in this department of Christian effort and improvement. I know of no means of intellectual and spiritual improvement, accessible to all, which will by any means compare with this. It furnishes a stimulus to intellectual effort, of great value to persons of all ages, and in every department of life. It is one of the best means of *self-education* which the times afford; for there is no study better adapted to develop, enlarge, and strengthen, the mind than the investigation of religious truth. And it has this peculiar advantage, that it combines moral and spiritual improvement with intellectual cultivation. There is perceptible in the minds of those who have been for a number of years connected with the Sabbath school, a wakefulness of mind, an acuteness of perception, and a definiteness in their views of truth, not often to be found among those who have not had this advantage. It creates the necessity for study, and obliges every one to learn something new every week; and this keeps the mind active, and secures a constantly progressive advancement in knowledge. It tends, also, to keep alive religious feeling, by keeping the truth before the mind, and bringing different minds together, to act upon one another. I can hardly persuade myself that it is necessary to advise young Christian females to become connected with the Sabbath school; for it would seem that their own feelings would lead them to a place of so great interest and improvement; and I suppose the majority of those into whose hands this book may fall, have been trained up in the Sabbath school, and have never left it. And I trust none of them will ever feel that they are too old to continue to attend as pupils. In many parts of the country, it is the custom for the whole congregation, both old and young, to be formed into a Sabbath school; and a most excellent custom it is. May I not hope that the young ladies for whom I am writing will be every where forward to encourage so good a custom?

But young Christian ladies ought to calculate upon qualifying themselves to teach in the Sabbath school, in case their services in this department shall be required. It may be personally more agreeable to sit as a learner; but duty requires that we should always prefer an opportunity of imparting, to that of receiving, a spiritual benefit. Indeed, this is the true way of securing a personal benefit; for our Lord has said, " It is more blessed to give than to receive ; " and he verifies his word, by pouring the richest spiritual blessings into the souls of those who lay themselves out most for the benefit of others. This is especially the case with Sabbath school teachers. They are excited, by the responsibilities of their station, to greater study in the preparation of their lessons, and in acquiring information to impart to those they teach; and this secures a greater intellectual benefit. Their pupils, also, give direction to their desires, prayers, and efforts, and thus their piety is cultivated, strengthened, and increased. If successful, too, they are permitted to rejoice in the fruit of their labors. Every faithful Sabbath school teacher, therefore, knows, from experience, that it is " more blessed to give than to receive." I may presume, therefore, that every young lady who loves the Savior will esteem it a privilege to be a Sabbath school teacher.

But, should you be called upon to engage in the interesting and responsible work of Sabbath school instruction, *enter upon it heartily.* If you cannot do this, I advise you not to attempt it. If you engage in such a work without being deeply interested in it yourself, and laying yourself out upon it, you will find neither pleasure, profit, nor success, therein. Presuming, therefore, that you will be desirous of using all the means in your power to qualify yourself for such a work, I offer for your consideration the following hints, which are given under the impression that your pupils are children or young persons : —

1. *Endeavor to obtain just views of the importance and responsibility of the work.* In a certain subordinate sense, the Sabbath school teacher is the pastor of a little flock. He is appointed, in his sphere, to watch for their souls, every one of which is of more value than the whole world. The influence which he exerts upon these souls may give direction not only to their character and influence in this life, but to their char-

14

acter and destiny throughout eternity. The responsibility is therefore fearful indeed.

2. Keep before your mind the *objects* to be attained by Sabbath school instruction, and pursue these objects with *directness* of purpose and effort. These objects are, the conversion of the souls of the pupils, if they are unconverted, and their sanctification, and preparation for usefulness, if converted. To attain either of these objects, it is necessary that they should have a clear and discriminating knowledge of those truths of God's word which teach them their lost and ruined condition by nature, and the way of salvation revealed in the gospel; because it is through these that the Holy Spirit operates in the conversion and sanctification of souls. These truths must, therefore, be so illustrated, simplified, and brought down to their capacities, that they will see their application to themselves, and learn from them their duty. But, to prepare them for usefulness, energy of mind, and habits of deep thought and close study, are of great importance, and must, therefore, be cultivated in the Sabbath school.

3. *Labor to obtain clear, full, and discriminating views of gospel truth yourself.* This is indispensable, if you would impress the same upon the minds of others. If your general views of truth are obscure, indefinite, and unsatisfactory to yourself, your instructions will be of the same character.

4. *Study to become skilful in the sacred art of communicating divine truth to the minds of children.*

Little as this may be esteemed, it is one of the most valuable talents you can possess. I know of no other which females can so profitably employ in the service of Christ. You must, therefore, *study the juvenile mind.* Endeavor to understand the philosophical principles of its early development, and reduce them to practice. Be familiar with children. Become acquainted with their language and modes of thinking, and strive to adapt yourself to their capacities. You may also obtain many valuable hints by reading some of the many excellent works which have been published on the subject of education, some of which are especially designed for Sabbath school teachers.

You must also *aim at drawing out the minds of the children, and teaching them to study, and to think, with clearness and precision, for themselves.* There is a great difference between *conversing with* children and *talking to* them. By the former, you call their minds into exercise, and get hold of their feelings. Thus you will secure their attention. But the latter will be much less likely to interest them; for, being the recipients of thought, instead of thinking for themselves, they participate less in the exercise. By engaging them in conversation, and leading that conversation in the investigation of truth, you teach them to *think.*

If we simply explain to a child the meaning of a passage of Scripture, the whole benefit lies in the instruction he receives at the time; but, if we show him practically how to ascertain the meaning himself, and bring him under the mental discipline which it requires, we give him a kind of key to unlock the mean-

ing of other passages. By an ingenious mode of catechizing, children's minds may be led to perceive and
understand almost any truth much more distinctly and
clearly than by any direct explanation which a teacher
can make. By *catechizing*, I do not mean the repeat-
ing of *catechisms*, but the calling out of their minds
upon any Scripture truth that may be before them, by
a series of simple questions, leading them to see the
truth as though they had discovered it themselves.
But it should be a leading object to secure the thorough
study of the lessons by themselves. The teacher
should never answer a question till it has passed
round the class; and remarks should be brief, and
directly to the point, intended either to bring out the
meaning of the Scripture more fully than their answers do, or else to impress the truth practically upon
their minds. But never forget that you are dependent
upon the Holy Spirit for the proper direction of the
powers of your mind. Pray, then, for clearness of
perception and discrimination of judgment, that you
may understand the truth, and for skill to communicate
it to your class. Study every Sabbath school lesson
in your closet, with these ends in view. Persevere in
your efforts till you become mistress of the art of
teaching.

5. To be a successful Sabbath school teacher, *you
must have a rich, fertile, and growing mind.* Nothing
else will compensate for the want of this. You cannot, for any length of time, sustain the interest of a
class, unless there is a constant growth in your own
mind. If there is a continued repetition of the same

thoughts, remarks, or exhortations, you will soon grow dull and uninteresting. But, in regard to the manner in which this is to be accomplished, I must refer you to a subsequent chapter, on mental improvement.

6. *Make yourself thoroughly acquainted with the lesson.* Study the portion of Scripture which is to be the subject of your lesson, with all the helps you can obtain, till you have satisfied your mind on every point involved in it, and till you can answer every question which you intend to propound to your scholars. Unless you do this habitually, you cannot be qualified for a teacher. If the teachers of the school with which you are connected hold a meeting of mutual consultation upon the lesson, never fail to attend, when it is in your power. These meetings are essential to a well-conducted and successful Sabbath school; and, when properly managed, they are both interesting and profitable to those who attend them. And you will contribute very much to this interest and profit, if you are always present, with your lesson thoroughly studied.

7. *Let your own heart be affected with the truth you are endeavoring to teach.* Upon this, so far as your instrumentality is concerned, greatly depends your success. Unless you *feel* the force of the truth yourself, it will be very difficult for you to convince your scholars that you are in earnest. While preparing the lesson in your closet, endeavor to obtain a realizing sense of the personal interest which you and your class have in the subject you are contemplating. See

14 *

what bearing it has upon their eternal destiny, as well as your own, and pray for the Holy Spirit to impress it powerfully upon your heart. Always, if possible, spend a little season in your closet, as an immediate preparation for the duties of the Sabbath school. Get your heart refreshed, in view of the practical truth contained in the lesson, and go before your class deeply impressed with its solemn import.

8. *Make a personal application of the practical truths contained in the lesson*, and embrace frequent opportunities of conversing separately and privately with every one of your scholars in regard to their religious feelings. If they give no evidence of piety, explain to them the duty of immediate repentance and submission to God, and urge them to perform it without delay. Do this under the solemn impression that it *may be* your last opportunity, and that you will soon meet them at the judgment-seat of Christ.

If you have reason to believe their hearts have been renewed, show them the importance of holy living. Urge upon them the duties of watchfulness, self-examination, studying the Scriptures, and prayer. Show them, also, the necessity of carrying out their religion into every action of their lives. Show them that the design of religion is to make them better, to give them better dispositions, to keep them humble, and make them more amiable, obedient, and dutiful, in every thing. Teach them, also, the great importance of improving their minds while young, to fit them for the service of Christ. You may have before you some future Harriet Newell, or Mrs. Judson, who may willingly surrender all the comforts of this life to carry the glad tidings of salvation to the benighted heathen.

9. *Be earnest and importunate for the Holy Spirit to bless your labors.* Without this, all your efforts will be in vain. Feel continually that you are but an instrument in the hand of God, and that all your success must depend upon him. Yet he has *promised* to give his Holy Spirit to them that ask him. Let no day pass without presenting before the throne of grace every individual of your class, rehearsing, as particularly as possible, the circumstances and feelings of each. Visit them as often as you can, and, if possible, persuade them to meet with you once a week for prayer. But make no effort in your own strength. Search well your motives, and see that self-seeking has no place in your heart. If you seek the conversion of your class, that you may be honored as the instrument, you will be disappointed. *God must be glorified in all things.*

PRIVATE SABBATH DUTIES.

There are duties that we owe to God *in private*, which ought to occupy a portion of the holy Sabbath. In the present age, when so much of the Lord's day is spent in attendance upon public worship and the Sabbath school, there is danger that secret communion with God will be neglected; and thus, like the tree with a worm at its root, the soul will wither under the genial rain and sunshine of the gospel. With a few practical directions on this point, I shall close this chapter.

1. *Spend as large a portion as possible of the intervals of public duties in your closet.* The time thus spent should be employed principally in the devotional reading of the Holy Scriptures; meditation upon divine truth, with the view of affecting the heart; self-examination; and prayer. If you have very much time to spend in this way, you may employ a part of it in reading some devotional book; but I think our reading, on the Sabbath, should be principally confined to the Scriptures. But *prayer* should be frequent, and mingled with every thing.

2. *Spend no part of the Lord's day in seeking your own ease or pleasure.* We are required to turn away our foot from finding our own pleasure on God's holy day. All our time is the Lord's; but the Sabbath is his in a peculiar manner. On other days of the week, he allows us to do *our own* work; but on this day, we must do *his work only.* There is no room, then, for the indulgence of idleness, indolence, or sloth, upon the Sabbath. The duties of this holy day are such as to require the active and vigorous exercise of all our faculties. That you may not, then, be tempted to indulge in sloth, use every means in your power to promote a lively state of your bodily energies. Make all your preparations on the afternoon of Saturday. Spend a portion of the evening in devotional exercises, for the purpose of banishing the world from your mind, and bringing it into a heavenly frame, and retire

to rest at an early hour. By this means, your animal powers will be refreshed, and you will be prepared early to meet the Lord, on the approach of his holy morning. But, in case of bodily infirmity, or the unforeseen interruption of rest on the night before the Sabbath, it is better to take time for rest, than to have all the duties of the day marred by lassitude or drowsiness. Yet great care should be taken not to drive the business of Saturday so far into the night, as to trespass on the hours of sleep, and thus rob God and your own soul of a portion of the holy Sabbath. If you will cast your eye forward down the stream of life, you will see that consequences of vast importance to your own soul, and to your influence upon those associated with you in life, may depend upon the early habits which you form in these respects.

3. *Watch over your thoughts.* The Sabbath is a season when Satan is exceedingly busy in diverting our thoughts from holy things. Evil thoughts also proceed from our own depraved hearts. But the Lord's day is as really profaned by vain and worldly thoughts as by the labor of our bodies. O, if we could realize this, how much food should we find for bitter repentance in the thoughts of a single Sabbath! Strive, then, to " bring into captivity every thought to the obedience of Christ." " I hate vain thoughts," says the Psalmist ; " but thy law do I love."

4. *Set a guard over your lips.* Conversing about the affairs of the world is a direct breach of the holy Sabbath. But we are not only required to refrain from worldly and vain conversation, but from *speaking*

our own words. All unprofitable conversation, even though it be about the externals of religion, should be avoided. It has a tendency to dissipate the mind, and to remove any serious impressions which the truth may have made. Our thoughts should be fixed on divine things, and our conversation should be heavenly. We are not only required to refrain from finding our own pleasure, speaking our own words, and doing our own ways, but we are to "call the Sabbath a delight. the holy of the Lord, honorable." And so will every one regard God's holy day who lives in the lively exercise of spiritual affections. Nor will the restrictions here proposed be regarded by such as burdensome, nor the sacred hours of the holy Sabbath drag heavily along; but the hours will pass too swiftly away, and the close of this blessed day will be followed by a feeling of regret that it was not longer, and that we have not accomplished all the good we hoped for and designed.

CHAPTER XI.

MEDITATION.

RELIGIOUS MEDITATION is a serious, practical, and
devout contemplation of divine things. It was the
delight of holy men of old, as it is now of all who set
their affections on things above. It is inseparably
connected with our growth in grace; for it is by
" beholding the glory of the Lord," that we are
" changed into the same image." And how can we
behold the glory of the Lord, but by the devout contemplation of his infinite perfections? The natural
tendency of our minds is to assimilate to those objects
which we contemplate. If, then, our thoughts are occupied with earthly things, our minds will be earthly.
Moreover, the word of God is " a lamp to our feet and
a light to our path;" but, if we do not open our eyes to
its truths, how can they guide our steps? It is by the
practical contemplation of the " lively oracles," that we
are to understand our duty; and, by a devout contemplation of them, that we are to drink into their spirit,
and hold communion with their Author.

Meditation should be constant. Divine truth is the
element in which the devout mind moves, as the fish
plays upon the bosom of the deep, and the bird mounts
aloft in the air; and, when deprived of its accustomed

element, it is in a condition not unlike that of the one
thrown upon the dry land, or the other pent up in a
cage.   Like the magnetic needle, when violently
turned from the pole, such a mind will revert to the
object of attraction, when the force which held it is
removed.   Its tendency is upward, as the needle to
the pole.   David says of the godly man, "His delight
is in the law of the Lord; and in his law doth he
meditate day and night;" and the writer of the 119th
Psalm says, "O, how love I thy law! it is my meditation *all the day.*"   This is true Christian feeling; and
we ought to be in such a frame continually that our
minds will dwell voluntarily upon the precious doc
trines, facts, precepts, and promises, of the word of
God.   But, so long as we are beset with temptations
without, and compelled to maintain a warfare with
indwelling corruptions, we must labor and watch, with
great diligence, to maintain a devout mind, and keep
our hearts affected with spiritual things.   Indeed,
nothing is to be attained, in the divine life, in our
present state, without great labor and strife; "for the
flesh lusteth against the Spirit, and the Spirit against
the flesh; and these are contrary, the one to the other;
so that ye cannot do the things that ye would."   One
of the most difficult matters in Christian experience
is to keep the mind habitually upon heavenly things,
while engaged in worldly employments, or surrounded
by objects which affect the senses.   Satan will be
continually seeking to divert your mind, and indwelling corruptions will rebel.   Vain thoughts will intrude; but if you hate them, and love the law of the

Lord, you will not suffer them to lodge with you. The Bible saints were fervent in spirit, even while engaged in business; and we have accounts of pious persons in every age, who have been like them. This is for our encouragement; for what they have done, we, by the grace of God, may do likewise. A heavenly mind is worth the labor of many years. Rest not till you attain it.

Meditation should be mingled with all our devotional reading, particularly with our reading of the Holy Scriptures. And it is well, in the morning, to fix upon some subject, or some passage of Scripture, for the mind to dwell upon, while we are engaged in our ordinary pursuits. But, in addition to this, it is profitable to set apart particular seasons every day, or as often as practicable, for fixed and holy meditation. We have examples of this among the saints of old; and they embraced the most favorable opportunities for this devout exercise. Isaac went out into the field to meditate in the stillness and solemnity of the evening. David sometimes chose the calmness of the morning. At other times, he fixed his thoughts in holy meditation during the wakeful hours of the night. "I remember thee *upon my bed*, and meditate on thee in the night-watches." "Mine eyes prevent the *night-watches*, that I might meditate in thy word." But this is a work of so much difficulty, requiring such abstraction of mind, that it is probable you will neglect it, unless you set apart stated and regular seasons for the purpose, and consider them as devoted to this sacred exercise. Select some subject, and think upon

15

it deeply, systematically, practically, and devoutly.
System is a great assistance in every thing. We can
never obtain clear views of any complex object without
separately viewing the various parts of which it is
composed. We cannot see the beautiful mechanism
of a watch, nor understand the principles which keep
it in motion, without taking it in pieces, and viewing
the parts separately. So, in contemplating any great
truth which contains many different propositions, if we
look at them all at once, our ideas will be confused
and imperfect; but, if we separate them, and examine
one at a time, our views will be clear and distinct.

Our meditation must be *practical*, because every
divine truth is calculated to make an impression upon
the heart; and, if it fails of doing this, our labor is
lost. Make, then, a direct personal application of the
truth on which your thoughts are fixed. But our meditations must also be *devout*. They must be mixed
with prayer. As an example of what I mean, I refer
you to the 119th Psalm. The Psalmist, in the midst
of his meditations, continually lifts up his soul in
prayer. His devout aspirations are breathed forth
continually. And in proportion as you follow his
example, will you succeed in this heavenly employment.

As for the *subjects of meditation*, the word of God
furnishes an endless variety. You may, however,
find advantage, in your seasons of fixed and solemn
meditation, by fastening your mind on some particular
portion of divine truth, and carrying it out in its various relations and applications. In my little work

entitled " THE CLOSET," which has grown out of a sense of my own wants, I have selected and arranged a considerable variety of topics, from which you may find some assistance. These are, however, intended as mere suggestions, and are, therefore, both imperfectly stated and partially carried out. One great difficulty in this exercise is, always to be able to fix the mind on some portion of truth in such a manner as to secure variety, and to contemplate truth in its proper proportions. I have arranged these subjects in such a manner, that, if taken in course, they will lead to the contemplation of divine truth, with some reference to its proper proportions, although they do not completely cover the ground. But any particular topic can be selected, according to your circumstances or inclination. Many of the subjects are divided under various heads ; and, in some cases, one or two heads may be found sufficient for one season of meditation. But no mere mechanical attention to the matter, as a task imposed upon yourself, will be of any avail. Your *heart* must be in it ; and then it will be an easy and delightful service.

CHAPTER XII.

ON HEALTH.

A HEALTHY and vigorous state of the body is important to a high degree of usefulness. The services which God requires of us, as laborers in his vineyard, are such as to call for vigor of body and strength of mind. A feeble state of health, other things being equal, must be a hinderance in the divine life. True, the Lord may make use of it as a chastisement, and so overrule it for our spiritual growth. But, with an equal degree of faithfulness, the healthy person has a great advantage over the unhealthy and feeble, in the religious life. When the animal powers are prostrated, the mind suffers with them; and many of the supposed spiritual maladies, which afflict the people of God, probably arise from bodily infirmity. But especially do we need bodily health, in our endeavors to benefit others. Works of usefulness are generally attended with laborious effort, either of body or of mind, or both; and frequently they require the sacrifice of personal ease, and those comforts of life which are necessary to the invalid. It is true that some individuals have lived very devoted lives, and been eminently useful, with frail and sickly bodies. But this does not prove that, with the same degree of faithfulness, and a sound body, they might not have made much higher attainments, and been much more useful. I think no one can read the memoirs of Baxter, Brainerd, Martyn, and Payson, without receiving the impression that, with the spirit which they possessed, in strong and vigorous bodies, they might have done much more good than they did, and perhaps arrived at a much higher degree of personal sanctification. During much of their lives, they were borne down and depressed by feeble health, and all but one of them died in the prime of life. But suppose them to have been as devoted as they were, with strong and vigorous constitutions, until they had arrived at the period of old age ; might they not have brought forth much more fruit ? Then God would have been so much the more glorified in them ; for Christ says, " Herein is my Father glorified, *that ye bear much fruit.*"

Is it not our duty, then, to use all proper means for maintaining a sound, healthful, and vigorous bodily constitution ? True, life and health, as well as every other blessing, come from God ; but he does not bestow them without the intervention of second causes. He has made our animal nature subject to certain fixed laws ; and when even his own children violate these laws, he will work no miracle to preserve their health or save their lives. We have no right to act on the supposition that our lives are our own ; and that the injury we bring upon our bodies, by imprudence and neglect, concerns nobody but ourselves. Our *bodies*, as well as our spirits, belong to God, by virtue of creation, preservation, redemption, and per-

15 *

sonal consecration.   We are, therefore, bound to use
all lawful means for the preservation of life and
health, that both may be prolonged for the glory of
God and the benefit of our fellow-creatures.   But,
when I speak of the means to be used for the preservation of health, I do not intend that excessive attention to *remedies* which leads so many people to resort
to *medicine* upon every slight illness.   But I mean the
study of the laws or principles of our animal existence,
and a diligent care to live according to those laws.
In short, I mean living *according to* nature.   *Disease*
is the natural consequence of living *contrary to* nature ; and probably a large proportion of the sickness
which prevails might be directly traced to the violation of the great laws which govern our present mode
of existence.

Within the compass of a single chapter I cannot be
very particular on this subject.   But I would recommend to you to read approved writers on physiology,
and endeavor to understand the *principles* upon which
this truly wonderful machine is kept in motion.   You
will find the subject interesting.   You will see the
evidence of a mighty intellect in the construction of
the human body.   You will also be able to draw from
it practical lessons to guide you in the most common
concerns of life.   I am the more earnest in this rec-
ommendation, because I think you will discover that
many of those habits and customs of society, which
are peculiarly under the control of ladies, need re-
forming.   I am seriously of the opinion that the general health of society depends far more upon the *la-*

dies than upon the *physicians.* The former direct the preparation of the daily supplies of food designed to sustain, refresh, and keep in motion the human system. The latter can only give prescriptions for regulating this delicate machinery, when, by mismanagement, it has got out of order.

But, in advising you to read on physiology, I would caution you against taking up medical writers, containing the description of diseases and their symptoms, and, comparing these descriptions with your own feelings, to ascertain whether you have the symptoms of the diseases of which you are reading. Such a course would almost certainly work on your imagination, and make you hypochondriac, if not actually induce the diseases themselves.

But, without further prologue, I will give a few simple rules for the preservation of health, which, though incomplete, will be of great benefit, if faithfully followed. From experience, study, and observation, you will, no doubt, be able to add to them many improvements.

I. *Make attention to health a matter of conscience, as a religious duty.* Pray for wisdom and self-denial, that you may be able to avoid whatever is injurious, and to persevere in the judicious use of such means as are necessary to promote sound health and energy of body.

II. *Maintain habitual cheerfulness and tranquillity of mind.* Perhaps few persons are fully aware of the influence which this has upon the health of the body. The opinion has been advanced that the stomach is affected chiefly by the influence of the brain on the nervous system. If this theory is correct, it adds very much to the importance of the suggestions under this head. If you are constitutionally inclined to *melancholy*, endeavor to avoid it as a *sin* dishonoring to God and destructive of your own health and happiness. It is dishonoring to God, because it is calculated to give the world a gloomy and repulsive idea of religion. It is sinful, because it destroys confidence in God, and leads to repining. Melancholy differs entirely from sorrow for sin, sympathy for distress, and concern for the perishing. Godly sorrow is a melting exercise, which softens the heart, and brings it low before God ; while a sight of the cross of Christ, and a sense of pardoning love, bring a holy calm and heavenly peace over the soul. But despondency comes over us like the withering blasts of winter. It congeals the tender emotions of the heart, and casts an icy gloom over every object. It hides from our view every thing lovely. It makes us insensible to the mercies of God which he is daily lavishing upon us. It shuts up the soul to brood alone, over every thing dark and hideous. It is no less unfriendly to the exercise of holy affections, than levity of conversation and manners. Although often created by bodily infirmity, it reacts, and renders disease doubly ferocious. Yet it is so far under the control of the will, that grace will enable us to subdue it. There is a very intimate connection between the mind and body. The one acts upon the other. Depression of spirits enfeebles all the animal powers, and particularly disturbs digestion, thereby deranging the whole system. If, therefore, you ever feel a gloomy depression of spirits, try to bring your mind into a serene and grateful frame, by meditating on the mercies you enjoy, and exercising a cheerful submission to the will of God. Remember that God directs all your ways, and that you have just as much of every comfort and blessing as he sees fit to give you, and infinitely more than you deserve. Rise above yourself, and think of the infinite loveliness of the divine character. But, if this is not sufficient, walk out and view the works of nature, and try to forget yourself in contemplating the wisdom and glory of God, as manifest in them; and the bodily exercise will assist in driving away this disturber of your peace. Or seek the society of some Christian friend, who is not subject to depression of spirits, whose heavenly conversation may lead you to lose sight of yourself in the fulness and glory of God. But avoid, at such times, the society of those who, like yourself, are subject to depression, unless they have made so much progress in subduing this infirmity as to be able not only to sympathize with you, but to give you encouragement. Sympathy alone will but increase the evil. Any violent emotion of the mind, or exercise of strong passions of any kind, is likewise exceedingly injurious to the health of the body.

III. *Be* REGULAR *in all your habits.* Ascertain, as nearly as you can, from your own feelings and experience, how many hours of sleep you require. No general rule can be adopted on this subject. Some people need more sleep than others. The want of sleep, and excessive indulgence in it, alike operate to enervate both body and mind. Probably every con-

stitution may be safely brought between five and eight
hours.   Of this you will judge, by making a fair trial.
That period of sleep which renders both body and
mind most energetic and vigorous should be adopted.
Rev. John Wesley states that he was, in the early part
of his life, in the habit of sleeping late in the morning;
but that he found himself wakeful and restless in the
middle of the night, and nervous all day.   He commenced rising earlier every morning, until he could
sleep soundly all night, and found himself much improved
in health.   He went farther, and endeavored still more
to diminish his sleep; but the effect was to render him
weak and nervous.   He continued, through a long life,
to rise at four, with improved health and spirits.   But
young persons require more sleep than those in advanced life.   If possible, take all your sleep in the
night.   Fix upon an hour for retiring and an hour for
rising, and then conscientiously keep them.   Let
nothing but stern necessity tempt you to vary from
them in a single instance; for you may not be able in
a week to recover from the effects of a single derangement of your regular habits.   We are the creatures of
habit; but if we would *control* our habits, instead of
suffering them to control us, it would be greatly to our
advantage.   It is also important that the hours of retiring and rising should be *early.*   Upon the plan
proposed, early retiring will be necessary to early
rising, which is a matter of the first importance.
Early rising promotes cheerfulness, invigorates the
system, and in many other ways contributes to health.
It also assists devotion.   There is a solemn stillness

before the dawn of day, in a winter morning, peculiarly favorable to devotional feelings; and nothing is better calculated to fill the mind with grateful and adoring views of the beneficence of the Creator, than the refreshing sweetness of a summer morn. Whoever sleeps away this period, loses half the pleasures of existence. To sally forth and enjoy the calmness and serenity of such a season; to listen to the sweet warbling of the birds; to behold the sparkling dewdrops, and the gayety of the opening flowers, as all nature smiles at the approach of the rising sun; to join the music of creation, in lifting up a song of softest, sweetest melody, in praise of their great Author, is no common luxury.

IV. *Spend at least two hours every day in active exercise in the open air.* This time may be divided into such portions as you find most convenient. The proper seasons for exercise are, about an hour either before or after a meal. This you may do without regard to the weather, provided you observe the following precautions, when it is cold, damp, or wet: 1. Exert yourself sufficiently to keep moderately warm. 2. Do not stop on your way to get chilled. 3. On returning, change any garment that may be wet or damp, before sitting down. This course will not only keep up your regular habits, but produce a hardiness of constitution which will greatly increase your usefulness in life. It is a great mistake to suppose that exposure to a damp, vapory atmosphere is injurious to health. The danger lies in exposing yourself when the system is in a relaxed state, as it is during rest after exercise. But, while a general action is kept up by vigorous exercise, nature itself will resist the most unfriendly vapors of the atmosphere. There is a great and growing evil in the education of ladies of the middling and higher classes, at the present day. The tender and delicate manner in which they are bred enfeebles their constitutions, and greatly diminishes their usefulness in every station of life. Many of them are sickly, and few of them are able to endure the slightest hardships. To show that this is the fault of their education, we need only refer to the condition of those young women whose circumstances in life render it necessary for them to labor. In most cases, they possess hale and vigorous constitutions, and are even more capable of enduring hardships than most men of sedentary habits. There may be some exceptions to this remark; but, in these cases, we know not what other causes have contributed to a contrary result. As a general fact, I think the remark will hold good; though it is equally true that excessive labor and exposure, in the period of youth, often destroy the health. I do not see how the delicate training to which I have alluded can be reconciled with Christian principle. If we have devoted ourselves to the Lord, it is our duty not only to do all the good we can in the world, but to make ourselves *capable* of doing as much as possible. The man in the parable was condemned for not *improving* and *increasing* his talent. Any thing, then, which has a tendency to diminish our usefulness should be regarded as *sin*. Exposure to all kinds of weather has this advantage also, — it renders a person much less likely to take cold, and, of course, less subject to sickness ; for a great proportion of diseases owe their origin to common colds.

No part of a code of health is of more importance than exercise. Without it, every thing else will fail. And it is as necessary that it should be *regular*, every day, and at nearly the same hours every day, as it is that meals should be regular. We might as well omit eating for a day as to neglect exercise. The one is as necessary as the other to promote the regular operations of the animal functions.

But, when your situation will admit of it, I would advise you to take a portion of your exercise in those domestic employments which require vigorous exertion. If you open your windows, you will have the fresh air ; at the same time, you will enjoy the satisfaction of rendering your hours of relaxation useful.

Every lady, whatever may be her situation in life, ought to have a *practical* knowledge of household affairs ; and no one will be any the less respected by those whose opinion is worth caring for, on account of employing her hands in any department of housekeeping. Nor will any *young lady* be more highly esteemed for avoiding labors of this kind, *especially if the labors and cares of her mother should in consequence be increased.*

V. *Bathe frequently.* About five-eighths of the food taken into the stomach passes off, by insensible perspiration, through the pores of the skin ; and with it is thrown off whatever impure matter is found in any part of the system. When this perspiration is obstructed, general derangement succeeds. It is chiefly to

16

promote this, that exercise is required.   But the matter thrown off is of a very poisonous nature, and, if not removed, may be absorbed again into the system. It also collects upon the surface, and obstructs the regular discharge from the pores.   Frequent ablution is, therefore, highly necessary.

It is also essential to personal cleanliness.   There is an *odor* in this insensible perspiration, which becomes offensive when the impurities collecting upon the surface of the skin are not frequently removed.   The entire surface of the body should be washed every day ; and, if this is done, on rising in the morning, with cold water, and followed by brisk rubbing with a coarse towel, it will furnish an effectual safeguard against taking cold.   This, however, should be omitted when there is any danger to be apprehended from the sudden application of cold, or serious consequences may follow.   Warm water, with soap, should occasionally be used at night, in order to remove all impurities from the skin.

VI. *Pay attention to the quality and quantity of food taken into the stomach.*   Nothing more necessarily affects both the health of the body and the vigor of the intellect.   It is from this that the blood is formed, and the continual waste of the system supplied.   And through the blood it acts on the brain, which is supposed to be the seat of the intellect.   Yet, notwithstanding this, those whose peculiar province it is to direct the preparation of our food, seldom inquire into the chemical effect any such preparation may have upon the stomach, and, through it, upon the whole

system. Indeed, the business is generally left to persons entirely ignorant of chemistry and the principles
which govern the human constitution. It is no wonder, then, that a large proportion of our culinary preparations are decidedly unfriendly to it. But, in relation
to this matter, I cannot here be very particular. I
will only give some general rules, by which you may
discover the bounds of moderation, and what articles
of food ought to be avoided. The sensible effects
arising from food unsuitable to the state of the stomach
are generally the following: disagreeable eructations,
accompanied with risings of food; uneasy or burning
sensations of the stomach; or acidity, with flatulence;
and these symptoms are often succeeded by headache,
and vertigo, or dizziness. The effect of an excessive
quantity of food is first felt by an uneasiness and op-
pressive fulness of the stomach. These are succeeded
by a general distention or fulness of the blood-vessels,
particularly about the head, general lassitude, slug-
gishness and dulness of intellect, with a great aversion
to mental effort. These sensations are accompanied
by a general uneasiness throughout the whole system,
with more or less pain. It also seriously affects the
temper. It makes people fretful, impatient, and peevish. The best disposition may be ruined by the im
proper indulgence of the appetite. I have been particular in describing these symptoms, because people
are often subject to many uncomfortable sensations, for
which they cannot account, but which might be traced
to this source. A large share of our unpleasant feelings probably arise either from the improper quality or

excessive quantity of the food taken into the stomach;
and the bounds of moderation are more frequently
exceeded by all classes of people than many imagine.
But, for a more full examination of this subject, I must
again refer you to the works of judicious writers on
health, and the means of preserving it. This is a
matter so intimately connected with the sphere of a
lady's influence, that every female should give it a
careful examination.

Take care to observe those articles of food which
you find injurious, and avoid them. Observe, also, as
nearly as you can, the *quantity* which agrees with
your stomach, and see that you never exceed it.
Take no food between your regular meals. The
stomach is employed from three to five hours in di-
gesting a meal; and if more food is taken during that
time, it disturbs and impedes digestion, making it
more laborious. And, after one meal is digested, the
stomach needs rest before another is taken. In connection with these general hints, attention to the two
following rules will generally be sufficient: —

1. Avoid highly-seasoned food, fresh bread, heating
condiments, and stimulating drinks.

2. Select the simplest dishes, and make your meal
of a single course. Mixed dishes are more likely to
be injurious; and a second course will almost certainly lead to excess.

But do not give your attention so much to this subject as to become *splenetic*. The imagination has a
great influence upon animal feeling; and, if you are
always watching the digestion of your food, you will

be sure to find dyspeptic symptoms ; and, by humoring your stomach too much, you will weaken its capacity of accommodating itself to the kind of nutriment it receives. Having fixed your principles of regimen, adhere to them as rigidly as you can without inconvenience to others. But, having done this, let your mind dwell as little as possible on the subject, and do not make it a matter of frequent conversation. Especially do not make trouble to the friends who entertain you, when away from home, by excessive particularity. You may find some wholesome dish on the most luxurious table ; and, if the table is *lean*, you need not fear.

As we are commanded, whether we eat or drink, or whatsoever we do, to do all to the glory of God, it may not be amiss to inquire how we may *glorify God in eating and drinking.* 1. We may eat for the purpose of strengthening our bodies, to enable us to engage in the active service of the Lord. 2. When we partake, in moderation, of the bounties of Providence, it is right that our animal appetites should be feasted with the delicious taste of the fruits of the earth. But we must see the glory of God in it. Here the benevolence of his character shines forth in the wonderful provision which he has made for the gratification of our appetites. Hence we may argue the ineffable sweetness of the bread of life, — the food of the soul. This mortal body is but a tent pitched in the wilderness, for the residence of the soul during its pilgrimage. If, then, God has opened the treasures of the animal and vegetable kingdoms to please the taste of

16 *

this meaner part, how much more abundant the provision for feasting the soul with pure spiritual food,—with eternally-increasing knowledge of the divine character and perfections! But we cannot so partake of those rich and hurtful dainties invented by man. The delight thus experienced is the glory of man, not of God. And the effect produced is the destruction of those delicate organs of taste, which he has provided that we may discern the exquisite sweetness of the natural fruits of the earth. By the same means, also, we destroy our health, and unfit ourselves for his service. 3. But I suppose the apostle had in his mind chiefly the idea of *acknowledging God* when we partake of his bounty, and of *honoring him* by doing every thing *in obedience to his commands.* Strict and intelligent regard to these points would generally direct us aright in the matter of eating and drinking.

Do not, by any means, think this subject beneath your attention. The greatest and best of men have made it a matter of practical study. Those who have given us the brightest specimens of intellectual effort have been remarkable for rigorous attention to their diet. Among them may be mentioned Sir Isaac Newton, John Locke, and President Edwards. *Temperance* is one of the fruits of the Spirit. It is, therefore, the duty of every Christian to know the bounds of moderation in all things, and to practise accordingly. But it may be necessary to throw in a caution here against *excessive abstinence.* There is a strong tendency, especially in the ardor of youth, to carry every thing to extremes. It is a dangerous experiment to live so low as to enfeeble the animal powers. You may, from such imprudence, suffer through life; or, if attacked with an acute disease when the system is very much reduced, there is no room for depletion, and recovery is extremely difficult.

VII. *As much as possible, avoid taking medicine.* The practice of resorting to *remedies* for every unpleasant feeling cannot be too strongly reprobated. Medicine should be regarded as a choice of two evils: it may throw off a violent attack of disease, and save life; but it must inevitably, in a greater or less degree, impair the constitution. Medicine is unfriendly to the human system. Its very effect, which is to disturb the regular operation of the animal functions, proves this. But, when violent disease is seated upon any part, this may be necessary; and the injury received from the medicine may not bear any comparison with the consequences which would follow if the disease were left to take its course. In such cases, the physician should be called immediately, as delay may be fatal. But the great secret lies in avoiding such attacks by a scrupulous attention to the laws of nature. Such attacks may generally be traced either to violent colds, or the interruption of some of the regular functions of the body. The most important of these may, with proper attention, be brought almost entirely under the control of *habit*; and all of them may generally be preserved in healthy action by prudence and care, and proper attention to diet and exercise. But careless and negligent habits in these respects will ruin the most hardy constitution, and bring on a train of disorders equally detrimental to mind and body. But, in most cases of moderate, protracted disease, a return to the regular system of living *according to nature* will gradually restore lost health ; or, in other words, a strict examination will discover some violation of the principles of the human constitution as the cause of derangement ; and, by correcting this error, nature will gradually recover its lost energies, and restore soundness to the part affected.

It is proper, however, to remark, in qualification of the foregoing observations, that we are in a *world of death*. Sin has deranged the course of nature, and the very elements have turned against us. The seeds of disease are often propagated by hereditary descent ; and the exciting causes thereof are floating on the breeze, and concealed in the food and drink which we take to nourish our bodies. It is not always possible, therefore, to trace the origin of a particular disease ; nor is it always our own fault when we are sick. But our wisdom is, as much as possible, by the care we take of ourselves, not to excite the latent diseases which lurk within us, and to avoid every thing which we know tends to their development. It is, therefore, important that we study our own constitution. For this purpose, it may be of great benefit to consult a skilful physician, even in apparent health.

CHAPTER XIII.

MENTAL CULTIVATION. READING.

IN the parable of the talents, our Lord teaches us that we shall be called to account for all the means of usefulness he has bestowed upon us, and that we are under obligation not only to employ our talents in his service, but to *increase* them as we have opportunity. Among these talents stand foremost the powers of mind which he has given us ; and therefore, if we neglect the proper cultivation of our intellectual faculties, we shall come under the condemnation of the servant who hid his talent in the earth. But, when I speak of the improvement of the mind, I do not mean *reading* merely, but such discipline as will call into exercise the intellectual powers, and enable us to employ them in the investigation of the truth. This discipline is a necessary preparation for profitable reading. It is a great mistake to suppose that mental ability is entirely original, or that only a few possess intellectual faculties capable of searching into the deep recesses of knowledge. It is true, some have talents of a superior order ; but none, except idiots, are incapable of improvement ; and many of the greatest minds have been formed upon a foundation which appeared, in the early stages of their education, to consist of little else than dulness and stupidity. The most crooked and unpromising twig may, by proper care and culture, become a great and beautiful tree. The proper objects of education are, to give the ability of acquiring knowledge, and to prepare for usefulness. We are not to disregard ourselves; and knowledge is an object of intrinsic value to us. God is glorified in us in proportion as we are filled with knowledge and spiritual understanding. But we are to love others *as* ourselves, and seek their good *as* our own. Although our heads may be filled with knowledge, yet, if we have not the capacity of employing it for practical purposes, it will be comparatively of little value. Many persons excuse themselves for neglecting to improve their minds, upon the ground that they are incapable of doing any thing great or brilliant. But this arises from a foolish pride. If we have but a single talent, we are equally under obligation to improve it in the service of our Master as if we had ten. And it was upon this principle that the servant was condemned to whom but one was given.

The discipline of which I speak may be effected in many ways. But the method I shall propose is one that can be pursued without an instructor, while employed most of the time in active pursuits. The course already recommended in relation to meditation and the study of the Scriptures, will be found a valuable means of mental discipline. But other means should likewise be employed. I know of nothing which more effectually calls out the resources of the mind than writing. To a person unaccustomed to this exercise it appears very difficult; but a little practice will make it a pleasing and delightful employment. The mind is more deeply interested with its own discoveries or productions than it is with second-hand thoughts, communicated through the medium of the senses; and all the intellectual faculties are strengthened and improved by exertion.

I would therefore advise you to pursue a regular plan of written exercises. This will be very easy, if you only learn to think methodically. Select chiefly practical subjects; which your Sabbath school lessons, your subjects of meditation, and your daily study of the Scriptures, will furnish in great abundance. One reason why young persons find this exercise so difficult is, that they select abstract subjects, which have little to do with the common concerns of life. On this account, it will be greatly to your advantage to choose some Scripture truth as the subject of your exercise. The Bible is a practical book, and we have a personal interest in every thing it contains. When you have selected your subject, carefully separate the different parts or propositions it contains, and arrange them under different heads. This you will find a great assistance in directing your thoughts. If you look at the whole subject at once, your ideas will be obscure, indefinite, and confused. But this difficulty will be removed by a judicious division of its parts. Take time, as often as you can, to devote to this exercise; and rein up your mind to it, with the determination that you will succeed. Do not indulge the absurd notion that you can write only when you *feel like it*. Your

object is to *discipline* the mind, and bring it under
the control of the will; but this you will never accomplish, if you suffer your mind to be controlled by your
feelings in the very act of discipline. Finish one division of your subject every time you sit down to the
exercise, until the whole is completed; then lay it
aside till you have finished another. After this, review,
correct, and copy, the first one. The advantage of
laying aside an exercise for some time before correcting it is, that you will be more likely to discover its
defects than while your first thoughts are fresh in your
mind. But never commence a subject, and leave it
unfinished. If you do so, you will cherish a fickleness
of mind which will unfit you for close study and pa-
tient investigation. Finish what you begin, however
difficult you may find it, or however unsatisfactory
your performance may be when it is done. Scarce any
habit is of more practical importance than perseverance. Do not be discouraged, even if you should be
able to bring forth but one idea under each division of
your subject. You will improve with every exercise.
And you will permit me to say, for your encouragement, that, the first attempt I made at writing, with all
the study of which I was capable, I could not produce
more than five or six lines. Carefully preserve all
your manuscripts. By referring to them occasionally,
you will discover your progress in improvement. In
these exercises, you can make use of the knowledge
you acquire in reading, whenever it applies to your
subject. You will find advantage, if you have a
friend who is willing to take the trouble of criticising

your performances. But do not be discouraged, if the criticisms should make them appear mean in your own eyes; neither be displeased with your friend's severity. It will do you good; and, if you persevere, you will always be thankful for the advantage of having your defects pointed out. When you have practised so as to have acquired considerable facility of expression, it will be a stimulus to effort, occasionally, to send a piece to some periodical for publication. And, if you find your writings acceptable, it will increase your means of usefulness. In my early attempts at writing, I had no instruction, and no one to aid or encourage me; but, from the moment my first piece appeared in print, I felt a stimulus, leading me to exertion which I should never have made without it. — But, in every thing, remember your dependence upon God, and seek the direction of his Holy Spirit; and carefully guard against being elated with success, or puffed up with the idea that you possess extraordinary talents. Such a notion will only subject you to mortification when you discover your mistake. But, should it be true, it would be no ground of pride; for you have nothing but what you have received from God. What can be more contemptible than being proud of our talents? It is like a beggar being puffed up with the idea that he is rich, because some one has given him a few coppers.

Reading is likewise an important means of intellectual improvement. But you should never engage in reading for mere amusement or mental excitement; but have always in view the acquisition of knowledge

17

and the improvement of your mind. And, when you read, do not make your mind a mere reservoir, to hold the waters that are poured into it; but, when you read the thoughts which others have penned, think them over, and make them your own, if they are good, or mark their defects, and reject them, if they are bad. And, when you read history or intelligence, let it always be accompanied with reflections of your own.

But the first thing which claims attention is the *kind of books to be read.* It would hardly seem necessary to caution the class of persons I am addressing against the reading of pernicious books; because serious piety generates a chastened taste, which turns away from whatever contravenes its spirit. Yet, since the question as to what kinds of reading are pernicious is by no means settled in the Christian community, and as the "last new novel" finds a place on the centre-tables of many professedly religious people, I have thought it might be useful, in this place, to enter into a discussion of the tendencies of this kind of reading. I shall not stop to define the terms *novels* and *romances*, because their popular acceptation is sufficiently definite for my purpose. Nor is it necessary to inquire whether there may not be exceptions to the charges preferred against them; because the objections lie against the general character of a whole class of writings, and grow naturally out of this general character. It would be strange, indeed, if there were no gems of intellect, no fine sentiments, in the deluge of productions emanating from the exuberant imaginations of novel writers; but to attempt to separate the precious from the vile, would be like diving into a common sewer to hunt for pearls. " A judicious historian," says Mr. Hall,* " has said, respecting the fictitious works of the last century, — and those of the present are no improvement upon them, — that, if we should divide them into a *thousand parts*, five hundred of these parts must be at once condemned as so contemptibly frivolous as to render the perusal of them a most criminal waste of time. *Four hundred and ninety-nine* of the remaining *five hundred* parts he pronounces positively corrupting in their influence. He describes them as full of representations which can have no other tendency than to mislead, corrupt, and destroy, those who habitually peruse them, and especially those who give them a favorable reception. There remains, then, but the *thousandth* part, in defence of which any thing can be said. Even for these it is impossible to claim any higher character than that of 'innocent and amusing compositions.' *This merit*, small as it is, is greater than can be conceded. All works are not *innocent* which may be exempt from the charge of disseminating irreligion and licentiousness. If they convey false impressions of life, excite a distaste for its duties, and divert the mind from *real* scenes to images of its own creation, they are decidedly pernicious. This, to a greater or less extent, is the effect of all novels.

* Rev. S. R. Hall, late principal of the Andover Seminary for Teachers. I quote from his " *Lectures to Parents.*"

Every habitual reader of them *knows* it to be the fact."

But, without further preliminary remarks, I proceed to specify some of the objections to novel reading; and, in doing so, I shall endeavor to establish my positions by the testimony of competent witnesses.

1. First, then, I remark, that *novel reading produces an undue development of the imagination.* That profound thinker, the author of the " Natural History of Enthusiasm," * &c., in his invaluable treatise on " Home Education," remarks, that " The imagination and the imaginative sentiments are the very last to be developed, where nature takes her own course. It is the rich-colored chrysanthenum † of the intellectual parterre. So late in their appearance are the genuine imaginative emotions, and so nearly do they bear upon the confines of personal or adult mental culture, that, except in regard to certain commencements and preparations, the subject might altogether have been excluded, as not belonging to home education." An American medical writer, in a treatise on the influence of mental cultivation upon health, says, the nervous system, being connected with the brain, is early developed, and becomes the predominating system in youth; which predominance is necessary during the periods devoted to the increase of the body; but this great and early development very much increases the liability to disease. He therefore concludes that,

---

* Mr. Isaac Taylor.
† A flower that blooms late in the season.

during this period, strong excitement of the feelings is in danger of producing such a preponderance of the nervous system as to make it always easily excited, and disposed to sympathize with disorder in any part of the body; thus generating a predisposition to hypochondriasis and numerous afflicting nervous diseases. "Mental excitement," he says, "increases the flow of the blood to the head, and augments the size and power of the brain, just as the exercise of the limbs increases and strengthens the muscles of the limbs exercised." And Dr. James Jackson says, "Extra development and sensibility of the brain cannot take place but at the expense of some function or structure in the animal or organic system. When, therefore, an undue share of the vital energy of an individual is directed to a particular organ, a proportionate subduction is made from some other."

Any sort of light reading is supposed to be less injurious to health than close study. But, if these principles are correct, works of fiction, which strongly excite the imagination and feelings, must be much more injurious than study, and, in the period of youth, highly dangerous. As the predominance of the nervous system is necessary during the growth of the body, the opinion of Mr. Taylor, as to the late development of the imagination, agrees with the analogy of nature; for it is the imagination which acts most directly on the nervous system; and we should naturally conclude that the wisdom of the Creator would delay its development during the predominance of the nervous system. What, then, must be the physical

17 *

effects of strong stimulants applied to the imaginative powers of girls in their teens? for this is generally the period when the taste for novels is acquired, and when their deleterious influence, in the permanent deterioration of character, is most severely felt. The danger is very great, at this critical period, as to the health of females, either that fatal diseases will be induced, or that such a permanent preponderance of the nervous system will be created, as greatly to enfeeble the constitution, and destroy all balance of character. Just such injurious excitement is furnished by novel reading; and we need not go far to find examples of just such ruinous effects. " That excessive predominance of feeling and imagination," says Mr. Hall, for which the infidel Rousseau was noted, is thought to have been chiefly owing to such a cause. Nearly his whole time, till eight years of age, was spent in listening to romances, read to him by his father."

The effects of this kind of reading upon girls, in the premature and disproportionate development of the imagination, is thus described by Hannah More, whose extensive acquaintance with fashionable society will give due weight to her opinions on such a subject: "Frivolous reading will produce its correspondent effect in much less time than books of solid instruction; the imagination being liable to be wrought upon, and the feelings to be set a-going, much faster than the understanding can be opened and the judgment enlightened. A talent for conversation should be the *result* of instruction — not its *precursor :* it is a golden fruit, when suffered to ripen gradually in the tree of knowledge; but, if forced in the hot-bed of a circulating library, it will turn out worthless and vapid, in proportion as it was artificial and premature. Girls who have been accustomed to devour a multitude of frivolous books, will converse and write with a far greater appearance of skill, as to style and sentiment, at twelve or fourteen years old, than those of a more advanced age, who are under the discipline of severe studies; but the former, having early attained to that low standard which had been held out to them, become stationary; while the latter, quietly progressive, are passing through just gradations, to a higher strain of mind; and those who early begin with talking and writing like women, commonly end with thinking and acting like children."

The following remarks of the same writer apply, with equal force, after the period of youth is passed. Speaking of the education of females, she says, " Though their imagination is already too lively, and their judgment naturally incorrect, in educating them we go on to stimulate the imagination, while we neglect the regulation of the judgment. They already want ballast, and we make their education consist in continually crowding more sail than they can carry. Their intellectual powers being so little strengthened by exercise, makes every little petty business appear a hardship to them; whereas serious study would be useful, were it only that it leads the mind to the habit of conquering difficulties. But it is peculiarly hard to turn at once from the indolent repose of light reading,

— from the concern of mere animal life, the objects
of sense, or the frivolousness of female chit-chat, — it
is peculiarly hard, I say, to a mind so softened, to
rescue itself from the dominion of self-indulgence, to
resume its powers, to call home its scattered strength,
to shut out every foreign intrusion, to force back a
sprig so unnaturally bent, and to devote itself to religious reading, to active business, to sober reflection,
to self-examination : whereas, to an intellect accustomed to think at all, the difficulty of thinking seriously is obviously lessened."

2. *Novel reading produces a morbid appetite for
excitement.* The object of the novelist generally is, to
produce the highest possible degree of excitement,
both of the mind and the passions. The effect is very
similar to that of intoxicating liquors on the body ;
hence the confirmed novel reader becomes a kind of
literary inebriate, to whom the things of *entity* have
no attractions, and whose thirst cannot be slaked even
with *the water of life.* And as intoxication enfeebles
the body and engenders indolent habits, so this unnatural stimulus enfeebles the intellectual powers,
induces mental indolence, and unfits the mind for
vigorous effort. Nothing less stimulating than its
accustomed aliment can rouse such a mind to action,
or call forth its energies ; and then, being under the
influence of mental intoxication, which dethrones reason and destroys the power of self-control, they are
always misdirected.

3. *Novel reading promotes a sickly sensibility.* A
medical writer, speaking of the too powerful excite-

ment of the female mind, says, " In them the nervous system naturally predominates. They are endowed with quicker sensibility, and far more active imagination, than men. Their emotions are more intense, and their senses alive to more delicate impressions. They therefore require great attention, lest this exquisite sensibility, which, when properly and naturally developed, constitutes the greatest excellence of woman, should either become excessive by too strong excitement, or suppressed by misdirected education." Novel reading produces just the kind of excitement calculated to develop this excessive and diseased sensibility; and the effect is, to fill the mind with imaginary fears, and produce excessive alarm and agitation at the prospect of danger, the sight of distress, or the presence of unpleasant objects; while no place is found for the exercise of genuine sympathy for real objects of compassion. That sensibility which weeps over imaginary woes of imaginary beings calls forth but imaginary sympathy. It is too refined to be excited by the *vulgar* objects of compassion presented in real life, or too excitable to be of any avail in the relief of real distress. It may faint at the sight of blood, but it will shrink back from binding up the wound. If you wish to become weak-headed, nervous, and good for nothing, read novels. I have seen an account of a young lady who had become so nervous and excitable, in consequence of reading novels, that her head would be turned by the least appearance of danger, real or imaginary. As she was riding in a carriage over a bridge, in company

with her mother and sister, she became frightened at
some fancied danger, caught hold of the reins, and
backed the carriage off the bridge, down a precipice,
dashing them to pieces.

This excessive sensibility renders its possessor ex-
quisitely alive to all those influences which are unfriendly to human happiness, while it diminishes the
power of endurance. Extreme sensibility, especially
in a female, is a great misfortune, rendering the ills
of life insupportable. Great care should therefore be
taken, that, while genuine sensibility is cherished, its
extremes should be avoided, and the mind fortified by
strengthening the higher powers. On this subject,
Mrs. More has the following sensible remarks: " Serious study serves to harden the mind for more trying
conflicts; it lifts the reader from sensation to intellect;
it abstracts her from the world and its vanities; it fixes
a wandering spirit, and fortifies a weak one; it di-
vorces her from matter; it corrects that spirit of
trifling which she naturally contracts from the frivolous turn of female conversation, and the petty nature
of female employments; it concentrates her attention,
assists her in a habit of excluding trivial thoughts, and
thus even helps to qualify her for religious pursuits.
Yes, — I repeat it, — there is to woman a Christian use
to be made of sober studies; while books of an opposite
cast, however unexceptionable they may be sometimes
found in point of expression, however free from evil in
its more gross and palpable shapes, yet, from their
very nature and constitution, they excite a spirit of
relaxation, by exhibiting scenes and suggesting ideas

which soften the mind and set the fancy at work; they take off wholesome restraints, diminish sober-mindedness, and, at best, feed habits of improper indulgence, and nourish a vain and visionary indolence, which lays the mind open to error and the heart to seduction."

4. *Novel reading gives erroneous views of life.* The testimony of Fenelon, on this point, is valuable, as showing that the influence of novels, a hundred years ago, in another country, was the same as it now is among us. He says, " Uninstructed and ignorant girls are always possessed of an erratic imagination. For want of solid nourishment, all the ardor of their curiosity is directed toward vain and dangerous objects. Those who are not without talent often devote themselves entirely to the perusal of books which tend to cherish their vanity; they have a passionate fondness for novels, plays, narratives of romantic adventures, in which licentious love occupies a prominent place; in fine, by habituating themselves to the high-flown language of the heroes of romance, their heads are filled with visionary notions. In this way, they even render themselves unfit for society; for all these fine sentiments, these adventures which the author of the romance has invented to gratify the imagination, have no connection with the true motives that excite to action and control the interests of society, or with the disappointments invariably attendant on human affairs. A poor girl, full of the tender and the marvellous, which have charmed her in the perusal of such works, is astonished not to find in the world real characters resembling these heroes: she would wish to live like

those imaginary princesses, who, in the fictions of romance, are always charming, always adored, always placed beyond the reach of necessary duties. What must be her disgust when compelled to descend from these flights of fancy to the humble details of domestic life!"

But the following testimony of Goldsmith is, if possible, still more valuable, as the writer's wisdom, like Solomon's, is experimental, he having written one of the least exceptionable novels in the English language. "Above all things," he says, in a letter to his brother, "*never let your son touch a romance or a novel.* These paint beauty in colors more charming than nature, and describe happiness that man never tastes. How delusive, how destructive, are those pictures of consummate bliss! They teach the young mind to sigh after beauty and happiness which never existed; to despise the little good which Fortune has mixed in our cup, by expecting more than she ever gave; and, in general, — take the word of a man who has studied human nature more by experience than precept, — take my word for it, I say, that such books teach us very little of the world."

5. *Novel reading strengthens the passions, weakens the virtues, and diminishes the power of self-control.* Multitudes may date their ruin from the commencement of this kind of reading; and many more, who have been rescued from the snare, will regret, to the end of their days, its influence in the early formation of their character. The novel writer, having no higher object in view than to amuse the reader, and

being deficient in moral principle, appeals to the imagination and the passions, as the readiest way of access to the heart. A love affair, of some sort, is indispensable to this species of writing. Indeed, both novel writers and novel readers seem to be worshippers at the shrine of an imaginary sentiment, denominated *love;* but which, if traced to its source, would be found to have a much more questionable origin than the sentiment which leads to conjugal union. To a very great extent, these works unite in the same person some of the noblest traits of character with secret or open immorality; thus clothing vice in a garb of loveliness, and insensibly undermining virtuous principle. Yet, in many of them, the subtle poison is so diffused as not to be seen by its victims till it is too late to apply a remedy. To substantiate this charge, I shall produce the authority of one whose literary character and position in society gave her the most ample opportunity of judging correctly. Though the principal drift of the following remarks of Mrs. Hannah More is directed against a particular class of these writings, yet, from the commencement, it will be seen that she meant to apply them indiscriminately to novels and romances of every description, at least in their ultimate tendencies. It may be true that, in regard to some of them, the picture is highly wrought; yet the more covert and insidious the poison, the greater is the danger. If there are any, of the whole tribe of novels and romances, which are not obnoxious to these charges, they all fall under those already enumerated; and they will all be found tending to-

18

wards the imminent dangers here portrayed; for the appetite, once created, will demand still stronger and stronger stimulus, till it has tasted the whole. It may, however, be safely asserted that no work of imagination, the incidents of which are interwoven with a love affair, can be wholly free from these dangers.

"Novels," says Mrs. More, "which chiefly used to be dangerous in one respect, are now become mischievous in a thousand. They are continually shifting their ground, and enlarging their sphere, and are daily becoming vehicles of wider mischief. Sometimes they concentrate their force, and are at once employed to diffuse destructive politics, deplorable profligacy, and impudent infidelity. Rousseau was the first popular dispenser of this complicated drug, in which the deleterious infusion was strong, and the effect proportionably fatal; for he does not attempt to seduce the affections but through the medium of the principles. He does not paint an innocent woman ruined, repenting, and restored; but, with a far more mischievous refinement, he annihilates the value of chastity, and, with pernicious subtlety, attempts to make his heroine almost more amiable without it. He exhibits a virtuous woman, the victim, not of temptation, but of reason; not of vice, but of sentiment; not of passion, but of conviction; and strikes at the very root of honor, by elevating a crime into a principle. With a metaphysical sophistry the most plausible, he debauches the heart of woman by cherishing her vanity, in the erection of a system of male virtues, to which, with a lofty dereliction of those that are her more peculiar and characteristic praise, he tempts her to aspire; powerfully insinuating that to this splendid system chastity does not belong; thus corrupting the judgment, and bewildering the understanding, as the most effectual way to inflame the imagination and deprave the heart.

"The rare mischief of this author consists in his power of seducing, by falsehood, those who love truth, but whose minds are still wavering, and whose principles are not yet formed. He allures the warmhearted to embrace vice, not because they prefer vice, but because he gives to vice so natural an air of virtue; and ardent and enthusiastic youth, too confidently trusting in their integrity and in their teacher, will be undone, while they fancy they are indulging in the noblest feelings of their nature. Many authors will more infallibly complete the ruin of the loose and ill-disposed; but perhaps there never was a net of such exquisite art, and inextricable workmanship, spread to entangle innocence, and ensnare inexperience, as the writings of Rousseau; and, unhappily, the victim does not even struggle in the toils, because part of the delusion consists in imagining that he is set at liberty.

"Some of our recent popular publications have adopted and enlarged all the mischiefs of this school; and the principal evil arising from them is, that the virtues they exhibit are almost more dangerous than the vices. The chief materials out of which these delusive systems are framed, are characters who practise superfluous acts of generosity, while they are trampling on obvious and commanded duties; who combine inflated sentiments of honor with actions the most flagitious; a high tone of self-confidence with a perpetual neglect of self-denial; pathetic apostrophes to the passions, but no attempt to resist them. They teach that chastity is only individual attachment; that no duty exists which is not prompted by feeling; that impulse is the main spring of virtuous actions, while laws and religion are only unjust restraints; the former imposed by arbitrary men, the latter by the absurd prejudices of timorous and unenlightened conscience. Alas! they do not know that the best creature of impulse that ever lived is but a wayward, unfixed, unprincipled being; that the best *natural* man requires a curb, and needs that balance to the affections which Christianity alone can furnish, and without which benevolent propensities are no security to virtue. And perhaps it is not too much to say, in spite of the monopoly of benevolence to which the mere philosopher lays claim, that the human duties of the second table have never once been well performed by any of the rejectors of that previous portion of the decalogue which enjoins duty to God.

"In some of the most splendid of these characters, compassion is erected into the throne of justice, and justice degraded into the rank of plebeian virtues. It is considered as a noble exemplification of sentiment that creditors should be defrauded, while the money due to them is lavished, in dazzling acts of charity, to some object that affects the senses; which paroxysms of charity are made the sponge of every sin, and the

substitute of every virtue ; the whole indirectly tending
to intimate how *very benevolent people are who are not
Christians.* From many of these compositions, indeed, Christianity is systematically, and always virtu-
ally, excluded ; for the law and the prophets, and the
gospel, *can* make no part of a scheme in which this
world is looked upon as all in all ; in which want and
misery are considered as evils arising solely from the
defects of human governments, and not as making part
of the dispensations of God ; in which poverty is represented as merely a political evil, and the restraints
which tend to keep the poor honest are painted as the
most flagrant injustice. The gospel can make no part
of a system in which the absurd idea of perfectibility
is considered as applicable to fallen creatures ; in
which the chimerical project of consummate earthly
happiness (founded on the mad pretence of loving the
poor better than God loves them) would defeat the
divine plan, which meant this world for a scene of
discipline, not of remuneration.

"But the part of the system most fatal to that class
whom I am addressing is, that, even in those works
which do not go all the length of treating marriage as
an unjust infringement on liberty, and a tyrannical
deduction from general happiness, yet it commonly
happens that the hero or heroine, who has practically
violated the letter of the seventh commandment, and
continues to live in the allowed violation of its spirit,
is painted as so amiable and so benevolent, so tender,
or so brave, and the temptation is represented as so
irresistible, (for all these philosophers are fatalists,)

18*

the predominant and cherished sin is so filtered and defecated of its pollutions, and is so sheltered, and surrounded, and relieved, with shining qualities, that the innocent and impressible young reader is brought to lose all horror of the awful crime in question, in the complacency she feels for the engaging virtues of the criminal."

The following remarks of the same writer are worthy of special attention, at a time when the country is deluged with foreign romances, and every steamship that arrives is freighted with new productions from the prolific pens of English novel writers, which, by another steam process, are multiplied, and sent out, not like the "leaves of the tree which were for the healing of the nations," but, like the fabled *Bohon Upas*, spreading moral death over the land : —

" Let not those to whom these pages are addressed deceive themselves by supposing this to be a fable ; and let them inquire most seriously whether I speak the truth in asserting that the attacks of infidelity in Great Britain are at this moment principally directed against the female breast. Conscious of the influence of women in civil society, — conscious of the effect which female infidelity produced in France, — they attribute the ill success of their attempts in this country to their having been hitherto chiefly addressed to the male sex. They are now sedulously laboring to destroy the religious principles of women, and in too many instances have fatally succeeded. For this purpose, novels and romances have been made the vehicles of vice and infidelity."

6. *Novel reading is a great waste of time.* Few
will pretend that they read novels with any higher end
in view than *mere amusement;* while, by the strong
excitement they produce, they impose a heavier tax on
both mind and body than any other species of mental
effort. If any thing valuable is to be derived from
them, it may be obtained with far less expense of time,
and with safety to the morals, from other sources. No
Christian, who feels the obligation of " redeeming the
time because the days are evil," will fail to feel the
force of this remark. We have no more right to
squander our time and waste our energies in frivolous pursuits, than we have to waste our money in
extravagant expenditures. We are as much the *stew-*
ards of God in respect to the one as the other.

7. *Novel reading is a great hinderance to serious*
piety. Such is the mental intoxication produced by it,
that we might as well attempt to reach the conscience
of the inebriate with the truths of God's word, as that
of the novel reader; and the heart that can be feasted
on such dainties cannot have sufficient relish for the
" sincere milk of the word " to " grow thereby." The
following testimony bears intrinsic evidence that the
writer speaks from experimental knowledge. Mr. Hall
says, " The fictions of a disordered fancy annihilate,
as it were, the *realities* of the *future* world, as well as
of the *present.* They place men, just so far as they
produce their legitimate influence, in the midst of ideal
scenes, as remote from the existence which *is to be*
as from that which is. There are objects of idolatry
in the *land of shadows*, which may as effectually ex-

clude the soul from heaven as the riches of the miser, or the pleasures of the sensualist. It is truly melancholy to think that any should be led by the *actual* concerns of time to neglect the interests of eternity. How much greater folly, then, to be diverted from so momentous an affair by mere phantoms of the imagination! That the productions of the novelist have precisely the tendency which I am attributing to them, cannot be denied. I make my appeal with confidence to those who have for a time indulged in such reading, but at length awakened from the spell of the enchantress. Say, did not you find your interest in religion *diminish* exactly in proportion as your attachment to works of fiction *increased*? Were not the hours which you devoted to them your hours of greatest stupidity in regard to your souls? Was not the Bible then a tedious and neglected book to you? Did you not shun the praying circle, and your closets, and the society of devout Christians? Were not your thoughts unfixed and wandering in the sanctuary? Could you relish, as delightfully as at other times, the sacred employments of the Sabbath? There will be, I am confident, but one answer to these questions. The experience of thousands will bear witness that the conscience never slumbers so profoundly as over the pages of the novelist. The mind is then insensible alike to the hopes and the fears of eternity. The ear is so full of other sounds, that God is unheard, though he speak. He may even whet his sword of vengeance, but the fascinated victim sees not its terrible gleam."

If such is the effect of novel reading, how can one, who has solemnly devoted himself to the service of God, spend the precious moments, given him here for discipline and preparation for a higher and nobler sphere, in thus counteracting the gracious designs of God towards his soul? How dangerous thus to parley with temptation! What an example to set before impenitent friends, which, if they follow it, will place an almost insurmountable obstacle in the way of their conversion! How ungrateful to Him who " died for all, that they which live should not henceforth live unto themselves, but unto Him which died for them and rose again! "

8. Before leaving this subject, a class of works denominated *religious novels* claim some attention. They may, perhaps, find more friends among religious people than common romances, because they profess to recommend religion. But, though they may be free from every thing gross and directly tending to irreligion or licentiousness, yet it is believed that the same general objections lie against them as against all others. All that has been said of the influence on the imagination and sensibility, of morbid excitement, and of erroneous views of life, lies equally against *religious novels;* and, besides these, there is another objection, of sufficient weight to counterbalance all that may be said of their unexceptionable *morals.* It is, that they *give false views of religion.* Mrs. More, in a note appended to her description of popular novels, says, " It is to be lamented that some, even of those more virtuous novel writers, who *intend* to espouse the cause

of religion, yet exhibit false views of it. I have lately seen a work of some merit in this way, which was meritoriously designed to expose the impieties of the new philosophy. But the writer betrayed his own im-perfect knowledge of the Christianity he was defending, by making his hero, whom he proposed as a pattern, *fight a duel !*"

On the same subject, Mr. Hall observes, " I would not except from these remarks those productions which, by a strange misnomer, are called *religious novels.* They have, in some instances, no doubt, been written by men of piety, and from good motives. Such persons have, however, it is but too manifest, in this case, misjudged, and done serious injury to the cause which they meant to advance. The objection which is so strong against other works of fiction, lies with equal weight against them. The views of life which the former give are not more erroneous than the representations of *religion* contained in the latter. Incalculable evil may be the consequence of this. The effect of turning from those *images* of Christian perfection, which the religious novel presents, to the mixed characters which even good men exhibit, must be either petulant censoriousness or distrust of all pre-tensions to piety. This is not all. Apply the test which should always determine your estimate of books. Do romances of this class increase your attachment to the Bible? Are you able, at any moment, to lay them aside, and resume the sacred volume with undiminished interest? Do they prepare your minds for more delightful communion with God? Do they dispose you to more frequent acts of sympathy and benevolence? If any have, even in a slight degree, experienced such effects, they are examples of an exception to the general law. The testimony on this subject bears with overwhelming preponderance the other way. All, except those who are fascinated to delusion, know that the mind may be full of the excitement which a religious novel awakens, while it is enmity itself against God. The danger that those who feel such emotion may substitute it for the subduing power of the gospel, is one which those only will think trifling who know little respecting the deceitfulness of the human heart."

But I would not advise you to read *any* books, merely because you can obtain no other, nor because there is nothing bad in them. There are many books which contain nothing particularly objectionable, which, nevertheless, are not the best that can be obtained. There are so many books, at the present day, that there is no necessity for wasting precious time upon crude, ill-digested, or unprofitable works. There is such a thing, also, as reading too much. The mind may be filled with ideas and facts which it cannot digest. You may likewise read in such a miscellaneous, desultory manner, as to derive little benefit from it. A house may contain abundance of rich furniture, yet, if it is all stowed away in the lumber-room, it will be of little use. The mind and character may also receive great injury from an undue proportion of such *light reading* as is useful in its place, but injurious when indulged to excess. The following remarks of

Mrs. More deserve serious attention, in this connection:
" I venture to remark, that real knowledge and real
piety, though they may have gained in many instances,
have suffered in others, from that profusion of little,
amusing, sentimental books, with which the youthful
library overflows. Abundance has its dangers, as well
as scarcity. In the first place, may not the multiplicity
of these alluring little works increase the natural re-
luctance to those more dry and uninteresting studies,
of which, after all, the rudiments of every part of
learning must consist? And, secondly, is there not
some danger (though there are many honorable exceptions) that some of those engaging narratives may
serve to infuse into the youthful heart a sort of spurious goodness, a confidence of virtue, a parade of
charity? and that the benevolent actions, with the
recital of which they abound, when they are not made
to flow from any source but feeling, may tend to
inspire a self-complacency, a self-gratulation, a ' Stand
by, for I am holier than thou'? May not the success
with which the good deeds of the little heroes are
uniformly crowned, the invariable reward which is
made the instant concomitant of well-doing, furnish
the young reader with false views of the condition of
life, and the nature of the divine dealings with men?
May they not help to suggest a false standard of
morals, to infuse a love of popularity, and an anxiety
for praise, in the place of that simple and unostentatious rule of doing whatever good we do, ' because it
is the will of God' "?

It is not my purpose, however, to condemn all

works of fiction, nor to censure the judicious cultivation of the imagination and the taste. Fictions of the allegorical and parabolical kind have their place in the illustration of truth, and are sanctioned by Scripture. Those of another class, which give just representations of life, without the accompaniment of a love story, may, to a limited extent, be allowed. You may, also, devote some time, pleasantly and profitably, to the best English classics, both in poetry and prose, which, for the want of a better term, I shall include under the head of *belles lettres*, for the purpose of cultivating the imagination, improving the taste, and enriching your style. These should be selected with great discrimination and care, with reference both to their style and their moral tendency. Poetry, to a limited extent, tends to elevate the mind, cherish the finer sensibilities of the heart, and refine the taste. But, if you cannot obtain books which furnish you a *profitable* employment for your hours of leisure, devote them to the study of the Bible. This you always have with you, and you will find it a never-failing treasure. The more you study it, the more delight it will afford. You may find new beauties in it, and " still increasing light," as long as you live; and, after death, the unfolding of its glorious mysteries will furnish employment for a never-ending eternity.

The selection of books to be read depends so much on the peculiar circumstances of each individual, that it is not an easy matter to recommend a *general list*

19

which will meet the wants of all. I have spent much
time and thought, and sought the aid of learned and
judicious friends, in preparing the list of books
which will be found in the Appendix; but with so little
satisfaction to myself, as to its practical utility, that I
have hesitated whether to insert it; but have con-
cluded to do so, thinking that it may be of use to
some who may read this book, in assisting them to
make a selection for themselves. I would advise
you, by all means, to consult your pastor in making
your selection. If you are able, it is better to
purchase than to borrow the books which you read.
You will not be able to keep borrowed books long
enough to read them thoroughly, especially if you
attempt to carry along together the various kinds, in
due proportions, as is desirable; and you can make
much more of your reading, if you possess your
books, so as to be able to refer to them again. If you
read your own books, I would recommend the use of
" Todd's Index Rerum," or a similar work by M. T.
C. Gould; the advantage of which is, that you will
then have an index to all that you have read, so that
you can at any time refer to any passage or incident
which recurs to your mind, or which you may desire
to use. As these works contain ample directions for
their use, I need not give any in this place. If you
read borrowed books, this will still be useful; but the
less so, as the trouble of referring to them again will
be much greater; and, in this case, the edition of the
book referred to should be stated in the reference.

Reading after this manner will, in the course of a few years, put one in possession of a vast fund of information, which may at any time be resorted to.

In order to read with profit, you must adopt some plan which will secure a suitable variety. To assist you in forming your plan, I shall arrange my remarks on the various kinds of reading, under the heads of *History*, *Biography*, *Doctrine*, and *Miscellany* ; and you should so regulate your reading as to keep along a suitable proportion of each. Either give to each kind particular days of the week ; or, if this does not suit your circumstances, read through one work on one of these branches, and then take a work on another, and so on, till you have read something on each ; and then begin again upon the branch where you commenced. But, if you have the books and the time at your command, I should recommend that you keep on hand something on each of these departments of knowledge, devoting stated times to each. Yet do not suffer your inability to carry out any definite plan which may be recommended, or which you may form, to prevent your attempting a systematic course of reading. Your plans must conform to your circumstances ; and you will never be able to accomplish all that you purpose. But never permit yourself to yield to discouragement. With these remarks, I proceed to speak of the several kinds of reading which I have mentioned, each by itself.

I. HISTORY. This is usually considered under three divisions, viz., *sacred*, *ecclesiastical*, and *profane*. The

first of these terms is applied to the Bible histories;
the second, to the history of the church since the
canon of Scripture was completed; and the third, to
the histories of the world, written by uninspired men.
But, as I have already treated of the first, I shall now
speak only of the others; both of which are highly
necessary to every one who desires an enlarged view
of the affairs of the world, and the dealings of God
with mankind in general, and with his church in particular. In reading profane history, observe, —

1. *The providence of God in directing the affairs
of men.* Look for the hand of God in every thing;
for he controls the actions even of wicked men, to
accomplish his own purposes. The Bible is full of this
great truth. Scarcely a page can be found where it is
not recognized. " The Most High ruleth in the kingdom of men, and giveth it to whomsoever he will."
He calls the king of Assyria the " rod of his anger,"
for chastising the hypocritical Jews; but adds, " How-
beit, he meaneth not so, neither doth his heart think
so; but it is in his heart to destroy and cut off nations
not a few." And, in a subsequent verse, he says,
when he has performed his whole work by this wicked
king, he will punish his stout heart, and the glory of
his high looks. But it is not in great matters alone
that the hand of the Lord is to be seen. He exercises
a particular providence over the least, as well as the
greatest, of his works. Even a single sparrow, says
our Lord, shall not fall to the ground without our
heavenly Father. And this is one of the brightest

glories of the divine character. He who fills immensity with his presence, condescends to care for the minutest beings in the universe.

2. *Observe the connection of the events recorded in history with the fulfilment of prophecy.* I do not, however, suppose you will be able to see this very clearly, without reading some authors who have made the prophecies their particular study. And this you will not be prepared to do with much profit, till you have the leading events of history fixed in your mind.

3. *Observe the depravity of the human heart, and the evil nature of sin*, as manifested in the conduct of wicked men, who have been left without restraint, and in the consequences resulting from such conduct.

4. *See the hatred of God towards sin*, as displayed in the miseries brought upon the world in consequence of it. In reading history, we find that individuals, whom God could have cut off by a single stroke of his hand, have been permitted to live for years, and spread devastation, misery, and death, every where around them. The infidel would pronounce this inconsistent with the character of a God of infinite benevolence. But the whole mystery is explained in the Bible : all this wretchedness is brought upon men for the punishment of their sins.

5. *Observe the bearing of the events recorded on the church of Christ.* One great principle in the divine administration appears to be, that the Lord overrules the affairs of men with reference to the kingdom of Christ. Often, events which seem, at first glance, to be foreign to the interests of his kingdom, appear,

19 *

upon a closer examination, to be intimately connected
with it. Instance the conquests of Alexander the
Great. As the life of this extraordinary man stands
out alone, unconnected with the subsequent history
of the church, we see nothing but the wild career of
mad ambition. But, on a more enlarged view of the
subject, we discover that he was the instrument which
God employed for spreading over a large portion of
the world one common language, and so to prepare
the way for the introduction of the gospel. Wherever
the arms of Alexander extended, the Greek language
and Greek literature were made known; thus preparing the way for the universal reception of the gospel, which was first published in that language. Who
knows but every event of history has a bearing, equally
direct, on the interests of Christ's kingdom?

But, in order to keep all these things before your
mind, you must maintain, in the midst of your reading,
a constant spirit of prayer.

In reading church history, you will have occasion
to observe the same things, because the history of the
church is necessarily connected with the history of the
world. But there are some things to be noticed,
wherein the history of the church differs from that
of the world. The dealings of God with his own
people differ from his dealings with his enemies. The
afflictions which he brings upon the former are the
wholesome corrections of a tender father, and designed
for their good; those he brings upon the latter are
either designed to lead them to repentance, or they are
just judgments, intended for the destruction of those

who have filled up the measure of their iniquities. But be careful, in reading church history, that you do not lose sight of the true church of Christ. Many of the histories which have been written are filled either with accounts of individuals, or of bodies of wicked men who could lay no claim to the character of the church of Christ. A church consists of a society of people professing the fundamental doctrines of the gospel, and practising them in their lives; or, in other words, having both the *form* and *power* of godliness. Without these, no body of men have any right to be called the church of Christ. If you observe this, you will relieve yourself from much perplexity of mind, which the careless reader experiences, from supposing that all the evils described in any period of the history of the nominal church do really exist in the *true* church. For, during many ages, of which church history treats, the true church appears to have been confined chiefly to small bodies of poor and persecuted people, who were regarded as heretics; while the nominal church had departed from both the faith and practice of the true gospel. I do not mean to say that there may not be many evils, and some wicked men, in the true church; but, when the body generally is corrupt, it cannot be acknowledged as the church of Christ. The church is compared to the human body; and, if the whole body is corrupt, all the limbs must be; though there may be some withered or decaying limbs, while the body is sound.

II. RELIGIOUS BIOGRAPHY is, perhaps, the best kind of practical reading. It is, in many respects, very

profitable. It furnishes testimony to the reality and
value of the religion of Jesus, by the exemplification
of the truths of revelation in the lives of its followers.
It also points out the difficulties which beset the Christian's path, and the means by which they can be sur-
mounted. , Suppose a traveller just entering a dreary
wilderness. The path which leads through it is exceedingly narrow, and difficult to be kept. On each
side it is beset with thorns, and briers, and miry pits.
Would he not rejoice to find a book containing the experience of former travellers who had passed that
way, in which every difficult spot is marked, all their
contests with wild beasts and serpents, and all their
falls, described, and a *guide-board* set up wherever
a beaten track turns aside from the true way? All
this you may find in religious biographies. There
the difficulties, trials, temptations, falls, and deliver-
ances, of God's people are described. You may profit
from their examples. Yet even these works must be
read with some caution. Bear in mind that you are
reading the history of fallible men, whose example and
experience are to be followed no farther than they
agree with the word of God. If you find any thing
contrary to this unerring standard, reject it. Satan is
ever busy, and may deceive even good men with false
experiences. Besides, there is, in every one's religious
experience, a great mixture of human infirmity. It is
seldom, and perhaps never, the case that these experiences are, in all respects, what they ought to be.
Some, whose lives have been written, dwell too much
on the dark side of their characters, and others too

much on the bright side; some are tinged with melancholy, and others may not show as much as they ought the depths of the human heart. Others are greatly marred by defective views of truth. They will be very profitable to you, if read with judgment and discrimination, and carefully compared with the Scriptures; but, if you take for granted that all their experiences were right, and therefore attempt to imitate them, they may lead you astray. You will find it profitable generally to keep on hand a volume of biography, and read a few pages at your daily seasons of devotion.

III. In relation to DOCTRINAL READING, I have already given general directions. I will only remark, in this place, that you must give it a prominent place in your systematic course of reading.

IV. Under the head of MISCELLANEOUS READING, I shall comprehend the following, viz.: Works on the prophecies, to be read in connection with history; practical works on Christian character, experience, and duty; on the instruction of the young; illustrations of Scripture; on the natural sciences; on health, belles lettres, travels; biographies not strictly religious, &c. You will need to exercise considerable judgment, in order to give a suitable proportion of time to these various subjects. Until you have the principal events of history in your mind, and until you have a tolerable knowledge of the doctrines of Christianity, miscellaneous reading should occupy a subordinate place. You may profitably keep on hand some approved practical work on Christian character, experience, or duty, to be read alternately with religious biography, as part of the devotional exercises of the closet. Illustrations of Scripture you will need in connection with the study of your Sabbath school lessons; and the lighter works, here recommended, you can take up as a relaxation from severe mental effort. You will need, likewise, to read newspapers and periodical publications sufficiently to keep in your mind the history of your own times, and to understand the subjects which interest the public mind, as well as to observe the signs of the times in relation to the progress of Christ's kingdom. But, if you are careful of your *shreds of time*, you may accomplish this at intervals when you could not sit down to a book. But do not suffer yourself to acquire a morbid appetite for this kind of reading, and by no means attempt to read every thing contained in these publications; but cast your eye over them, with the swiftness, dexterity, and skill, with which the bee lights on the flower; and in imitation of his industry and prudence, do not tarry where you find no *honey*. Newspapers and periodicals contain much trash; and you may fritter away all your leisure upon them, to the great injury of your mind and heart. Endeavor to acquire the habit of reading them rapidly, and of passing over at a glance what is not worth reading. But especially beware of the popular tales with which many of these publications abound. All the objections against novels lie equally against them; and if you begin to indulge in reading them, you know not where it will end. Religious papers, and periodicals containing missionary intelligence, are, however, generally worthy of an attentive perusal.

The work laid out in the foregoing pages may seem so great, at first sight, as to discourage you from making the attempt. But a little calculation will remove every difficulty. If you read but twenty pages in a day, at the close of the year you will have read more than six thousand; which would be equal to twenty volumes of three hundred pages each. Pursue this plan for ten years, and you will have read *two hundred volumes*, containing *sixty thousand pages.* You can, at least, read twenty pages in an hour; and I think you will not say it is impossible to spare this portion of time every day, for the purpose of acquiring useful knowledge. Think what a vast amount may thus be treasured up in the course of a few years.

You will find it a profitable exercise to keep a journal, and at the close of every day, or some time the next day, write the substance of what you have read briefly from memory, together with such reflections as occur to your mind while reading, particularly the several points to be noted in history, and the lessons which you learn from biography and other practical writings. But, to do this, or, indeed, to profit much by reading, you must take sufficient time thoroughly to understand what you read.

CHAPTER XIV.

WHEN you entered into solemn covenant with the Lord, you consecrated your whole being to his service. Your *time*, then, is not your own, but the Lord's. If you waste it, or spend it unprofitably, you *rob* God; for it is one of the talents which he has intrusted to you as his steward. You are not at liberty even to employ it exclusively for yourself; but you must glorify God in the use of it, which you will do by employing it in the way that will be most beneficial to your whole being, and to your fellow-creatures. I need not caution you against wasting your time in vain amusements or frivolous pursuits; for, addressing myself, as I do, to those who have commenced the religious life, I can hardly suppose it possible that they should have any inclination to do so. The Christian who properly considers the great work he has to perform in his own soul, as well as the wide field of benevolent exertion which opens every where around him, and reflects how exceedingly short his time is, will not be disposed to trifle away its precious moments. Hence we are exhorted to *redeem*, or *rescue*, the time, as it flies. A very common fault lies in not estimating the value of a moment. This leads to the waste of immense portions of precious time. It is with time as with an estate. The old adage is, "Take care of the *pennies*, and the *pounds* will take care of themselves." So, if we take care of the *moments*, the *hours* will take care of themselves. Our whole life is made up of moments. A little calculation may startle those who carelessly trifle away small portions of time. Suppose you waste *only ten minutes* at a time, six times in a day; this will make an hour. This hour is subtracted from that portion of your time which might have been devoted to active employments. Sleep, refreshment, and personal duties, generally occupy at least one half of the twenty-four hours. You have, then, lost one twelfth part of the available portion of the day. Suppose you live to the age of seventy years. Take from this the first ten years of your life. From the sixty remaining you will have thrown away *five years!* These five years are taken from that portion of time which should have been employed in the cultivation of the mind, and in the practical duties of religion ; the common excuse for neglecting the improvement of the mind and the cultivation of personal piety being *want of time.* Were you to employ one half of this time in reading, at the rate of twenty pages an hour, you would be able to read more than *eighteen thousand pages*, or *sixty volumes*, of three hundred pages each. If you employ the other half in devotional exercises, in addition to the time you would spend in this manner, upon the supposition that these five years are lost, what an influence will it have upon

your personal piety! Or, if you spend the whole of
it in the active duties of Christian benevolence, how
much good may you accomplish! Think what you
might do by employing five years in the undivided
service of your Master.

But the grand secret of *redeeming* time lies in *systematic arrangements.* The wise man says, " To
every thing there is a *season*, and a time for every
purpose under heaven." If we so divide our time as
to assign a particular season for every employment,
we shall be at no loss, when one thing is finished, what
to do next ; and one duty will not crowd upon another.
For want of this system, many persons suffer much
needless perplexity. They find a multitude of duties
crowding upon them at the same time, and they know
not where to begin to discharge them. Much of their
time is wasted in considering what they shall do.
They are always in a hurry and bustle ; yet, when the
day is gone, they have not half finished its duties. All
this would have been avoided, had they parceled out
the day, and assigned particular duties to particular
seasons. They might have gone quietly to their work,
pursued their employments with calmness and serenity,
and, at the close of the day, laid themselves down to
rest, with the satisfaction of having discharged every
duty. Form, then, a systematic plan, to regulate your
daily employments. Give to each particular duty its
appropriate place ; and, when you have finished one,
pass rapidly to another, without losing any precious
intervals between. Bear in mind that every moment
you waste will make your life, or the period of your

probation, so much shorter; and every moment you redeem will be adding so much to it. Yet do not try to crowd too much into the compass of a single day. You will always be liable to numerous and unavoidable interruptions. You have friends, who claim a portion of your time : it is better to interrupt your own affairs, than to treat them rudely. You have also many accidental duties, which you cannot bring into the regular routine of your employments. Give, then, sufficient latitude to your system to anticipate these, so that your affairs may not be thrown into confusion by their unexpected occurrence.

The duty of being systematic in our arrangements is enforced by several considerations : —

1. *By the example of our Creator.* In the first chapter of Genesis, you will see that God assigned a particular portion of the creation to each day of the week, and that he rested on the seventh day. He could as easily have made all things at once, by a single word of his power, as to have been occupied six days in the creation. As for resting the seventh day, the Almighty could not be weary, and therefore needed no rest. What, then, could have been his design, but to set us an example of order? Our Savior also set a beautiful example of *order*, on the morning of his resurrection. Those who first went into the sepulchre found the linen clothes lying in one place, and the napkin *folded* and laid by itself.

2. *This duty is also enforced by the analogy of the visible creation.* The most complete and perfect system, order, and harmony, may be read in every

page of the book of nature. From the minutest insect, up, through all the animal creation, to the structure of our own bodies, there is a systematic arrangement of every particle of matter. So, from the little pebble that is washed upon the sea-shore, up to the loftiest mountain, and even to the whole planetary system, the same truth is manifest.

3. *This duty is enforced by our obligation to employ all our time for the glory of God.* If we neglect it, we lose much precious.time, which might have been employed in the service of the Lord.

NATURE OF OBLIGATION.

The very idea of obligation supposes the possibility of the thing being done that is required. There can be no such thing as our being under obligation to do what is, in its own nature, impossible. This principle is recognized by our Lord in the parable of the talents. The man only required of his servants *according to their ability.* Nothing, then, is duty, except what can be done at the present moment. There are other things which may be duty hereafter; but they are not *present duty. The obligation of duty, therefore, rests on the present moment.* This is a principle of great importance in practical life. It lies at the foundation of all Christian effort. It is the neglect of it which has ruined thousands of immortal souls, who have sat under the sound of the gospel. It is the neglect of it which prevents Christians from rising to the true standard of personal piety. If it is the duty of a sinner to repent, it is his duty to do it *now;* and every moment's delay is a new act of rebellion against God. If it is the duty of a backslider to return and humble himself before God, it is his duty to do it *now;* and, every moment he delays, he is going farther from God, and rendering his return more difficult. If it is the duty of a Christian to live near to God, to feel his presence, to hold communion with him, to be affected with the infinite beauty and excellence of his holy nature, the obligation of that duty rests on the present moment. Every moment's delay is *sin.* And so of every other duty. Our first object, then, is to *know* present duty; our second, to *do* it. We cannot put off any thing which we ought to do *now,* without bringing guilt on our souls. An eminent living minister has said, " *What ought to be done can be done.*" When taken in connection with a proper sense of dependence upon God, this is true; and, when adopted as a principle of Christian conduct, it is a truth of great practical force. The person who acts constantly under the impression of this maxim, will never be moved by obstacles in his way, when he is satisfied that any thing *ought to be done.* He will always be efficient in action; nor will he live in vain, but his life will show that *something can be done.*

20 *

CHAPTER XV.

CHRISTIAN ACTIVITY.

THE spirit of Christianity, at the present day, is distinguished for its *enterprises of benevolence.* Whoever drinks deeply into the spirit of his Master, will find his soul going out in fervent desire for the melioration of human wretchedness, and the salvation of perishing souls. Whatever tends to the accomplishment of these objects will, therefore, be regarded as of deep interest. Indifference towards the enterprises of love, which the benevolent spirit of this age has brought into existence, must, therefore, indicate a destitution of the spirit of Christ, without which we are none of his. It is important, then, that we should know what we *can do* towards advancing these enterprises; for obligation is coëxtensive with ability. Christ commended the woman who poured the ointment on his head for doing "*what she could.*" If you do more than any within the circle of your acquaintance, and yet leave undone any thing that you can do, you do not discharge your obligations. You have entered into the service of the Lord, and he requires you to *do what you can.* It, then, becomes a matter of serious inquiry, " *What can I do ?* " It is an interesting fact that the benevolent operations to which I have alluded have, to a great extent, been sustained by the energy of *female influence*. This influence is felt in every department of society wherever Christianity has elevated your sex to the station which properly belongs to them. Yet, where correct principles prevail, it will be exerted in an unostentatious, noiseless manner, without assuming to act in a sphere which " nature itself teaches " does not belong to woman. I will, therefore, endeavor to point out some of the principal channels through which female influence may, with propriety, be put forth for the promotion of benevolent objects.

I. *You may make your influence felt in the Bible Society.* The object of this society is, as you know, to furnish the Holy Scriptures to the destitute. The spirit of Christ is a spirit of the most expansive benevolence. If you possess it, and value the sacred treasure contained in God's word as you ought, you will feel a thrilling interest in this cause ; your heart will overflow with compassion for those poor souls who have not the word of life. What, then, must be your emotions, when you consider that many hundreds of millions of your fellow-beings, as good by nature as yourself, are destitute of the Bible ? The population of the whole world is estimated at *seven hundred and thirty-seven millions.** Of these, *five hundred and nine millions* are heathen, and *one hundred and fifty-six millions* are Roman and Greek Catholics ; nearly

---

* This is the estimate of *Balbi*, which was made in 1826. It is probably much too low. From later discoveries as to the population of the Chinese empire and o'her parts of the world, there is reason to believe that 1,000,000,000 is nearer the truth.

all of whom are destitute of the word of God. This
leaves but *seventy-two millions* who are called Prot-
estants; but a vast number of these, even in our own
highly-favored land, are living without the Bible. Can
you say, with the Psalmist, " O, how love I thy law !
It is my meditation all the day " ?　How, then, must
your heart bleed, in view of these facts !　" But,"
perhaps you reply, " what can *I* do for these perishing millions ? "　I answer, *Do what you can.*　This is
all that God requires of you.　You can become a
member of the Bible Society ; you can contribute, at
least, your mite ; you can act as a visitor and collector,
both to ascertain and supply those families which are
destitute of the word of life, and to obtain the means
of supplying others ; and you can exert an influence
upon others, to induce them to enlist in this heavenly
enterprise.　This may seem to you very insignificant ;
but it will not appear so, if you contemplate the aggregate of similar benefactions.　In a mountainous
region, in the south-western part of the state of New
York, there are innumerable little rills, running in
different directions, some, whose sources are within
a mile of each other, taking opposite courses.　In-
terspersed throughout the same region are a multitude
of little lakes, opening their placid bosoms to the sun,
as his rays fall obliquely upon them through the
mountains, converting the little ripples which play
upon their surface into the appearance of a thousand
sparkling gems.　The careless observer, as he gazes
with rapture upon the broad surface of the lovely lake,
takes no notice of the little rill that murmurs its quiet

way through the forest. Yet, while the beautiful lake, in apparent self-complacency, opens its fair bosom to the admiring gaze of the passing stranger, the modest rill is patiently pursuing its unwearied course along the sides of the mountains, through deep ravines, and across the verdant vale, mingling with sister rills, increasing in size, swelling into streams, till stream meets stream, and river meets river, forming, in one direction, the noble Susquehannah, in another, the majestic St. Lawrence, and, in a third, the mighty Mississippi, — pouring incessantly a flood of waters into the ocean. So, while a few splendid acts of charity may, like the quiet lake, contribute to the self-complacency of their authors, and draw upon them the admiring gaze of the multitude, it is the aggregate of the *little rills* that must form the great streams of benevolence, which are to flow on and fertilize the earth, and fill it with the knowledge of the Lord, as the waters cover the face of the great deep.

II. *You can make your influence felt in the Tract enterprise.* The circulation of religious tracts has been greatly owned and blessed of God. It seems to be almost the only means of reaching some particular classes of people, who never wait upon God in his house. It is a cheap method of preaching the gospel both to the rich and the poor. For a quarter of a cent, a sermon may be obtained, containing a portion of divine truth sufficient, with God's blessing, to lead a soul to Christ. Engage actively in the various forms of this department of benevolent labor.

The distribution of a tract to every family in a town once a month, when properly conducted, may be the means of doing great good. It furnishes an easy introduction into families where God is not acknowledged; and the matter contained in the tract will assist in the introduction of religious conversation. It will enable you to ascertain and relieve the wants of the poor, without seeming to be obtrusive. It will soften your own heart, and excite your compassion, in view of the objects of distress with which you meet. It also furnishes a convenient opportunity for collecting children into Sabbath schools. In distributing tracts, endeavor, as far as courtesy and propriety will admit, to engage those with whom you meet in direct personal conversation with regard to the concerns of their own souls; and when you meet only with the female members of the family, and circumstances favor it, pray with them. Thus you may be the instrument of saving many precious souls. Your labor will also reflect back upon yourself, and warm your own heart. You will get a deeper sense of the dreadful condition of impenitent sinners; and this will be the means of exciting a spirit of prayer in their behalf. Those engaged in this work should meet every month, after finishing the distribution, report all cases of interest, and spend a season in prayer for the divine blessing upon their labors. If you are a tract distributor, where the monthly distribution is sustained, begin your distribution early in the month, and always finish it before the middle; and never neglect to make a written report to the superintendent, as soon as you have finished it. But endeavor always to have these little messengers of truth in your possession, whether at home, abroad, or on a journey, so that you may avail yourself of every opportunity that presents of scattering the " good seed." I was instructed, recently, by an anecdote of that benevolent lady, Mrs. Fry, who, having taken a coach to visit a friend, and forgetting her tract, stopped the coachman at her friend's door till she could obtain a tract for him. This shows the persevering principle with which she carried out her benevolent desires for the good of immortal souls.

III. *You can make your influence felt in the Missionary cause.* This cause must be near the heart of every Christian. The spirit of missions is in unison with every feeling of the new-born soul. It is the spirit of universal benevolence, — the same which brought our Lord from heaven to suffer and die for perishing sinners. His last command to his disciples, before ascending up again into heaven, was, that they should follow his example, in the exercise of this spirit, until the whole world should be brought to a knowledge of his salvation. But more than eighteen hundred years have passed away, and yet, at least, two thirds of the inhabitants of this fallen world have never heard the gospel ; and probably not more than one seventieth part of them have really embraced it. This is a mournful picture, and calculated to call forth every feeling of Christian sympathy, and awaken a burning zeal for the honor and glory of God. O, think how Jesus is dishonored by his own people, who thus disregard his last, parting request! But here, again, you may inquire, "What can *I* do?" You can do much. Perhaps you may go yourself on this errand of mercy; but, if not permitted this privilege, you can help them that do go. Although your means may be limited, yet there are many ways in which you can do much for this cause with little means. By regulating your expenses upon Christian principle, you may save much, even of a small income, for benevolent purposes. But you may also exert an influence upon others. In your intercourse with other Christians, you may stir up a missionary spirit. To aid you in this, become acquainted with what has been done, and what is now doing, for the conversion of the heathen. Read missionary intelligence. Make yourself familiar with the arguments in favor of the cause. By this means, you may become a zealous and successful advocate of the claims of hundreds of millions of perishing heathen. As an opportunity occurs once a month for all to contribute to this cause, you know not what effect such efforts may have upon the amount contributed. There are other ways in which you can advance this cause; but, for further suggestions on the subject, I would refer you to an interesting little work, published by the Massachusetts Sabbath School Society, entitled "*Louisa Ralston,*" which presents the subject of missions to the heathen in an interesting light, and furnishes examples of various methods of promoting the cause.

IV. *You can make your influence felt in behalf of the poor.* By frequenting the abodes of poverty and distress, you may minister to the wants of the afflicted, and call into exercise the feelings of Christian sympathy in your own bosom. By this means, also, you will be prepared to enlist others in the same cause. In large towns, much is done for the poor by the aid of benevolent associations; and you may assist in this department. But perhaps there is no way in which you can do so much for them as by assisting them with your own hands in their afflictions, and aiding them with your advice. Be careful, however, that you do not make them feel that you are conferring an obligation.

It is often objected against rendering assistance to the poor, that they are improvident, wanting in industry and economy; and that relieving their necessities has a tendency to make them indolent, and prevent them from helping themselves. This may be true to some extent; for intemperance has brought ruin and distress upon many families, and we cannot expect either industry, economy, or any other virtue, in a drunkard. But there is much suffering even among the virtuous poor. Sickness and misfortune often bring distress upon deserving people.

The only way we can realize the sufferings of the poor is to suppose ourselves in their situation. Let a wealthy gentleman and lady, with five or six small children, be suddenly deprived of all their property, and compelled to obtain a support for their family by daily labor, in the lowest employments; would they think they could live comfortably upon a laboring man's wages, with perhaps the addition of a trifle laboriously earned with the mother's needle? Yet

21

such is the situation of thousands of families, even in
this land of plenty.   I have met with families of small
children, in the severity of winter, destitute of clothing
sufficient to cover them, and without shoes.   And,
upon inquiry into their circumstances and means of
support, I could not see how the parents could make
any better provision.   But, even supposing the wretchedness of the poor is brought on them by their own
vices, is it agreeable to the spirit of Christ to refuse to
relieve their distresses ?   Has not sin brought upon us
all our wretchedness ?   If the Lord Jesus had reasoned
and acted upon this principle, would a single soul have
been saved ?   But he has commanded us to be merciful, *even as our Father which is in heaven is merciful.*
And how is he merciful ?   " He is kind unto the *unthankful* and to the *evil.*"   And are we to suppose
that the poor in our day are any worse than they were
when Christ was upon earth ?   Yet he greatly honored the poor, in appearing himself in a condition of
extreme poverty.   At his birth, his parents could provide him no better bed than a manger ; and while
wearing out his life in the service of a lost world, he
had no place to lay his head !   Yet, poor as he was,
he set an example of giving.   At the last supper,
when he told Judas, " That thou doest, do quickly,"
his disciples supposed he had sent him to give something to the poor ; from which we may infer that he
was in the habit of alms-giving.   He also exhorted
others to give to the poor ; and similar exhortations
are frequent in the apostolical writings.   But, even on
the principle upon which the world acts, shall we neg-

lect the sufferings of a deserving woman, because her husband is intemperate and vicious? Or should we suffer the children to grow up without instruction, in ignorance and vice, because their parents are vicious? Be, then, the devoted friend of the poor; and seek to relieve distress wherever you find it, or whatever may be its cause.

It may be necessary, however, to use some caution against indiscriminate giving; so as not thereby to encourage idleness and dissipation. As a general principle, it is not best to give to *beggars ;* as, by so doing, we encourage a practice that is demoralizing in the extreme. The more deserving poor are retiring, and unwilling to make known their wants. It is better to seek out such, as the objects of your charity, than to give indiscirminately to those that ask for it. Still, it may be well to follow those who seek your charity to their places of residence, and ascertain their circumstances, lest there might be suffering which you could relieve. But there is not much confidence to be placed in those whose sensibilities have been blunted by the habit of begging; and we are very liable to be imposed upon by them. The best way in which you can help such persons is to furnish them with employment ; and this will test their honesty. If they are deserving aid, they will be willing to labor for it.

V. *You may make your influence felt in the cause of Temperance.* A false delicacy prevails among many ladies in relation to this subject. They seem to think that, as intemperance is not a common vice of their own sex, they have no concern with it. But this is a great mistake. No portion of society suffer so much from the consequences of intemperance as females. On them it spends its fury. The heart sickens when we contemplate the condition of the drunkard's wife. We turn from the picture with horror and disgust. But is there no danger that females themselves may fall under the power of this monstrous vice? Does not every town, village, and hamlet, furnish appalling evidence that they are not proof against it? But, independent of this, it is scarcely possible to dry up the secret elements of this wasting pestilence without the aid of *female influence*. If the curtain were lifted from the domestic history of the past generation, it would doubtless appear that many of the intemperate appetites which have exerted such a terrific influence upon society were formed in the nursery. But, besides the formation of early habits, females exert a controlling influence over the public sentiment of the social circle. Here is the sphere of your influence. If young ladies would, with one consent, set their faces against the use of all intoxicating liquors, their influence could not fail to be felt throughout society. Make yourself acquainted with the subject, and lose no suitable opportunity of advocating the cause, or of doing whatever is right and proper for a lady to do in advancing it.

VI. *You may make your influence felt in every circle in which you move, by directing conversation towards profitable subjects.* The ability to converse is a talent put into our hands to cultivate for the glory of God; and we shall be called to account for the manner in which we improve it. To be able to converse well upon important subjects is an attainment worthy of great effort. And to give a right direction to the conversation of any circle in which we move, requires some skill, along with a spiritual and prayerful frame of mind. It is well, before going into company, to seek the aid of the Holy Spirit, that our social intercourse may be profitable both to ourselves and others. And, by imitating the example of the Savior, we may improve circumstances and occasions, to direct the conversation in which we engage towards profitable subjects. Endeavor, by your own conversation, to give the lie to the sentiment that ladies cannot be interested in any thing but frivolous *chit-chat.* But more of this hereafter.

VII. *You may make your influence felt in bringing people within the sound of the gospel.* There are multitudes, even in this Christian land, who live like the heathen. They do not appreciate the privileges they might enjoy. They live in the habitual neglect of public worship and the means of grace. This is especially the case with the poor in large towns. Poverty depresses their spirits, and they seem to feel that "no man cares for their souls." It is impossible to conjecture how much good one devoted female may do by gathering these people into places of worship. A lady can much more readily gain access to such families than a gentleman ; and, by a pleasing address, and an humble and affectionate demeanor, she may secure their confidence, and persuade them

21 *

to attend public worship. In this way she may be the means, under God, of saving their souls.

VIII. *You may, with God's blessing, make your influence felt by those who are living in a careless state.* That it is the duty of Christians to warn such of their danger, and direct them to the Savior, will appear from several considerations.

1. The apostle Peter says, " Christ suffered for us, *leaving us an example that we should follow his steps.*" And what was his example with reference to the subject under consideration? The spirit of Christ, in the great work of redemption, manifests itself in COMPASSION FOR SINNERS, and ZEAL FOR THE GLORY OF GOD. " While we were yet sinners, Christ died for us." And in the near prospect of his agonies, his prayer was, " Father, glorify thy name." It was, that mercy might be extended to the guilty, consistently with the honor of God, that he laid down his life. Behold him, deeply feeling the dishonor done to God by ungrateful and rebellious men, constantly reproving sin, weeping over the impenitence and obstinacy of his countrymen, and even exerting his power to drive out those who were profaning the temple. And he says, " If any man will come after me, let him deny himself, and take up his cross, and *follow* me." To *follow* Christ is to imitate his example. Hence, unless we follow Christ in his general spirit, we have no right to be called after his name. And this we must do *to the extent of our ability*, and at the expense of any personal sacrifice, not excepting, if

need be, even *our own lives.* This is the true spirit of the gospel ; and, if it were carried out in the life of every professor of the religion of Jesus, who can estimate the results which would follow ?

2. *We are required to love God with all our heart, soul, mind, might, and strength.* When we love a friend, we are careful of his honor. If we hear him defamed, or lightly spoken of, or see him ill-treated, it gives us pain. We take part with him, and vindicate his character. But we see God dishonored, and his goodness abused, continually. Multitudes around us habitually cast off his authority, and refuse to honor him as the moral Governor of the universe. What can we do more for his honor and glory than to seek to reclaim these rebellious subjects of his government, and bring them back to loyalty and obedience ?

3. *We are required to love our neighbor as ourselves.* We profess to have seen the lost condition of impenitent sinners. We think God has taken our feet from the " horrible pit and miry clay." We profess to believe that all who have not embraced Christ are every moment exposed to the horrors of the second death. Can we love them *as ourselves,* and make no effort to open their eyes to their awful danger, and persuade them to flee from it ?

4. *The business of reclaiming a lost world is committed to the church, in conjunction with the Holy Spirit.* It is the business of the church to apply " the truth " to the consciences of the impenitent. It is the office of the Spirit to make it effectual to their salvation. " The Spirit and the *bride* [the church] say,

Come." And even the hearer of the word is allowed to say, "*Come.*" The Scriptures recognize the conversion of the sinner as the work of the Christian. "*He which converteth a sinner* from the error of his way, shall save a soul from death, and shall hide a multitude of sins." "Others *save* with fear, *pulling them* out of the fire." "Then will I *teach transgressors* thy ways, and sinners *shall be* converted unto thee." It is true, we cannot, of our own power, convert souls. But, if we are faithful in the use of the means of God's appointment, he may employ us as instruments for accomplishing this great work. Every one, who has truly come to Christ, *knows the way*, and can direct others to him. And in no way, perhaps, can the truth be rendered more effectual than by personal application to the conscience. David did not understand Nathan's parable till the prophet said, " Thou art the man! "

As this is a plain, positive duty, it cannot be neglected with impunity. God will not bless his children while they refuse to obey him. " If I regard iniquity in my heart, the Lord will not hear me." Were you to spend all your time on your knees, while living in the neglect of a plain duty, I do not see how you could obtain a blessing. We cannot expect to enjoy the presence of God while we refuse to point sinners to Christ. It is probable that the neglect of this duty is one of the principal causes of spiritual barrenness in the church. If, then, Christians wish their own hearts revived, they must persuade others to come to Christ. " He that watereth shall be watered also himself." If we wish to maintain constant communion with God, we must live in the habitual exercise of the spirit of Christ.

The primitive Christians carried out the example of Christ, in this particular, in a manner worthy of our imitation. In the eighth chapter of Acts, we read that the church at Jerusalem were all scattered abroad, except the apostles. " And they that were scattered abroad *went every where, preaching the word.*" And afterwards, in the eleventh chapter, nineteenth verse, we hear of them as far as Phenice and Cyprus, where they had travelled, preaching (in the Greek, *talking*) the word as they went. It is to be particularly remarked that these, or at least most of them, were the private members of the church; for the apostles still remained at Jerusalem. And what was the result of these joint labors of the whole church? Revivals of religion immediately spread all over the land of Judea and its vicinity. And so might we see revivals spreading over this land, and continuing with increasing power, and multitudes of sinners converted, if the church, *as one*, united in Christ, would come up to her duty. Nor would it stop here: the fire thus kindled would burn brighter and brighter, and extend, with increasing rapidity, till it spread over the whole world. Should not all Christians, then, consider themselves placed, to some extent at least, in the situation of watchmen upon the walls of Zion? And, if they neglect to warn sinners, will they be guiltless of the blood of souls? How can they meet them at the bar of God? (Ezek. xxxiii. 1—9.)

Few persons are aware of what they might accomplish, if they would *do what they can.* I once knew a young lady, who was the moving spring of nearly every benevolent enterprise in a town of seven or eight thousand inhabitants. The Bible Society of the town appointed a number of gentlemen as visitors, to ascertain who were destitute of Bibles, and make collections to aid the funds of the society. But the time passed away in which the work was to have been accomplished, and nothing was done. The books were handed over to this lady. She immediately called in the assistance of a few friends in whom she could confide; and, in a very short time, the whole town was visited, collections made, and the destitute supplied. She imparted life and energy to the tract cause, putting into operation and sustaining, with the aid of a few friends, the monthly distribution. There had been, for some time, a small Temperance Society in the town; but its movements were slow and inefficient. She undertook to impart to it new life and vigor. The plans and efforts which she, in conjunction with her friends, put in operation, produced a sensation which was felt in every part of the town; and, in a few months, the number of members was increased from about fifty to three hundred.

The amazing influence of one Christian, who lives out the spirit of Christ, is illustrated, in a still more striking manner, in the life of a lady who died, not long since, in one of the principal cities of the United States. I am not permitted to give her name, nor all the particulars of her life; but what I relate may be relied upon, not only as *facts*, but as far below the *whole truth.* She had been, for a long time, afflicted with a drunken husband. At length, the sheriff came, and swept off all their property, not excepting her household furniture, to discharge his *grog-bills.* At this distressing crisis, she retired to an upper room, laid her babe upon the bare floor, kneeled down over it, and offered up the following petition : " O Lord, if thou wilt *in any way* remove from me this affliction, I will serve thee, *upon bread and water,* all the days of my life." The Lord took her at her word: her besotted husband immediately disappeared, and was never heard of again till after her death. The church would now have maintained her, but she would not consent to become a charge to others. Although in feeble health, and afflicted with the sick headache, she opened a small school, from which she obtained a bare subsistence ; though it was often no more than what was contained in the condition of her prayer, — literally *bread and water.* She had also another motive for pursuing some regular employment : she wished to avoid the reproach which would have arisen to the cause of Christ, from her being maintained upon the bounty of the church, while engaged in the system of Christian activity which she adopted. She remembered the duty of being *diligent in business,* as well as fervent in spirit. She was a lady of pleasing address, and of a mild and gentle disposition. " In her lips was the law of kindness." Yet she possessed an energy of character, and a spirit of perseverance, which the *power of faith* alone can impart. When she undertook any Christian enterprise, she was discouraged by no obstacles, and appalled by no difficulties. She resided in the most wicked and abandoned part of the city, which afforded a great field of labor. Her benevolent heart was pained at seeing the grog-shops open on the holy Sabbath. She undertook the difficult and almost hopeless task of closing these sinks of pollution on the Lord's day, and succeeded. This was accomplished by the mild influence of persuasion, flowing from the lips of kindness, and clothed with that power which always accompanies the true spirit of the gospel. But she was not satisfied with seeing the front doors and windows of these moral pest-houses closed. She knew that little confidence could be placed in the promises of men whose consciences would permit them to traffic in human blood. She would, therefore, upon the morning of the Sabbath, pass round, and enter these shops through the dwellings occupied by the families of the keepers, where she often found them engaged secretly in this wickedness. She would then remonstrate with them, until she persuaded them to abandon it, and attend public worship. In this manner she abolished almost entirely the sale of liquors on the Sabbath, in the worst part of the city.

She also looked after the poor, that the gospel might be preached to them. She carried with her the numbers of those pews in the church which were unoccupied; and, upon Sabbath mornings, she made it her business to go out into the streets and lanes of the city, and persuade the poor to come in and fill up these vacant seats. By her perseverance and energy, she would remove every objection, until she had brought them to the house of God, She was incessant and untiring in every effort for doing good. She would establish a Sabbath school, and superintend it until she saw it flourishing, and then deliver it into the hands of some suitable person, and go and establish another. She collected together a Bible class of apprentices, which she taught herself. Her pastor one day visited it, and found half of them in tears, under deep conviction. She was faithful to the church and to impenitent sinners. She would not suffer sin upon a brother. If she saw any member of the church going astray, she would, in a kind, meek, and gentle spirit, yet in a faithful manner, reprove him. She was the first to discover any signs of declension in the church, and to sound the alarm, personally, to every conscience. It was her habitual practice to reprove sin, and to warn sinners wherever she found them. At the time of her death, she had under her care a number of pious young men preparing for the ministry. These she had looked after, and brought out of obscurity. As soon as their piety had been sufficiently tested, she would bring them to the notice of her Christian friends. She persuaded pious teachers to give them gratuitous instruction, and pious booksellers to supply them with books. In the same way, she procured their board in the families of wealthy Christians ; and she formed little societies of ladies, to supply them with clothing. There was probably no person in the city whose death would have occasioned the shedding of more tears, or called forth more sincere and heartfelt grief. Her memory was long and deeply cherished in the heart of her pastor ; * who declared that he should not have felt as severely the loss of six of the most devoted men in his church.

And why may you not " go and do likewise " ? It is amazing to see what can be accomplished by a single individual, by earnest effort and untiring perseverance, accompanied with a simple and hearty dependence upon God. If the individual members of the church would do *what they can*, what a tremendous shock would be felt in Satan's kingdom ! What a glorious triumph would await the church ! Therefore, " whatsoever thy hand findeth to do, do it with thy might ; for there is no work, nor device, nor knowledge, nor wisdom, in the grave, whither thou goest."

But the work of directing sinners to Christ is one of vast responsibility. How distressing the consequences, when the weary traveller is directed in the wrong way ! How deeply so, if his way lie through the forest, where he is exposed, if night overtake him, to stumble over precipices, sink in the mire, or be devoured by wild beasts ! Yet what is this, in comparison with leading astray the soul that is inquiring for the way of salvation ? " He that winneth souls is wise." I cannot, however, pursue this subject here ; but must refer you

---

* Rev. Mr. Patterson, of Philadelphia, who has gone to that "better land," where he has, no doubt, met the hearty greetings, not only of this dear fellow-laborer, but of scores whom he has been instrumental in plucking as "brands from the burning."

to a little work, entitled " Friendly Counsel," in which
I have given directions more in detail.

CAUTIONS.

1. *Avoid every appearance of ostentation.* Suppress
every rising of self-complacency on account of what
you do, and of the success which attends your efforts.
Such feelings are abominable in the sight of God;
and, if indulged, will make you appear contemptible
in the eyes of men. The Pharisees were active in
many religious duties. They made long prayers, and
were so particular in outward things as to pay tithes
of the most common herbs. They also gave to the
poor. But all this they did that they might have
praise of men. They chose public places to pray;
and when they were about to give any thing to the
poor, they caused a trumpet to be sounded before
them, to give notice of their approach. All this was
done to feed the pride of the carnal heart; and, notwithstanding their loud professions, and apparent good
deeds, the heaviest curses the Lord Jesus ever pronounced were directed against them. Be modest, un-
obtrusive, and courteous, in all you do and say. Let
the love of Jesus animate your heart, and the glory of
God be your object. Make as little noise as possible,
in every thing you do. Never speak of what you
have done, unless you see that some good can be accomplished by it. " When thou doest thine alms, let
not thy left hand know what thy right hand doeth."
Keep yourself out of view, and give all the glory of
your success to God.

2. *Great prudence and discretion are necessary in every thing.* Do nothing rashly. When you have any enterprise in view, first sit down and consider the matter seriously. Pray over it. Look at it in all its bearings, and inquire what good will be likely to result from it. When you have satisfied yourself on this point, inquire whether you have reasonable ground to hope for success. Then summon all your wisdom to contrive a judicious plan of operations. When this is done, proceed with energy and perseverance, till you have either accomplished your object, or become convinced that it is impracticable. Pay especial regard to the feelings and advice of those who act with you. Keep as much in the background as you can without embarrassing your efforts ; and, whenever you can do it, put others forward to execute the plans you have devised. This will save you from becoming the object of jealousy, and also serve to mortify your pride.

3. *Be resolute and persevering.* When satisfied you are in the way of duty, do not be moved by ridicule. If some good people disapprove your conduct, thinking that you attempt too much, let it lead you to a candid and impartial reëxamination of your course. If by this you become convinced that you are wrong in the particular matter in question, confess it, and change your conduct. But, if this review of the affair confirms you in the opinion that your course is right, pursue it with decision and firmness. There are some well-meaning people, of limited views, and excessive carefulness, who disapprove the best of measures, if they happen to be at variance with their long-established customs; or, more frequently, if they were not *consulted* before the particular enterprise was undertaken.

4. BE MUCH IN PRAYER. Upon this will greatly depend your success in all things. Feel that of yourself you can do nothing, but that you can do all things through Christ strengthening you. Before undertaking any thing, pray that God would give you wisdom to direct, and strength to perform ; and if it is any thing in which the efforts of others will be required, pray that he would incline their hearts to engage in the work. Before you go out on an errand of mercy, first visit your closet, and commit yourself to the direction of the Lord. Pray that he would give you wisdom, courage, and discretion ; and that he would keep down the pride of your heart, and enable you to do all things for his glory.

22 *

CHAPTER XVI.

DRESS.

I AM far from considering attention to dress as a matter of so great importance as many attach to it; and it is remarkable that so little is said about it in the Bible, while false systems of religion, as well as enthusiastic or fanatical sects, generally prescribe the form of dress, or vehemently proscribe certain fashions. This is false zeal. Nevertheless, the subject is one of sufficient consequence to be carefully considered, and regulated upon Christian principle.

In the third chapter of Genesis, we learn that the object of dress at first was, to provide a decent covering for the body. It was the shame brought upon man by transgression which made this covering necessary. And it is in consequence of sin that the elements have been turned against him, so as to make clothing a necessary defence against the hostile influence of heat and cold. The immediate discovery of their nakedness, by our first parents, after their disobedience, is probably intended to show the nakedness and shame which sin has brought upon our souls; and the consequent exposure to the hostile elements aptly represents the exposure of the naked soul to the wrath of God. The invention of fig-leaf aprons may,

perhaps, represent the self-righteousness of the natural
heart; which leads unrenewed men to seek, by some
invention of their own, to save themselves from the
consequences of sin. But all their self-righteousness
will be no better defence against the storms of God's
wrath than fig-leaf aprons against the withering influence of a vertical sun, or the perpetual frosts of the
arctic regions. The coats of skin which the Lord
made for our first parents, seem well adapted to represent the righteousness of Christ, with which he
would clothe his people. This opinion appears the
more probable from the common use of this figure,
when the righteousness of Christ is spoken of as im-
puted to Christians: "He hath *clothed* me with the
garments of salvation, he hath *covered* me with the
robe of righteousness." "And to her [the church]
was granted that she should be arrayed in fine linen,
clean and white; for the linen is the righteousness of
the saints." The design of clothing, then, is, to furnish
a modest covering for the body; to provide a defence
against the hostile elements; and perhaps to remind us
of our spiritual nakedness and exposure to the wrath
of God, and our need to be clothed with the righteousness of Christ. From these ends we ought not to
pervert it to the gratification of pride and vanity.
But, if you will observe the following things in regard
to your apparel, you will probably not go far astray: —

1. *All that we have is the Lord's.* We have nothing but what he has given us; and this we have
solemnly promised to employ in his service. We
have no right, therefore, needlessly to squander it

upon our persons. The apostle Paul directs women to adorn themselves with modest apparel, and discountenances the wearing of costly ornaments and jewelry. Peter also says that, instead of these, their adorning should be the "hidden man of the heart." The love of finery, or a fondness for gay apparel, is contrary to the spirit of these passages; nor is it easy to see how Christians can reconcile so much needless expense as is often lavished upon their persons with the spirit of benevolence which the gospel breathes, when so many millions of precious souls are perishing without any knowledge of the only way of salvation, or while so many around them are suffering from penury and want. This is certainly contrary to the spirit of Christ. He who for our sakes became poor, who led a life of self-denial, toil, and suffering, that he might relieve distress and make known the way of salvation, could never have needlessly expended upon his person what would have sent the gospel to the destitute, or supplied the wants of poverty. Extravagance in dress is, therefore, obviously inconsistent with the Christian character. But no precise rule can be laid down in relation to this matter. It must be left to the sober judgment of Christians; and a sanctified conscience will readily discern the bounds of propriety. By asking yourself two or three questions, whenever you think of purchasing a new article of dress, you may very easily decide upon the path of duty — "Do I need this? Is it necessary for my comfort, or for my decent appearance in society? Can I glorify God in wearing it?"

2. *Your time is the Lord's.* You have no right to

waste it in useless attention to dress. One of the greatest evils of extravagant modes of dress is, that so much precious time is consumed at the toilet. I have already shown the value and importance of time, and the obligations of Christians to spend it in the most profitable manner. I need not here advance any new arguments to show that it is wrong to con-sume your time needlessly in the adjustment of your apparel.

3. *It is duty to pay some regard to personal ap-pearance.* A Christian lady, by making herself a *slattern*, brings reproach upon the cause of Christ, instead of glorifying God. The apostle enjoins upon women to adorn themselves with *modest* apparel. Modesty signifies *purity of sentiment and manners.* When this idea is applied to dress, it immediately suggests to the mind a neatness, taste, and simplicity, alike opposed both to extravagance and finery, and to negligence and vulgar coarseness. The exercise of a refined taste, in the adaptation and adjustment of ap-parel, may also be justified by the analogy of nature. Look abroad over the landscape, and see with what exquisite taste God has clothed the flowers of the field. There is a symmetry of proportion, a skilfulness of arrangement, and a fitness and adaptation of colors, which strike the eye with unmingled pleasure. And if God has shown a scrupulous regard to the pleasure of the eye, we may do the same. This opinion is also confirmed by the practical influence of the gos-pel. This is particularly observable among the poor in our own land. Just in proportion as the religion of

Jesus prevails among this class of people, you will see a scrupulous attention to personal appearance. By this, I do not mean the *pride of appearance*, but a decency, modesty, and propriety, opposed to negligence, coarseness, and vulgarity. But this is more strikingly manifest among those people who have been but recently raised, by the influence of the gospel, from the lowest depths of heathenism. Of this you will be convinced by examining the history of the missions among the North American Indians, and in the South Sea Islands. The same principles will also apply to equipage and household arrangements. Such regard to comfort and decency of appearance as will strike the eye with pleasure, and shed around an air of cheerfulness, doubtless contributes to moral improvement, and is not only authorized, but required, by the spirit of the gospel.

But this is a dangerous point. There is so much temptation to the indulgence of pride and vanity, and such a disposition to make dress the means of attracting the attention and seeking the admiration of others, that you have need of constant watchfulness. Pray that you may not be led into temptation in this matter; and especially at those times when you are most in danger.

4. *Have a regard to health.* Among the means of preserving health, attention to dress is not the least important. Great care should always be taken that it be suited to the season, and a defence against the inclemency of the weather. This is a Christian duty; and any pride of appearance, or carelessness of habit, which leads you to neglect it, is *sin*. But, above

all things, avoid the compression of any part of the body for the purpose of improving the appearance. It is astonishing that intelligent ladies can so blindly follow the mandates of fashion as to indulge a habit so destructive of comfort and life. There is no part of the system — not even the extremity of a limb — which can suffer violent compression without interrupting the regular circulation of the blood. But, when this pressure is about the chest, the effect is most destructive. The lungs, subject as they are to alternate distention and compression, from receiving and discharging both the blood and the breath, require the most perfect freedom. But, when the chest is compressed by tight clothing, the vitals are removed from their natural position, the free play of the lungs is prevented, and the whole system of respiration and circulation is deranged. The consequences are, shortness of breath and faintness; impeded circulation, producing listlessness and languor; and inclination of the blood to the head, producing headache and distressing dizziness. And, if this course is long persisted in, destruction of health is the inevitable consequence; and often the poor deluded victim of a barbarous fashion pays the forfeit of her life. I have heard of many cases of death from this cause, three of which occurred *in one family*, within the circle of my acquaintance. I need use no argument, then, to convince a Christian lady that it is her duty to avoid this species of conformity to the world, which can be regarded in no other light than as a palpable violation of the sixth commandment. Yet, such is the delusive

influence of habit, that there is great difficulty, often-
times, in convincing young ladies that they err in this
matter, when the fact appears obvious to all their
friends.

5. *Do not make too much of the matter of dress.*
It is our duty to avoid every species of conformity to
the world which requires the sacrifice of religious
principle.   But, in things indifferent, we are allowed
to conform to the customs of society.   I do not think
there is much danger of excessive plainness of apparel, but there is danger of making so much account
of it as to cultivate a self-righteous spirit.   As I have
already remarked, in almost every system of false religion, precise forms of dress are prescribed, especially
for those who are devoted to what is termed a *religious
life ;* whereas, in the Bible, it is left to be regulated by
the general principles and spirit of Christianity, with an
occasional caution against extravagance ; and it does
not appear that Christ and the apostles, or the early
Christians, adopted any peculiarity of dress.   From the
description given of the garments distributed among the
soldiers, it would appear that our Lord wore the common dress of a religious teacher.   There is such a
thing as a pride of singularity ; and this is often manifested in the preparation and adjustment of the ward-
robe.   Satan is ever on the alert to observe the bent
of the mind, and carry it to extremes.   Be not ignorant
of his devices ; but watch and pray, that you may be
secure against all his wiles.

CHAPTER XVII.

SOCIAL AND RELATIVE DUTIES.

MAN is a social being. Whoever, therefore, lives to himself, violates an established law of nature. A numerous train of duties arises out of our social relations, entering more or less into the common concerns of life, according as these relations are more or less remote. The first relation is that of the *family*. This was established by the Creator in Paradise; and it has been preserved, in all ages of the world, and in all countries, with more or less distinctness, according to the degree of moral principle which has prevailed. It lies at the foundation of all human society; and just in proportion as the original principles upon which it was constituted are observed, will society be good or bad. The Scriptures are very particular in describing this relation, as it existed in the patriarchal ages. It has its foundation in the fitness of things; and hence the duties arising out of it are very properly classed as *moral* duties. Of such consequence does the Lord regard it, that he has given it a place in the decalogue; three of the ten commandments having respect to the family state. From the first institution of this relation, we learn that the father and mother are to constitute the united head of the family. *"They twain shall be one flesh.*" Authority is, therefore, vested in them both, to exercise jointly. But, since the fall, mankind having become perverse and self-willed, the nature and fitness of things seem to require that there should be a precedence of authority, in case of a division of the united head. This precedence the Scriptures distinctly indicate. One of the curses pronounced upon the woman, after the fall, was, that her husband should rule over her. This principle was carried out in the families of the patriarchs. The apostle Peter says that the holy women of old adorned themselves with a meek and quiet spirit, and were in subjection to their own husbands; and particularly notices the conduct of Sarah, the mother of the Jewish nation, who *obeyed* Abraham, calling him lord. The same principle is repeatedly taught in the New Testament. "Wives, submit yourselves unto your own husbands, as unto the Lord." "As the church is subject unto Christ, so let the wives be to their own husbands in every thing." "Let the wife see that she reverence her husband." "Likewise, ye wives, be in subjection to your own husbands."

The apostle Paul, moreover, intimates that this subordination of the woman to the man was originally indicated by the manner in which she was created: "He" — that is, the *man* — "is the image and glory of God; but the woman is the glory of the man. For the man is not of the woman, but the woman of the man; neither was the man created for the woman, but the woman for the man." The body of the woman was not created originally of the dust, as the man was, nor was her soul, like his, formed directly after the divine image ; but the former was constructed of a portion of the flesh and bone of the man, while the latter was modeled after his soul, so as to bear his image, rather than that of the Creator. While this may intimate that both the matter of the body, and the faculties and dispositions of the soul, are more refined, as almost every thing is which is remodeled and made over, it, nevertheless, clearly indicates subordination to man as the head. Yet the same apostle, by declaring the relation between man and woman to be similar to that between Christ and the church, has shown that the exercise of arbitrary or tyrannical authority, on the part of the man, was never contemplated, and is, therefore, a usurpation. The basis of the union between the man and the woman, as between Christ and the church, is *love ;* and where Christian principle prevails, there will rarely, if ever, be occasion to exercise authority. But the attempt of some recent *reformers* to confound all distinction between the respective place, duties, and sphere of action, of *man* and *woman*, is a sin against nature, the offspring of an infidel spirit, which disregards the teachings both of nature and of inspiration.

The fifth commandment teaches the duty of subordination to the head of the family, not only on the part of the children themselves, but of every member of the household. So far as the general interests of the family are concerned, persons residing in it are regarded in the same light as children, — subject to all its laws, rules, and regulations. Thus the Lord speaks of Abraham: "I know him, that he will command his children *and his household* after him, and they shall keep the way of the Lord." The principle is here recognized, that Abraham had a right to *command*, not only his own children, but all his household. And the same may also be inferred from the language of the fourth commandment. It is addressed to the head of the family, and enjoins upon him to see that no labor is performed on the Sabbath by any of his household, not even excepting the *stranger* that is within his gates.

The duty of the younger members of the family to respect the elder, may be inferred, — 1. From the nature and fitness of things. The elder brothers and sisters are the superiors of the younger, not only in age and experience, but generally in wisdom and knowledge. They are better qualified to take the lead, and therefore entitled to respect and deference. 2. The same may also be inferred from the precedence always given in Scripture to the first-born.

But the great household duty is LOVE. If this is properly discharged, it will set all other matters right. If this is wanting, there will be a lack of every thing else. The Scriptures insist much upon the duty of brotherly love. "Behold how good and how pleasant it is for brethren to dwell together in unity!" Christ, in his Sermon on the Mount, severely rebukes the indulgence of anger, and the want of kindness and courtesy, among brethren. And the apostle John says, "Whosoever hateth his brother is a murderer." A kind, tender-hearted, affectionate, and peaceful temper should be maintained in all the intercourse of different members of the same family.

But, as mankind began to multiply, it became necessary that the social relations should be extended. A number of families, residing near each other, formed a neighborhood, or community. This gave rise to the new relation of neighbor, from the necessity of intercourse between families. This was again extended to the formation of nations and kingdoms. But all these various relations are subject to the same general laws as those of the family; for they have grown out of them. The same principle which requires subordination to the head of the family, requires, also, deference to the elders of a community, and subordination to the rulers of the nation. And the same principle which requires the exercise of kindness, gentleness, meekness, forbearance, condescension, and love, between the members of the same family, requires the exercise of similar dispositions between individuals of the same community and nation. The principle is also still farther extended, embracing the whole world as one great family, and requiring the exercise of love, and the practice of benevolence, towards all mankind. "Submit yourselves to every ordinance of man, for the Lord's sake." "Thou shalt love thy neighbor as thyself."

But, in consequence of the fall, another most interesting relation has been established. Out of this apostate world God has chosen himself a family. Of this family Christ is the head, and his people are the members. Here are the same relations as in the

23 *

natural family; but they are different in their nature.
They are spiritual, and, of course, of higher obligation.
We are required to love Christ more than father or
mother. And the Lord Jesus says, with emphasis,
"This is my commandment, that ye love one another."
When grace is in full exercise, the love which Christians bear towards one another is stronger than the
natural affection which exists between brothers and
sisters of the same family.

RULES.

1. *Render to all the members of the family in which
you reside just that degree of deference and respect
which belongs to them.* Conscientiously regard the
rules and regulations introduced by the head of the
family, unless they are contrary to the word of God.
In such case, you should leave the family; because
your relative duties would interfere with your duty to
God.* It is in the domestic circle that your character
is to be formed. It is here that your disposition is to
be tried, and your piety cultivated. Endeavor, then,
to maintain, in your family intercourse, the same dignity and propriety of deportment which you wish to
sustain in society. Never descend to any thing at the
fireside which you would despise in a more extended

---

* This direction would not be proper for a minor in her
father's house, or in the place provided by a guardian. In
such cases, it would be duty to remain, and submit to the
penalty of disobedience; remembering that it is a blessing to
be persecuted for righteousness' sake.

circle. Bring the most minute actions of your daily
life to the test of Christian principle. Remember that,
in the sight of God, there are no *little sins*. The least
transgression, unrepented of and unforgiven, is sufficient to condemn the soul forever. " He that offendeth
in one point is guilty of all." Especially avoid the
indulgence of a selfish disposition. Be always ready
to sacrifice your own feelings, when, by so doing, you
can give pleasure to others. Study their wishes and
feelings, and prefer them to your own. Strive to be
helpful to others, even at the expense of personal feeling and interest. " Look not every man on his own
things, but every man on the things of others."
" Charity seeketh not her own." Be kind to all ;
respectful towards superiors, courteous to equals, and
condescending to inferiors. Be particularly careful
not to trample upon the feelings of servants — a
meanness of which it is scarcely possible to speak
in terms of undue severity. If you cultivate the dispositions and principles which I have here recommended, habitually, in the domestic circle, they will
become natural and easy in every other ; and this will
endear you to all your acquaintances. It will bring
honor upon your profession, increase your influence,
and thereby enable you to do more for the glory of
God.

2. *There are special duties growing out of your
relation to the church.* Some of these I have considered in former chapters. But I have particular
reference now to *social* duties. You are to regard all
the members of the church as brethren and sisters.

You are to love them in proportion as they are like Christ. It is the appearance of his image in them which excites our love. " He that loveth him that begat, loveth him also that is begotten of him." Brotherly love is much insisted on in the Scriptures, being repeatedly enjoined by our Lord and his apostles. It is so essential a part of the Christian character, that it is mentioned by the beloved disciple as one of the principal evidences of the new birth. And how do we manifest our love to our brothers and sisters? We delight in their society. We love to meet them, and to converse with them of the things which concern ourselves and the family of which we are members. So, if you love your brethren and sisters in the church, you will delight in their society; you will love to meet with them; to interchange kind offices; to talk of the difficulties, trials, hopes, fears, joys, and sorrows, of the way to the heavenly Canaan; and to speak of the interests of the great spiritual family to which you belong. This is the spirit alluded to by the prophet Malachi, when he says, " Then they that feared the Lord spake often one to another; and a book of remembrance was written before him for them that feared the Lord, and that thought on his name." Would that this " book of remembrance " were always kept in view when Christians speak to one another! How would it chasten their hearts, exclude injurious and unprofitable conversation, and lead them upward, to hold intercourse with heavenly things, as they commune with one another!

In addition to the general obligation of social intercourse among Christians, there are some particular duties which they owe to one another. They are to exercise mutual forbearance and tenderness towards each other's faults; and, at the same time, to watch over and admonish one another. Whenever you see a brother or a sister out of the way, it is your duty, with meekness, tenderly and kindly to administer reproof. "If a man be overtaken in a fault, ye which are spiritual, restore such an one in the spirit of meekness." "With all lowliness and meekness, with long-suffering, *forbearing one another in love.*" In all cases, where one is to be selected for the performance of a particular duty which may seem to confer honor, prefer others to yourself. "In honor, preferring one another." "In lowliness of mind, let each esteem other better than themselves." "Yea, all of you be subject one to another, and be clothed with humility." "Submitting yourselves one to another in the fear of God." Yet do not carry this principle so far as to refuse to act where duty calls. A disposition to be backward in such matters is often a serious hinderance to benevolent effort. Be always ready to engage in any enterprise for doing good; but prefer the office which requires the most labor with the least honor. Christians ought also to take delight in assisting each other, and to feel personally interested in each other's welfare. In short, the feeling that pervades the church should be preëminently a FAMILY FEELING.

3. *There are also some duties growing out of your relations to general society.* Be ever ready to interchange kind offices with every one who maintains a

decent moral deportment; and be kind and compassionate, even to the vicious, so far as you can, without associating with them on terms of equality. By this means, you may win the affections of the impenitent, and thereby secure their attention to direct efforts for the salvation of their souls. But you should never suffer your feelings of complacency and good-will towards those who are destitute of piety, to lead you to conform to the spirit of the world which influences their conduct. Your social intercourse with them should be regulated upon this principle — *Never go any farther into their society than you can carry your religion with you.* " Be not conformed to this world."

4. *Although it be your duty to visit, yet, in this matter, be careful to be governed by religious principle.* There is in the human mind a tendency to extremes in every thing. Against this you need especially to be on your guard in social intercourse. When visiting is excessive, it dissipates the mind, and unfits it for any vigorous effort. When this state of mind becomes habitual, a person is never easy except when in company. The most gifted mind may thus be rendered comparatively inert and powerless. But, on the other hand, by shutting yourself out from society, you will dry up the social feelings, acquire a monkish love of solitude, and become soured in your temper towards your fellow-beings. You must, therefore, give to visiting its proper place in the routine of Christian duty. That place is just the one which it can occupy without encroaching upon more important duties. It should be the Christian's *recreation*. Seasons of relaxation from

the more laborious duties of life are undoubtedly necessary ; and I know of nothing which can better answer this end than the intelligent and pious conversation of Christian friends. Your friends have claims upon your time and attention; but these claims can never extend so far as to encroach upon more important duties, or to impair your ability to do good to yourself and others. As soon as you discover a secret uneasiness when out of company, or whenever you find that the demands of the social circle have led you to neglect other duties, it is time to diminish the number of your visits. But do not, on such occasions, violate Christian sincerity, by inventing excuses to satisfy your friends. Tell them frankly your reasons. If they are true and valuable friends, they will see the propriety of your conduct, and be satisfied. But, if they seek your friendship for their own selfish ends, they will be offended; in which case, you will lose nothing.

5. *Never go into any company where the spirit and maxims of the world predominate.* This may cut you off from a large portion of society ; but it is a rule founded on the word of God. If we would not be conformed to the world, we must not follow its maxims, nor partake of its spirit. It may be said that we should go into such society for the purpose of exerting a religious influence. But the practical result is directly the contrary. The spirit which prevails in such company is destructive of all religious feeling : it freezes up the warm affections of the Christian's heart. The consequence is, he is ashamed to acknowledge his Master, and avow his principles, where the prevailing current

is against him. He therefore moves along with it, to
the injury of his own soul, and the wounding of his
Master's cause. His worldly companions see no difference between his conduct and their own, and conclude, either that all is right with themselves, or that
he is a hypocrite. Large parties, as a general rule,
are unfriendly to the health both of body and soul.
The most profitable kind of social intercourse is the in-
formal meeting of small circles, of which a sufficient
number are religious people, to give a direction and
tone to conversation. Nevertheless, we should not
carry this rule so far as to exclude ourselves wholly
from the society of our unconverted friends ; but let
them see, by the chastened tone of our conversation,
our kindness, courtesy, and conscientiousness, that religion has improved our character.

6. *When in company, labor to give a profitable
direction to conversation.* If there are elder persons
present, who introduce general discourse, of a profitable character, let your words be few : it is generally
better, in such cases, to learn in silence. But when an
opportunity offers for you to say any thing that will
add interest to the conversation, do not fail to improve
it. Yet let your ideas be well conceived, and your
words well chosen. " A word fitly spoken is like ap-
ples of gold in pictures of silver." The interest of
conversation does not depend so much upon the multitude of words, as upon the matter they contain, and
their appropriateness to the subject. But, when no
other person introduces profitable conversation, take it
upon yourself. If you will study to be *skilful* in the

matter, you may turn any conversation to good account. This was one of the peculiar beauties of our Savior's discourse. Whatever subject was introduced, he invariably drew from it some important lesson. If you are on the alert, you may always give a proper turn to conversation, in this way. I do not say that conversation should always be exclusively religious; but it should be of a kind calculated to improve the mind or the heart, and it should at all times partake of the savor of piety. "Let your speech be always with grace, seasoned with salt." No proper opportunity, however, should be lost, of making a direct religious impression. If the solemn realities of divine things were always present to our minds, as they ought to be, we should never be at a loss to speak of them in a becoming manner. When you meet with persons who are living without hope, lose no proper occasion to warn them of their danger, and show them the sinfulness of their lives, and the guilt of rejecting the Savior. But this should be done as privately as possible. Speaking to them abruptly, in the presence of company, often has a tendency to provoke opposition, and harden their hearts. However, this caution is not always necessary. If there is much tenderness of conscience, admonition will be well received, even in the presence of others. Great care should be taken, on both sides, that you neither injure them by your imprudence, nor neglect your duty to their souls through excessive carefulness. Study wisdom, skilfulness, and discretion, in all things. "He that winneth souls is wise."

7. *Set your face against the discussion of absent*

24

characters. Never allow yourself to say any thing to
the disadvantage of any person, unless your duty to
others may require it. This, however, will rarely
happen ; though it may sometimes be your duty to
caution others against being ensnared by one whose
character you know to be bad. The Scriptures condemn backbiting and evil-speaking, in the most pointed terms. " Speak not evil one of another, brethren.
He that speaketh evil of his brother, speaketh evil of
the law." " Speak evil of no man." " Let all bitterness, and wrath, and anger, and clamor, and *evil-speaking*, be put away from you." " Debates, envyings,
wrath, strifes, *backbitings*, *whisperings*, swellings, tu-
mults." " *Whisperers*, *backbiters*, haters of God, de-
spiteful." Here we see how the Lord regards this
sin ; for he has classed it with the exercise of the most
abominable passions of the human heart. It is a great
sin, and productive of much evil in the church and in
society. It creates heart-burnings, jealousies, and
strife, and furnishes employment for *tale-bearers*, —
that most despicable set of mischief-makers. But this
sin is often committed without saying any thing directly against another. A sly insinuation is often productive of more mischief than direct evil-speaking : it
leaves a vague but strong impression upon the mind of
the hearer, against the character of the person spoken
of, and often creates a prejudice which is never removed. This is unjust and unfair, because it leaves
the character of the injured person resting under suspicion, without his having an opportunity to remove it.
This is probably what the apostle means by *whisperers*.

Solomon, also, speaking of the naughty person and wicked man, says, "He *winketh with his eyes*, he *speaketh with his feet*." " He that *winketh with the eye* causeth shame." How often do we see this winking, and speaking by gestures and knowing looks, when the characters of others are under discussion! Open and unreserved evil-speaking is unchristian ; but this winking, this speaking with the feet, is mean and dishonorable. Whenever you perceive a disposition to make invidious remarks about others, refuse to join in the conversation, and manifest your decided disapprobation. " The north wind driveth away rain ; so doth an angry countenance a backbiting tongue." Bear in mind the words of the apostle James: " If any man among you seemeth to be religious, and *bridleth not his tongue*, but deceiveth his own heart, this man's religion is vain." Thus the habitual indulgence of this sin will cut off the hope of the loudest professors.

8. *Avoid speaking of yourself.* Vanity and selfishness lead people to make themselves and their own affairs the principal topics of conversation. This is treating others with great disrespect, — as though one's self were of more consequence than the whole company. Endeavor to keep yourself as much as possible out of view, and to direct the thoughts and conversation of the company away from personal affairs to intellectual, moral, and religious subjects. But, when any of your friends make known their difficulties to you, manifest an interest in their affairs, sympathize with them, and render them all the assistance in your power.

9. *Never indulge a suspicious disposition.* Many

persons destroy their own peace, and gain the ill-will of others, by the exercise of this unhappy temper. You have no right to think others dislike you until they have manifested their dislike. Accustom yourself to repose confidence in your associates. It is better to be some-times deceived, than never to trust. And, if you are always jealous of those around you, be sure you will soon alienate their affections. In your intercourse with others of your own age and sex, be willing always to advance at least half way; and with those whose habits are very retiring, you may even go farther. Many persons of sterling worth have so low an opinion of themselves as to doubt whether even their own equals wish to form an acquaintance. "A man that hath friends must show himself friendly." Always put the best construction upon the conduct of others. Do not attach more meaning to their language and conduct than they properly express. If at any time you really believe yourself slighted, take no notice of it. Yet be careful never to intrude yourself into society where you have good reason to believe your company is not desired.

10. *Be cautious in the formation of intimate friend-ships.* Christians should always regard one another as friends. Yet peculiar circumstances, together with congeniality of sentiment and feeling, may give rise to a personal attachment much stronger than the common bond which unites all Christians. Of this we have a beautiful example in the case of David and Jonathan. This appears to be a perfect pattern of Christian friend-ship. They both, doubtless, loved other pious people;

but there was existing between them a peculiar personal attachment. Their souls were "*knit together*."
Friendships of this kind should not be numerous, and the objects of them should be well chosen. Long acquaintance is necessary, that you may be able to repose unlimited confidence in the friend to whom you unbosom your whole heart. Form no such friendships hastily. Think what would have been the consequence if David had been deceived in this friend. He would certainly have lost his life.

11. *Before going into company, visit your closet.*
Pray that the Lord would so direct your steps that you may do all things for his glory ; that he would enable you to spend the time profitably to yourself and others ; that he would keep you from evil-speaking, levity, foolish jesting, and every other impropriety ; and that he would enable you to honor him, and exert a good influence upon others. Endeavor to go out in a serious, devout, and tender frame of mind ; and then you may expect the Lord will go with you. But, if you go with a careless, undevout spirit, you will return with a wounded soul.

24 *

CHAPTER XVIII.

MARRIAGE.

SOME young persons indulge a fastidiousness of feeling in relation to the subject of marriage, as though it were indelicate to speak of it. Others make it the principal subject of their thoughts and conversation; and yet seem to think it must never be mentioned but in jest. Both these extremes should be avoided. Marriage is an ordinance of God, and therefore a proper subject of thought and discussion, with reference to personal duty. It is a matter of great importance, having a direct bearing upon the glory of God and the happiness of individuals. It should, therefore, never be approached with levity. But, as it requires no more attention than what is necessary in order to understand present duty, it would be foolish to make it a subject of constant thought, and silly to make it a common topic of conversation. It is a matter which should be weighed deliberately and seriously by every young person. In reference to the main subject, two things should be considered.

I. *Marriage is desirable.* It was ordained by the Lord at the creation, as suited to the state of man as a social being, and necessary to the design for which he was created. There is a sweetness and comfort in the bosom of one's own family, which can be enjoyed nowhere else. In early life, this is supplied by our youthful companions, who feel in unison with us. But, as a person who remains single advances in life, the friends of his youth form new attachments, in which he is incapable of participating. Their feelings undergo a change, of which he knows nothing. He is gradually left alone. No heart beats in unison with his own. His social feelings wither for want of an object. As he feels not in unison with those around him, his habits also become peculiar, and perhaps repulsive, so that his company is not desired: hence arises the whimsical attachment of such persons to domestic animals, or to other objects which can be enjoyed in solitude. As the dreary winter of age advances, the solitude of this condition becomes still more chilling. Nothing but that sweet resignation to the will of God, which religion gives in all circumstances, can render such a situation tolerable. But religion does not annihilate the social affections; it only regulates them. It is evident, then, that, by a lawful and proper exercise of these affections, both our happiness and usefulness may be increased.

II. *On the other hand, do not consider marriage as absolutely indispensable.* Although it is an ordinance of God, yet he has not positively enjoined it upon all. The apostle Paul intimates that there may be, with those who enter into this state, a greater tendency of the heart towards earthly objects, as well as an increase of care: "The unmarried woman careth for the things of the Lord, that she may be holy both in body

and spirit; but she that is married careth for the things
of the world, how she may please her husband." But
much more has been made of this than the apostle
intended. It has been greatly abused and perverted
by the church of Rome. It must be observed that, in
the same chapter, he advises that " every man have
his own wife, and every woman have her own husband." Whatever may be our condition in life, if
we seek it with earnestness and perseverance, in the
way of duty, God will give us grace sufficient for our
circumstances. But, though it is no sin to marry,
nevertheless, he says, " Such shall have trouble in the
flesh." It is undoubtedly true that the enjoyments of
conjugal life have their corresponding difficulties and
trials ; and, if these are enhanced by an unhappy connection, the situation is insufferable. For this reason,
I would have you avoid the conclusion that marriage is
indispensable to happiness. Single life is certainly to
be preferred to a connection with a person who will
diminish, instead of increasing, your happiness. Yet
I suppose the remark of the apostle, " Such shall have
trouble in the flesh," had reference chiefly to the
peculiar troubles of those times, when Christians were
exposed to persecution, the loss of goods, and even of
life itself, for Christ's sake ; the trials of which would
be much greater in married than in single life.

Bearing in mind the foregoing remarks, you will be
prepared calmly to consider what qualifications are requisite in a companion for life. These I shall divide
into two classes — those which are *indispensable*, and

those which are *desirable*. Of the first class, I see none which can be dispensed with, without so marring the character of a man as to render him an unfit associate for an intelligent Christian lady. But, although the latter are very important, yet, without possessing all of them, a person may be an agreeable companion and a man of real worth.

FIRST CLASS.

1. *The first requisite in a companion for life is* PIETY. I know not how a Christian can form so intimate a connection as this with one who is living in rebellion against God. You profess to love Jesus above every other object, and to forsake all, that you may follow him. How can you, then, unite your interests with one who continually rejects and abuses the object of your soul's delight? I am at a loss to understand how a union can be formed between the carnal and the renewed heart. They are in direct opposition to each other. The one overflows with love to God; the other is at enmity against him. How, then, can there be any congeniality of feeling? Can fire unite with water? And, " Can two walk together, except they be agreed? " A desire to form such a union must be a dark mark against any one's Christian character. The Scriptures are very clear and decided on this point. The intermarrying of the righteous with the wicked was the principal cause of the general corruption of the inhabitants of the old world, which provoked God to destroy them with the flood. Abra-

ham, the father of the faithful, was careful that Isaac, the son of promise, should not take a wife from among the heathen. The same precaution was taken by Isaac and Rebecca, in relation to Jacob. The children of Israel were also expressly forbidden to make marriages with the heathen, lest they should be turned away from the Lord to the worship of idols. And we see a mournful example of the influence of such unholy connections in the case of Solomon. Although he had been so zealous in the service of the Lord as to build him a temple, and had even been inspired to write portions of the Holy Scriptures, yet his strange wives turned away his heart, and persuaded him to worship idols. Though we are now under a different dispensation, yet *principles* remain the same. The union of a heathen and a Jew was, as to its effect on a pious mind, substantially the same as the union of a believer and an unbeliever; and the former would be no more likely to be drawn away from God by it than the latter. Hence we find the same principle recognized in the New Testament. Paul, speaking of the woman, says, " If her husband be dead, she is at liberty to be married to whom she will, only in the Lord." The phrase *in the Lord* denotes being a true Christian; as will appear from other passages where the same form of expression is used. " If any man be *in Christ*, he is a new creature." It is plainly implied, then, in this qualifying phrase, that it is unlawful for a Christian to marry one that is unconverted, or *out of Christ*. The same doctrine may also be inferred from the passage, " Be not ye, therefore, unequally yoked with unbelievers." Although the apostle had no particular reference here to this subject, yet he lays down a general principle, which applies to all intimate associations with unbelievers. And what connection could be more intimate than this? I conclude, therefore, that it is contrary both to reason and Scripture for a Christian to marry an impenitent sinner. And, in this respect, look not only for an outward profession, but for evidence of deep and devoted piety. Look for a person who makes religion the chief concern of his life; who is determined to live for God, and not for himself. Make this the test. Worldly-minded professors of religion are worse associates than those who make no profession. They exert a more withering influence upon the soul. And, in considering the evidences of devoted piety, you may well take into the account the question whether he indulges in the use of intoxicating liquors. If he does not practise rigidly the principle of abstinence from all intoxicating drinks, you ought to reject him at once. No lady is safe in the hands of a man, who, at this day, will parley with such an enemy to all that is lovely and of good report. Nor will you have much reason to repose confidence in him, if he is not a hearty friend to the Temperance Reformation.

2. *Another indispensable requisite is an* AMIABLE DISPOSITION. Whatever good qualities a man may possess, if he is selfish, morose, sour, peevish, fretful, jealous, or passionate, he will make an uncomfortable companion. Grace may do much towards subduing these unholy tempers; yet, if they were fostered in the heart in childhood, and suffered to grow up to maturity

before grace began to work, they will often break out in the family circle. However, you will find it exceedingly difficult to judge in this matter. The only direction I can give on this subject is, that, if you discover the exercise of a bad temper in a man, with the opportunity you will have of observation, you may consider it conclusive evidence of a disposition which would render you miserable.

3. *The person of your choice must possess a* WELL-CULTIVATED MIND. In order to produce a community of feeling, and maintain a growing interest in each other's society, both parties must possess minds well stored with useful knowledge, and capable of continued expansion. We may love a person for his piety alone, but we cannot long enjoy his society, as a constant companion, unless that piety is mingled with intelligence. To secure your esteem, as well as your affections, he must be capable of intelligent conversation on all subjects of general interest. And it is especially necessary in a husband, that he be not your *inferior*. You cannot entertain suitable feelings of respect and deference towards the man who is to be your *head*, if he is inferior to yourself in mental capacity and intelligence.

4. *His sentiments and feelings, on general subjects, must be* CONGENIAL *with your own.* This is a very important matter. Persons of great worth, whose views and feelings in relation to the common concerns of life are opposite, may render each other very unhappy. Particularly, if you possess a refined sensibility yourself, you must look for delicacy of feeling in a

companion. A very worthy man may render you unhappy by an habitual disregard of your feelings. And there are many persons who seem to be utterly insensible to the tender emotions of refined delicacy. A man who would subject you to continual mortification by his coarseness and vulgarity, would be incapable of sympathizing with you in all the varied trials of life. There is no need of your being deceived on this point. If you have much delicacy of feeling yourself, you can easily discover the want of it in others. If you have not, it will not be necessary in a companion.

5. *Another requisite is* ENERGY OF CHARACTER. Many people think some worldly prospects are indispensably necessary. But a man of energy can, by the blessing of God, make his way through this world, and support a family, in this land of plenty, by his own industry, in some lawful calling. And you may be certain of the blessing of God, if you obey and trust him. A profession or calling, pursued with energy, is, therefore, all the estate you need require. But do not trust yourself with a man who is inefficient in his undertakings. This would be leaning upon a broken staff.

6. *The person of your choice must be* NEARLY OF YOUR OWN AGE. Should he be younger than yourself, you will be tempted to look upon him as an inferior; and old age will overtake you first. But I should suppose the idea of marrying a man advanced in years would be sufficiently revolting to the feelings of a young female to deter her from it. Yet such things often happen. But I consider it as contravening the

25

order of nature, and therefore improper. In such case, you will be called upon rather to perform the office of a daughter and nurse, than a wife.

SECOND CLASS.

1. *It is desirable that the man with whom you form a connection for life should possess a* SOUND BODY. A man of vigorous constitution will be more capable of struggling with the difficulties and trials of this world, than one who is weak in body. Yet such an erroneous system has been pursued in the education of the generation just now coming upon the stage of action, that the health of very few sedentary persons remains unimpaired. It would, therefore, be cruel selfishness to refuse to form a connection of this kind, on this ground alone, provided the individual has no settled disease upon him. A person of feeble constitution requires the comfort and assistance of a companion more than one in vigorous health. But it certainly would not be your duty to throw yourself away upon one already under the influence of an incurable disease.

2. REFINEMENT OF MANNERS *is a very desirable quality in a companion for life.* This renders a person's society more agreeable and pleasant, and may be the means of increasing his usefulness. Yet it will not answer to make it a test of character; for it is often the case that men of the brightest talents, and of extensive education, — who are in every other respect amiable and worthy, — have neglected the cultivation of their manners; while there are very many, destitute

alike of talent and education, who seem to be adepts in the art of politeness. However, this may be cultivated, by a person of good sense, who appreciates its importance.

3. A SOUND JUDGMENT is also very necessary to enable a man to direct the common affairs of life. But this, also, may be cultivated by experience, and therefore cannot be called indispensable.

4. PRUDENCE *is very desirable.* The rashest youth, however, will learn prudence by experience. After a few falls, he will look forward before he steps, that he may foresee and shun the evil that is before him; but, if you choose such a one, take care that you do not fall with him, and both of you break your necks together.

5. It is a matter of great importance that the person with whom you form a connection for life, should belong to the same denomination of Christians with yourself. The separation of a family, in their attendance upon public worship, is productive of great inconvenience and perplexity; and there is serious danger of its giving rise to unpleasant feelings, and becoming an occasion of discord. I think it should be a very serious objection against any man, that he belongs to a different communion from yourself.

In additien to these, your own good sense and taste will suggest many other desirable qualities in a companion for life.

Upon receiving the addresses of a man, your first object should be to ascertain whether he possesses those prominent traits of character which you consider

indispensable. If he lack any one of these, you have
no further inquiry to make. Inform him openly and
ingenuously of your decision; but spare his feelings,
as far as you can consistently with Christian sincerity.
He is entitled to your gratitude for the preference he
has manifested for yourself. Therefore, treat him
courteously and tenderly; yet let him understand that
your decision is conclusive and final. If he possess
the feelings of a gentleman, this course will secure for
you his esteem and friendship. But, if you are satisfied with respect to these prominent traits of character, next look for those qualities which you consider
desirable, though not *indispensable*. If you discover
few or none of these, it will be a serious objection
against him. But you need not expect to find them
all combined in any one person. If you seek for
a perfect character, you will be disappointed. In
this, as well as in every other relation of life, you
will need to exercise forbearance. The best of
men are compassed about with imperfection and
infirmity. Besides, as you are not perfect yourself,
you have no right to look for perfection in a
companion.

While deciding these points, keep your feelings
under control. Suffer them to have no influence
upon your judgment. A Christian should never be
governed by impulse. Many persons have, no doubt,
destroyed their happiness for life, by suffering their
feelings to get the better of their judgment. Seek
wisdom from above. The Lord directs all our ways,
and we cannot expect to be prospered in any thing

wherein we neglect to acknowledge him and seek his direction. But, when you have satisfied yourself in relation to these things, and the person whose addresses you are receiving has distinctly avowed his intentions, you may remove the restraint from your feelings; which, as well as your judgment, have a deep concern in the affair. A happy and prosperous union must have for its basis a mutual sentiment of affection, of a peculiar kind. If you are satisfied that this sentiment exists on his part, you are to inquire whether you can exercise it towards him. For, with many persons of worth, whom we may esteem, there is often wanting a certain undefinable combination of qualities, not improperly termed the *soul of character;* which alone seems to call out the exercise of that peculiar sentiment of which we are speaking. But I seriously charge you never to form a connection which is not based upon this principle. Such depraved creatures as we are need the aid of the warmest affection to enable us to exercise that mutual forbearance, so indispensable to the peace and happiness of the domestic circle. That the conjugal relation should be cemented by a principle of a peculiar kind, will moreover appear from the superiority of the soul over the body. When two human beings unite their destinies, there must be a union of soul, or else such union is but partial. And the union of soul must be the foundation of the outward union, and of course precede it. The same may likewise be inferred from the existence of such a principle in the human breast. When Adam first saw Eve, he declared the nature of

25 *

this union, and added, " For this cause shall a man
leave his father and mother, and cleave unto his
wife; " implying that the affection between the parties to this connection should be superior to all other
human attachments.   The frown of God must, then,
rest upon a union founded upon any other principle;
for by it the order of nature is contravened, and therefore the blessings of peace and happiness cannot be
expected to attend it.

But love is not a principle which is brought into
existence as it were by magic.   It must always be
exercised in view of an object.   Do not, therefore,
hastily decide that you cannot love a man who possesses the prominent traits of character necessary to
render you happy.   You ought, however, to be fully
satisfied that such a sentiment, of a permanent character, does really exist in your own bosom, before you
consent to a union.

In your ordinary intercourse with gentlemen, much
caution should be observed.   Always maintain a dignity of character, and never condescend to trifle.   But,
in your conversation upon general subjects, you may
exercise the same sociability and freedom which you
would with ladies; not seeming to be sensible of any
difference of sex.   Indignantly repel any improper
liberties; but never decline attentions which are considered as belonging to the rules of common politeness,
unless there should be something in the character of
the individual which would justify you in wishing
wholly to avoid his society.   Some men are so dis-

agreeable in their attentions, and so obtrusive of their company, that they become a great annoyance to ladies. I think you would be justifiable in refusing ordinary attentions from such men, till they learn better manners. Pay the strictest regard to propriety and delicacy, in all your conduct; yet do not maintain such a cold reserve and chilling distance, as to produce the impression, in the mind of every one you meet, that you dislike his society. No gentleman of refined and delicate feelings will intrude his company upon ladies, when he thinks it is not desired; and you may create this impression, by carrying your reserve to an extreme. But the contrary extreme, of an excessive fondness for the society of gentlemen, is still more to be avoided. By cultivating an acute sense of propriety in all things, with a nice discrimination of judgment, you will be able generally to direct your conduct aright in these matters.

Never indulge feelings of partiality for any man until he has distinctly avowed his own sentiments, and you have deliberately determined the several points already mentioned. If you do, you may subject yourself to much needless disquietude, and perhaps the most unpleasant disappointments. And the wounded feeling thus produced may have an injurious effect upon your subsequent character and happiness.

CAUTIONS.

1. *Do not suffer this subject to occupy a very prominent place in your thoughts.* To be constantly

ruminating upon it, can hardly fail of exerting an injurious influence upon your mind, feelings, and deportment; and you will be almost certain to betray yourself, in the society of gentlemen, and, perhaps, become the subject of merriment, as one who is anxious for a husband.

2. *Do not make this a matter of common conversation.* There is, perhaps, nothing which has a stronger tendency to deteriorate the social intercourse of young people, than the disposition to give the subject of matrimonial alliances so prominent a place in their conversation, and to make it a matter of jesting and mirth. There are other subjects enough, in the wide fields of science, literature, and religion, to occupy the social hour, both profitably and pleasantly; and a dignified reserve, on this subject, will protect you from rudeness, which you will be very likely to encounter, if you indulge in jesting and raillery in regard to it.

3. *Do not speak of your own private affairs of this kind*, so as to have them become the subject of conversation among the circle of your acquaintances. It certainly does not add to the esteem of a young lady, among sensible people, for her to be heard talking about her beaux. Especially is this caution necessary in the case of a matrimonial engagement. Remember the old adage, —

> "There's many a slip
> Between the cup and the lip;"

and consider how your feelings would be mortified, if,

after making such an engagement generally known among your acquaintances, any thing should occur to break it off. In such case, you will have wounded feeling enough to struggle with, without the additional pain of having the affair become a neighborhood talk.

4. *Do not make an engagement a long time before you expect it to be consummated.* Such engagements are surrounded with perils. A few years may make such changes in the characters and feelings of young persons as to destroy the fitness and congeniality of the parties ; while, if the union had been consummated, they would have assimilated to each other.

In short, let me entreat you to cultivate the most delicate sense of propriety, in regard to every thing having the most distant relation to this matter ; and let all your feelings, conversation, and conduct, be regulated upon the most elevated principles of purity, refinement, and religion ; but do not carry your delicacy and reserve to the extreme of *prudery*, which is an unlovely trait of character, and which adds nothing to the strength of virtue.

CHAPTER XIX.

SUBMISSION. DEPENDENCE. CONTENTMENT.

THE secret of true happiness lies in a cordial acquiescence in the will of God. It is

> " Sweet to lie passive in his hand,
> And know no will but his."

The doctrine of a particular providence is precious to the Christian's heart. It enables him to see the hand of God in every event. Hence the sinfulness of a repining, discontented, unsubmissive temper. It is difficult to reconcile the habitual indulgence of such a disposition with the existence of grace in the heart. The first emotion of the new-born soul is *submission to the will of God.* We are prone to lose sight of the hand of God in the little difficulties and perplexities which are of every-day occurrence, and to look only at second causes. And so we often do in more important matters. When we are injured or insulted by others, we are disposed to murmur and complain, and give vent to our indignation against the immediate causes of our distress ; forgetting that these are only the instruments which God employs for the trial of our faith or the punishment of our sins. Thus God permitted Satan to try the faith of Job. Thus he permitted

Shimei to curse David. But the answer of this godly man is worthy of being imitated by all Christians under similar circumstances : " Let him curse, *because the Lord hath said unto him, Curse David*." Thus, also, the Lord employed the envy of Joseph's brethren to save the lives of all his father's family. " But as for you, ye thought evil against me ; but God meant it unto good, to bring to pass, as it is this day, to save much people alive." The principal reason why the histories of the Bible are so much more instructive than other histories is, that the motives of men, and the secret agency of divine Providence, are brought to light. Hence, also, the reason why the events recorded in Scripture appear so marvellous. If we could see how the hand of God is concerned in all things that occur within our observation, they would appear no less wonderful.

In this doctrine, we have the strongest motive for a hearty and cheerful resignation to all the crosses and difficulties, trials and afflictions, which come upon us in this life, whatever may be their immediate cause. We know that they are directed by our heavenly Father, whose " tender mercies are over all his works," and who " doth not afflict willingly, nor grieve, the children of men." And, whether we are Christians or not, the duty of submission is the same. When we consider the relation which we sustain to God, as guilty rebels against his government, we must see that, whatever may be our afflictions, so long as we are out of hell, we are the monuments of his mercy.

" Wherefore doth a living man complain, — a man for the punishment of his sins ? "

But, if we have evidence that we are the children of God, his promises furnish abundant consolation in every trial. We are assured " that *all things* work together for good to them that love God." And of this we have many examples in the Holy Scriptures, where the darkest providences have proved, in the end, to be fraught with the richest blessings. It was so in the case of Joseph, already mentioned. We are also taught to look upon the afflictions of this life as the faithful corrections of a kind and tender Parent. " For whom the Lord loveth, he chasteneth, and scourgeth every son whom he receiveth." How consoling the reflection that all our sufferings are designed to mortify and subdue our corruptions, to wean us from the world, and lead us to a more humble and constant sense of dependence upon God! Besides, the people of God have the most comforting assurances of his presence in affliction, if they will but trust in him. " *In all thy ways acknowledge him*, and he shall direct thy steps." " Cast thy burden upon the Lord, and he shall sustain thee : *he shall never suffer the righteous to be moved.*" " God is our refuge and strength, *a very present help in trouble :* therefore will not we fear, though the earth be removed, and though the mountains be carried into the midst of the sea ; though the waters thereof roar and be troubled, though the mountains shake with the swelling thereof." " *The steps of a good man are ordered* by the Lord ; and he delighteth in his way. Though he fall, he shall not be utterly cast down; for the Lord upholdeth him with his hand." How ungrateful for a child of God to repine at the dealings of such a tender and faithful Parent! O, the ingratitude of unbelief! Who can accuse the Lord of unfaithfulness to the least of his promises? Why, then, should we refuse to trust him, when the assurances of his watchful care and love are so full and so abundant?

We have not only strong ground of confidence in the Lord, under the pressure of afflictions in general, but we are particularly directed to look to him for the supply of our temporal wants. If we have evidence that we are living members of the body of Christ, growing in grace and in the knowledge of him, we have the assurance that all things needful for this life shall be supplied. Our Savior, after showing the folly of manifesting an anxious concern about the supply of our temporal wants, since the Lord is so careful in feeding the fowls of the air, and clothing the lilies and the grass of the field, says, "But seek ye first the kingdom of God, and his righteousness, and all these things shall be added unto you." By this, however, we are not to understand that the Lord will give us every earthly blessing which we *desire*. We are so shortsighted as often to wish for things which would prove injurious to us. But we are to understand that he will give us all that he sees best for us. And surely we ought to be satisfied with this; for he who sees the end from the beginning, must know much better than we what is for our good. The Scriptures abound with

26

similar promises. " O, fear the Lord, ye his saints;
for *there is no want* to them that fear him.   The young
lions do lack and suffer hunger ; but they that seek the
Lord *shall not want any* good thing."   " Trust in the
Lord, and do good, and *verily thou shalt be fed.*   I
have been young, and now am old ; yet have I not seen
the righteous forsaken, nor his seed begging bread."
" *No good thing will he withhold* from them that walk
uprightly."   " But my God shall *supply all your need,*
according to his riches in glory by Christ Jesus."
" Godliness is profitable unto all things, having promise
of the *life that now is,* and of that which is to come."
It must, then, be a sinful distrust of the word of God,
to indulge in anxious fears about the supply of our
necessities.   If we believed these promises, in their
full extent, we should always rest in them, and never
indulge an anxious thought about the things of this life.
This God requires of us.   " And seek not ye what ye
shall eat, or what ye shall drink, *neither be ye of
doubtful* mind."   " Therefore take no thought, saying,
What shall we eat ? or what shall we drink ? or where-
withal shall we be clothed ? "   " Be careful for
nothing."   And what can be more reasonable than this
requirement, when he has given us such full and repeated assurances that he will supply all our wants ?
The silver and the gold, and the cattle upon a thousand
hills, belong to our heavenly Father.   When, therefore,
he sees that we need any earthly blessing, he can
easily order the means by which it shall be brought
to us.

From the precious truths and promises which we

have been considering, we infer the *duty of contentment* in every situation of life. If God directs all our ways, and has promised to give us just what he sees we need, we surely ought to rest satisfied with what we have; for we know it is just what the Lord, in his infinite wisdom and unbounded goodness, sees fit to give us. But the apostle Paul enforces this duty with direct precepts. " But godliness *with contentment* is great gain." " Having food and raiment, let us be therewith *content*." " *Be content with such things as ye have;* for he hath said, I will never leave thee, nor forsake thee." Here he gives the promise of God as a reason for contentment. It is, then, evidently the duty of every Christian to maintain a contented and cheerful spirit in all circumstances. This, however, does not forbid the use of all lawful and proper means to improve our condition. But the means must be used with entire submission to the will of God. The child of God should cast all his care upon him; and, when he has made all suitable efforts to accomplish what he considers a good object, he must commit the whole to the Lord, with a perfect acquiescence in his will, even to the utter disappointment of his own hopes.

CHAPTER XX.

SELF-EXAMINATION.

In view of the positive injunctions of Scripture, no argument is necessary to show that self-examination is a duty. Paul says, " Examine yourselves, whether ye be in the faith; prove your own selves." But, if the word of God had been silent upon the subject, the importance of self-knowledge would have been a sufficient motive for searching into the secret springs of action which influence our conduct. A person ignorant of his own heart is like a merchant who knows not the state of his accounts, while every day liable to become a bankrupt; or like the crew of a leaky vessel, who are insensible to their danger. The professed follower of Christ, who knows not whether he is a true or false disciple, is in a condition no less dangerous. Although we may be Christians without the assurance of our adoption, yet we are taught in the Holy Scriptures that such assurance is to be attained. Job, in the midst of his affliction, experienced its comforting support: " I *know*," says he, " that my Redeemer liveth." David says, with confidence, " I *shall* be satisfied when I awake with thy likeness." Paul expresses the like assurance : " I *know* whom I have believed, and am persuaded that he is able to keep that which I have committed unto him against that day." All Christians are taught to expect the same, and exhorted to strive after it: " And we desire that *every one of you* do show the same diligence to the *full assurance of hope,* unto the end." " Let us draw near with a true heart, in *full assurance of faith.*" " Beloved, if our heart condemn us not, then have we *confidence* toward God." " He that believeth on the Son of God hath the witness in himself." " For ye have not received the spirit of bondage again to fear; but ye have received the spirit of adoption, whereby we cry, Abba, Father. The Spirit itself beareth witness with our spirit that we are the children of God." " Grieve not the Holy Spirit of God, whereby ye are *sealed* unto the day of redemption."

But, as gold dust is sometimes concealed in the sand, so grace in the heart may be so mingled with remaining corruption, that we cannot clearly distinguish its motions. It might not be for the benefit of a person of such low attainments in the divine life to receive an assurance of God's favor until these corruptions have been so far subdued as to give the principle of grace the ascendency. Hence God has wisely directed that the sure evidence of adoption can be possessed only by those who have made such progress in holiness as to be able to discern the fruits of the Spirit in their hearts and lives. The *witness of the Spirit* must not be sought in any sudden impulses upon the mind, but in the real work of grace in the heart, conforming it to the image of God. Even if God should indulge us with such impulses or impressions, they

26 *

would not be certain evidence of our adoption, because Satan can counterfeit experiences of this kind. Hence we may account for the *strong confidence* which is sometimes expressed by young converts who afterwards fall away. But when the image of God can be seen in our hearts and lives, we may be *certain* that we are his children. That this is the true witness of the Spirit, may be inferred from the passage last quoted. When this Epistle was written, it was the custom of princes to have their names and images stamped upon their seals. These seals, when used, would leave the impression of the name and image of their owners upon the wax. So, when God sets his seal upon the hearts of his children, it leaves an impression of his name and image. The same thing may be intended in Revelation, where Jesus promises to give him that overcometh " a white stone, and in the stone a *new name* written." A figure somewhat similar is also used in the third chapter of Malachi. Speaking of the Messiah, the prophet says, " He shall sit as a refiner and purifier of silver." A refiner of silver sits over the fire, with his eye steadily fixed upon the precious metal in the crucible, until he sees *his own image* in it, as we see our faces in the glass. So the Lord will carry on his purifying work in the hearts of his children, till he sees his own image there. When this image is so plain and clear as to be distinctly discerned by us, then the Spirit of God bears witness with our spirits that we are his children. As *love* is the most prominent and abiding fruit of the Spirit, it may be the medium through which the union between

God and the soul is seen, and by which the child of God is assured of his adoption. A strong and lively exercise of a childlike, humble love may give a clear evidence of the soul's relation to God as his child. "Love is of God; and every one that loveth is born of God, and knoweth God. He that loveth not, knoweth not God; for *God is love.*" As God is love, the exercise of that holy principle in the heart of the believer shows the impression of the divine image. "God is love; and he that dwelleth in love dwelleth in God, and God in him." Hence the apostle John says, "We *know* that we have passed from death unto life, because we love the brethren." But, if this love is genuine, it will regulate the emotions of the heart, and its effects will be visible in the lives of those who possess it. The same apostle says, "By this we know that we love the children of God, when we love God and *keep his commandments.*" So that, in order to have certain evidence of our adoption into the blessed family of which Jesus is the Elder Brother, all the fruits of the Spirit must have grown up to some degree of maturity.

From the foregoing remarks, we see the great importance of *self-examination.* We must have an intimate acquaintance with the operations of our own minds, to enable us to distinguish between the exercise of gracious affections, and the selfish workings of our own hearts. And, unless we are in the constant habit of diligent inquiry into the character of our emotions, and the motives of our actions, this will be an exceedingly difficult matter. The Scriptures specify several objects for which this inquiry should be instituted, viz.

I. *To discover our sins, that we may come to Christ for pardon, and for grace to subdue them.* David prays, " Search me, O God, and know my heart; try me, and know my thoughts; and *see if there be any wicked way in me;* and lead me in the way everlasting." The prophet Jeremiah says, " Let us search and try our ways, and *turn again* unto the Lord." This examination should be a constant work. We should search into the motives of our actions, and examine our religious feelings, to know, if possible, whether they come from the Spirit of God, or whether they are a fire of our own kindling. We must be cautious, however, lest, by diverting our attention from the truth, to examine the nature of the emotions produced by it, we should lose them altogether. This can better be determined afterwards, by recalling to recollection these emotions, and the causes which produced them. If they were called forth by correct views of truth, and if they correspond, in their nature, with the descriptions of gracious affections contained in the Bible, we may safely conclude them to be genuine.

But, as we are often under the necessity of acting without much deliberation; as we are so liable to neglect duty; and as every duty is marred by so much imperfection, — it is not only proper, but highly necessary, that we should have stated seasons for retiring into our closets, and calmly and deliberately reviewing our conduct, our religious exercises, and the prevailing state of our hearts, and comparing them with the word of God. There are two very important reasons why this work should be performed at the close of every day. 1. If neglected for a longer period, we may forget both our actions and our motives. It will be very difficult for us afterwards to recall them, so as to subject them to a thorough examination. 2. There is a great propriety in closing up the accounts of every day. "Sufficient unto the day is the evil thereof." Every day will bring with it work enough for repentance. Again, when we lie down, we may awake in eternity. What, then, will become of those sins which we have laid by for the consideration of another day? Let us, then, never give sleep to our eyes till we have searched out every sin of the past day, and made fresh application to the blood of Christ for pardon. This is, indeed, a very difficult work; but, by frequent practice, it will become less so. By sitting down in your closet, after finishing the duties of the day, and seriously and prayerfully engaging in this exercise, you may try your conduct and feelings by the rules laid down in the word of God. You may thus bring to remembrance the exercises of your heart, as well as your actions, and be reminded of neglected duty, and of those great practical truths which ought ever to be kept before your mind. You may bring up your sins, and set them in order before you, and discover your easily-besetting sins. You may be led to the exercise of penitence, and be driven anew to the cross of Christ for pardon, and for strength to subdue indwelling corruption. Whenever you discover that you have exer-

cised any correct feeling, or that your conduct has in
any respect been conformed to the word of God, acknowledge with gratitude his grace in it, and give him
the glory.   Wherein you find you have been deficient,
confess your sin before God, and apply afresh to the
blood of Christ, which " cleanseth from all sin."   But
be cautious that you do not put your feelings of regret,
your tears and sorrows, in the place of the great sacrifice.   Remember that no degree of sorrow can atone
for sin ; and that only is *godly sorrow* which leads to
the blood of Jesus.   Any peace of conscience obtained
from any other source must be false peace.   It is *in
believing*, only, that we can have *joy and peace.*

You will find advantage from varying this exercise.
When we frequently repeat any thing in the same
form, we are in danger of acquiring a careless habit,
so that it will lose its effect.   Sometimes take the ten
commmandents, and examine your actions and motives by them.   And, in doing this, you will find great
help from the explanation of the commandments, contained in the "Assembly's Shorter Catechism."   This
shows their spirituality, and brings them home to the
heart.   Again, you may take some portion of Scripture which contains precepts for the regulation of the
conduct, and compare the actions of the day with
them.   Or you may take the life of Christ as a pattern, compare your conduct and motives with it, and
see whether in all things you have manifested his
spirit.

But do not be satisfied till the exercise, however
performed, has taken hold of the heart, and led to

penitence for sin, and a sense of pardon through the blood of Christ, which accompanies true contrition; for " the Lord is nigh unto them that are of a broken heart, and saveth such as be of a contrite spirit."

II. *Another object of self-examination may be, to ascertain the reason why the Lord does not answer our prayers.* This reason may generally be found in ourselves. I know of but two exceptions. One is, when the thing we ask is not agreeable to the will of God. The other is, when the Lord delays to answer our prayers for the trial of our faith. The obstacles which exist in ourselves, to prevent his granting our requests, are generally some of the following: 1. We may be living in the practice of some sin, or the neglect of some duty. "If I regard iniquity in my heart," says the Psalmist, "the Lord will not hear me." "He that turneth away his ear from hearing the law, even his prayer shall be abomination." We may weep day and night on our knees before God; yet, if we are living in the habitual neglect of duty, or if any sin cleaves to us for which we have not exercised repentance and faith in the atoning blood of Christ, we have no reason to expect that he will hear our prayers. 2. We may not be sufficiently humble before God. " Though the Lord be high, yet hath he respect unto the lowly; *but the proud he knoweth afar off.*" "God resisteth the proud, but giveth grace unto the humble." " Humble yourselves in the sight of the Lord, and he shall lift you up." " Whosoever shall exalt himself shall be abased; and he that shall humble himself shall be exalted." Hence, if our hearts are proud, and we refuse to humble ourselves before God, he will not answer our prayers. 3. We may not desire the things we ask that God may be glorified, but that it may minister to our own gratification. "Ye ask, and receive not, because ye ask amiss, that ye may consume it upon your lusts." When we ask with such motives, we have no right to expect that God will hear our prayers. 4. We may not be asking in faith. "But let him ask in faith, nothing wavering. For he that wavereth is like a wave of the sea, driven with the wind and tossed. For *let not that man think that he shall receive* any thing of the Lord." "Without faith, it is impossible to please God." 5. We may be exercising an unforgiving temper; and if so, the Lord has declared that he will not hear our prayers. (Matt. xviii. 35; Mark xi. 25, 26.)

When, therefore, you have been for some time praying for any particular object, without receiving an answer, carefully examine yourself with reference to these points, and wherein you find yourself deficient, endeavor, in the strength of Christ, immediately to reform. If your circumstances will permit, set apart a day of fasting and prayer for this object. And, if the answer is still delayed, repeat the examination, until you are certain that you have complied with all the conditions of the promises.

III. *Another object of self-examination is, to ascertain the cause of afflictions, whether spiritual or temporal.* If the Lord sends distress upon us, or hides from us the light of his countenance, he has some good reason for it. By reading the book of Haggai, you will discover the principles upon which God deals with his people; and there he says, " In the day of adversity *consider.*" If, therefore, the work of your hands does not prosper, or if the Lord has withdrawn from you his special presence, be sure that something is wrong: it is time for you to " consider your ways." In the book referred to, the Lord informs the Jews of the cause of their poverty and distress. They had not built the house of God. He also tells them that the silver and the gold are his, and that he will bless them as soon as they do their duty. We are as dependent upon God's blessing now as his people were then. If we withhold from him what he requires of us for advancing the interests of his kingdom, can we expect temporal prosperity? If we refuse to do our duty, can we expect his presence? These, then, should be the subjects of inquiry, in such circumstances. In such cases, also, it may be very proper to observe a day of fasting and prayer.

IV. *Another object of self-examination is, to know whether we are Christians.* " Examine yourselves whether ye be in the faith." This is a very important inquiry. It is intimately connected with every other, and should enter more or less into all. In order to prosecute this inquiry, you must make yourself acquainted with the evidences of Christian character. These are clearly exhibited in the Holy Scriptures. Study the Bible diligently and prayerfully, for the purpose of ascertaining the genuine marks of saving grace. You may also find benefit from the writings of men of great personal experience, who have had much opportunity of observing the effects of true and false religion. In particular, I would recommend to you the careful study of President Edwards's " Treatise on Religious Affections." He was a man of great piety, who had attained to the *full assurance of hope.* He had also passed through a number of revivals of religion. The work of which I speak contains a scriptural view of the evidences of the new birth ; and also points out, with great clearness and discrimination, the marks of false religion. He distinguishes between those things which may be common both to true and false religion, and those which are the certain marks of true conversion. But, in reading this work, especially the first part of it, you need, perhaps, to be cautioned against discouragement. While you allow the truth its most searching effect upon your heart, do not suffer it to drive you to despair. You will, however, find the latter part of the book more encouraging. In the former part, where he is pointing out the marks of false religion, of selfishness, and of spiritual pride, it would seem as if none could escape being stripped of all their claims to true religion ; but, in the latter part, where he describes the effects of true piety, the marks of humility, &c., the reading of it will be likely to discover to you the marks of a saving change, if you have any.

Self-examination, for this object, should be habitual.

In reading the Bible, in meditation, in hearing the word, — wherever you see an evidence of Christian character, inquire whether you possess it. But you ought, also, frequently to set apart seasons for the solemn and prayerful consideration of the important question, "*Am I a Christian?*" A portion of the Sabbath may be very properly spent in this way. You should enter upon this work with the solemnities of the judgment day before you. The Scriptures furnish abundant matter for self-examination. Bring the exercises of your heart, and the conduct of your life, to this unerring standard. You will also find much assistance in this exercise by the use of the following tracts, published by the American Tract Society: No. 21, entitled "A Closet Companion;" No. 146, entitled "Helps to Self-Examination;" and No. 165, entitled "True and False Conversions distinguished." You have likewise probably noticed several chapters in Doddridge's "Rise and Progress" admirably adapted to this object. I mention these because it is advantageous frequently to vary the exercise. Take time to perform the work of self-examination thoroughly, bringing to your aid all the information you can obtain from these and other sources, — varying the exercise at different times, that it may not become superficial and formal.

I have prepared some questions, in my little work entitled "*The Closet*," both for the general purpose of inquiring as to the main question whether we are Christians, and also for particular occasions, as the close of the day, Sabbath evening, before communion, &c., to which I must refer you, instead of pursuing this part of the subject further, in this place.

Should you, at any time, come to the deliberate conclusion that you are resting upon a false hope, give it up, but do not abandon yourself to despair. Go immediately to the cross of Christ. Give up your heart to him, as though you had never come before. There is no other way. This is the only refuge, and Jesus never sent a soul empty away. "Him that cometh to me I will in no wise cast out." Persevere, even though you find scarce evidence enough to give a faint glimmering of hope. Continually renew your repentance and faith in Christ. Diligence in self-examination may be a means of growth in grace; and if you are really a child of God, your evidences will increase and brighten, till you will be able to indulge "a good hope through grace." "For, in due time, we shall reap, if we faint not." And "The path of the just is as the shining light, that shineth more and more unto the perfect day."

V. *Another object of self-examination is, to ascertain whether we are prepared to approach the Lord's table.* "But let a man examine himself, and so let him eat of that bread, and drink of that cup." Here the duty of self-examination, before partaking of the Lord's supper, is evidently taught. And, in the next verse, we are told what is requisite to enable us to partake of this ordinance in an acceptable manner. It is, that we have faith to discern the Lord's body. A backslider in heart, even though a real Christian, is not prepared to partake of this spiritual feast, without renewing his repentance and faith. In this examination, two subjects of inquiry present themselves. 1. "Am I a Christian?" 2. "Am I growing in grace?" In regard to the first of these inquiries, enough has already been said. To answer the second, you will need consider, 1. Whether you were living in the exercise of gracious affections at the last communion; 2. Whether you have since made any progress in the divine life. For questions, I must again refer you to "The Closet."

If you have time to keep a journal, you may find some advantage from reviewing it on such occasions. It will aid your memory, and help you to give your past life a more thorough examination. You will thereby be the better able to judge whether you are making progress. It should, however, be written solely for your own private use, without the remotest idea of having it ever seen by others; or else it may become a snare to you. But, however unfit this examination may find you, do not let Satan tempt you to stay away from the Lord's table. It is your duty to commemorate his dying love. It is your duty, also, to do it with a suitable preparation of heart. Both these duties you will neglect by staying away. In doing so, you cannot expect God's blessing. But set immediately about the work of repentance. Come to the cross of Christ, and renew your application to his atoning blood. Give yourself away to God anew, and

27 *

renew your covenant with him. In doing this, he will bless your soul ; and the Lord's table will be a season of refreshing. But, if this preparation be heartfelt and sincere, its fruits will be seen in your subsequent life. Remember who has said, " BE THOU FAITHFUL UNTO DEATH, AND I WILL GIVE THEE THE CROWN OF LIFE."

APPENDIX.

A COURSE OF READING.

[THIS course of reading is proposed for young ladies, not with the expectation that they will be able to read all this catalogue of books during the course of their education, but that they will commence, and form the habit of reading systematically, at this period, and prosecute the course, as they shall have opportunity, in subsequent years. The selection has been made with considerable care; yet it may be capable of improvement and adaptation to particular circumstances, under the direction of judicious friends.]

I. HISTORY.

1. *Sacred and Ecclesiastical History.* Jahn's Hebrew Commonwealth; Milner's Church History; (Mosheim's do., if practicable, to be kept on hand for occasional comparison, in doubtful cases;) Scott's Continuation of Milner; * Gilpin's Lives of the Reformers, (to be read in connection with the history where their names occur;) Life of Knox; Fuller's and Warner's Ecclesiastical History of England, or Bur-

---

* Those who prefer a course somewhat more condensed, without learned discussions, can substitute, so far as it goes, the author's Sabbath School Church History.

net's History of the Reformation of the Church of
England; Neale's History of the Puritans; Mather's
Magnalia; The Great Awakening; Choules's Origin
and History of Missions; (this latter might well be
commenced simultaneously with the first named, and
carried along with the course.)

2. *Secular or Profane History.* Neale's History
of New England; Guizot's History of Civilization in
Europe; Rollin's Ancient History; Bancroft's History
of America; Russell's Egypt; Russell's Palestine;
Plutarch's Lives, (to be kept on hand, and read when
the names occur in history;) Winthrop's Journal;
Ramsay's American Revolution; Sparks's American
Biography, (to be kept on hand, and read as the names
occur in history;) Mitford's Greece; Ferguson's His-
tory of the Roman Republic; Josephus's Works;
Marshall's Life of Washington; Sismondi's Decline of
the Roman Empire; Hallam's History of the Middle
Ages; Mills's History of the Crusades and Chivalry;
Turner's History of England; James's Life of Charle-
magne; Robertson's History of Scotland; Robertson's
Charles V.; Sismondi's History of the Italian Repub-
lics, (abridged in Lardner's Cabinet of History;)
Irving's Life of Columbus; Ferdinand and Isabella;
Robertson's History of America; Sparks's Life of
Washington; Scott's Napoleon.

II. CHRISTIAN DOCTRINE.

Gallaudet's Youth's Book on Natural Theology;
Todd's Truth made simple; Blunt's Veracity of the

Gospels; Alexander's Evidences; The Four Pillars; Attributes of God, (Mass. S. S. Society;) Brown's Compendium of Natural and Revealed Religion; Scott's Essays; Watts's Ruin and Recovery; Edwards's History of Redemption; Griffin on Divine Efficiency; Colquhoun on the Covenants; Owen on the Spirit; Owen on the Death and Satisfaction of Christ; Griffin on the Atonement; Doddridge's Ten Sermons on Regeneration; Scott's Treatise on Repentance; Watts on Death and Heaven; Mitchell's Guide; Dr. Woods on Infant Baptism; The Baptized Child.

III. RELIGIOUS BIOGRAPHY.

Humphrey's Christian Memoirs; Burder's Memoirs; Memoirs of Mrs. Graham, Mrs. Huntington, Mrs. Eleanor Emerson, Mrs. Savage, Mrs. Newell, Mrs. Paterson, Mrs. S. L. Smith, Mrs. Edgerton, Mrs. Allen, Mrs. Judson, Mrs. Winslow; Philip Henry, Oberlin, Francke, Neff, Payson, Martyn, Howard, Dr. Hopkins, Edwards, Brainerd, Pres. Davies, Maclaurin, Baxter, Doddridge, Owen, Watts, Howe, Mather, Dwight, Gill, Bunyan, Robinson, Andrew Fuller, Robert Hall, Fletcher, Asbury, Dr. A. Clarke, John and Charles Wesley, Whitefield, Watson, Cecil, Fenelon, J. B. Taylor, Emerson, Parsons and Fisk, Gordon Hall, Schwartz. (Convenience may be consulted, as to the order in which these are read; and any other approved biographies may be substituted or added.)

IV. MISCELLANEOUS.

1. *On the Prophecies.*   Newton's Dissertations; Keith on the Prophecies; Keith's Demonstration of Truth; Smith's Key to the Revelation.

2. *On Christian Character, Experience, and Duty.* Doddridge's Rise and Progress; Pilgrim's Progress; Edwards on Affections; Scougal's Life of God in the Soul; Bellamy's True Religion Delineated; Abbott's Young Christian; Owen on Spiritual-Mindedness; Flavel on Keeping the Heart; Gallaudet's Every-Day Christian; Philip's Guides; Hannah More's Practical Piety and Christian Morals; Owen on Indwelling Sin; Howe's Blessedness of the Righteous; Leighton on Peter; Flavel's Touchstone; American Tract Society's Evangelical Family Library, which includes some of the above.

3. *On the Discipline, Instruction, &c., of the Young.* Todd's Sabbath School Teacher; Abbott's Teacher; Mother at Home; Hannah More on Female Education; Mother's Friend; Father's Book; Fenelon on the Education of Daughters; Babington on Education; Hall's Lectures; Home Education; Book for Parents.

4. *Illustrations of Scripture.*   The Comprehensive Commentary, and Bush's and Barnes's Notes, (to be referred to in connection with the study of the Bible;) Townsend's Bible, (for its chronological information and Notes.)

5. *Health.*   Catechism of Health; Combe on the Constitution; Cornaro on Temperance.

6. *Travels.*   Bruce's Travels in Abyssinia; Denon's

Travels in Egypt; Clarke's Travels in Russia; Mackenzie's Travels in Iceland; Mungo Park's Mission to Africa; Lander's Journal; Rome in the 19th Century; Buchanan's Researches; the Christian Brahmin; Tyerman and Bennet's Journal; Williams's Missionary Enterprise; De Tocqueville's Democracy in America; Journals of the Missionaries, in the Missionary Periodicals.

7. *The Sciences.* Brown's Lectures on the Philosophy of the Mind; Day on the Will; Degerando on Self-Education; Dick's Christian Philosopher; Mrs. B.'s Conversations on Philosophy and Chemistry; Wayland's Moral Science and Political Economy; Douglas on the Advancement of Society; The Bridgewater Treatises.

8. *Belles Lettres.* Works of Jane Taylor and Madame De Staël; Johnson's Rasselas; Selections from the Spectator; Poems of Milton, Young, Dryden, Cowper, Thomson, Wordsworth, Montgomery, Hemans, Tappan; Southey's Cowper; Ripley's Specimens of Foreign Literature.

9. *Promiscuous.* Hannah More's Essays to Young Ladies; Miss Jewsbury's Letters to Young Ladies; Mrs. Farrar's Young Ladies' Friend; Daily Duties; Pastor's Daughter; The Listener; Way to do Good.

A Pastor's Sketches 1 & 2
by Dr. Ichabod Spencer

"*A Pastor's Sketches* is a sobering and challenging reminder that the Holy Spirit is the true agent of conversion. This book is urgently needed today when so much of our evangelism is patterned after current marketing methods. It has deeply convicted me to always seek to be in tune with the Holy Spirit as I minister to others." **Jerry Bridges**

"Dr. Spencer's *Sketches*, reprinted after a lapse of many years, are a veritable treasury of pastoral wisdom. They will amply repay careful reading by pastors and serious Christians in our day." **Maurice Roberts**

"The Spencer extracts are superb and will be of great benefit when printed. This is very sobering but enlightening material. It is quite contrary to much of today's practice and all pastors need to read it." **Peter Jeffery**

"Spencer is a master at flushing sinners out of hiding and directing them to Jesus Christ for salvation through Spirit-worked, simple faith. The responses he makes to inquirers is, in the main, biblical, doctrinal, practical, and experiential. His perceptive counsel certainly has produced much fruit. *A Pastor's Sketches* is a compelling read for pastors and Christian workers; its pages contain the nuts and bolts of biblical evangelism." **Joel R. Beeke**

"The republication of Spencer's sketches gives a rare opportunity for contemporary pastors, who have few if any models of pastors who understand the 'work of evangelism.' These sketches show a doctrinal depth and an experiential savvy perfectly meshed in one who had the cure of souls as his passion." **Tom Nettles**

"Ichabod Spencer was gifted by God with a passion for the pastoral care of souls. Any pastor desiring to shepherd the sheep, or to see God's elect drawn to Christ, will find page after page of wise and sage counsel in this work. It is practical, pious, personal, and precious." **James White**

List Price for each volume **$12.95**
Purchase both from SGCB for **$22.00**

Solid Ground Christian Books
Call us toll free at **1-877-666-9469**
E-mail us at **sgcb@charter.net**
Visit us on the web at **solid-ground-books.com**

SGCB Classic Reprints Series

In addition to *The Young Lady's Guide* that you hold in your hands, SGCB is excited to announce our intention to bring back several classic volumes that have been out of print for too long. Here are our present titles:

Christ in Song: Hymns of Immanuel from All Ages is a remarkable volume compiled by Philip Schaff best known for his "History of the Christian Church." In this volume Schaff has gathered the greatest hymns beginning in the early centuries. Of this rare volume Charles Hodge of Princeton said,

After all, apart from the Bible, the best antidote to all these false theories of the person and work of Christ, is such a book as Dr. Schaff's 'CHRIST IN SONG.' The hymns contained in that volume are of all ages and from all churches. They set forth Christ as truly God, as truly man, as one person, as the expiation for our sins, as our intercessor, saviour, and king, as the supreme object of love, as the ultimate ground of confidence, as the all-sufficient portion of the soul. We want no better theology and no better religion than are set forth in these hymns.

First Things by Gardiner Spring is a two volume set that is also very rare. These volumes set before our minds the foundation upon which all life is built, as recorded in the opening chapters of Genesis. In a day in which these chapters are being challenged even in so-called evangelical churches and seminaries, Spring takes us back with absolute assurance that we are reading genuine history. Every page is filled with pure spiritual gold.

The Church Member's Guide by John Angell James was once the most popular book in both the UK and the USA for instructing Christian's in their privileges and responsibilities as members of the body of Christ. Many are familiar with Calvary Press' booklet *The Duties of Church Members to their Pastors*, which is simply one chapter from this invaluable book. It would be a great tool for those who teach New Member's Classes, or Discipleship Training classes, and all seeking to serve in the Church of Jesus Christ.

The Life and Sermons of Dr. Ichabod Spencer is a three volume set that introduces the life and sermons of the author of the remarkable volumes called *A Pastor's Sketches*. The First Volume contains a very helpful sketch of the life of Dr. Spencer written by a dear friend, as well as 20 examples of Spencer's preaching called Practical/Experimental Sermons. Volume Two contains 35 Doctrinal Sermons, and Volume Three has 26 Sacramental Discourses delivered at the Lord's Table. A feast awaits all who love Christ.

Solid Ground Christian Books
Call us toll free at **1-877-666-9469**
E-mail us at **sgcb@charter.net**
Visit us on the web at **solid-ground-books.com**